Logistics: an Integrated Approach

about the author
Michael R Quayle

Michael is a member of the Chartered Institute of Purchasing and Supply, member of the Institute of Management, and member of the Institute of Training and Development. He has a masters degree in Industrial Relations, a first degree in Business Management, is a qualified Further Education lecturer and holds a Diploma in Training Management.

After several years experience in the electronics industry, in the fields of production, planning and purchasing, he has gained extensive purchasing logistics and project management experience within the UK and Central European Defence industry; this experience encompasses international, national and collaborative military aircraft and other defence related projects. Michael is now employed by Suffolk College Management Development Centre as their Director of Studies and has prime responsibility for their Master of Business Administration (MBA) programmes.

He has combined this career with extensive guest lecturing at University, Polytechnic and Regional Management centres and has tutored a wide variety of business courses. Similarly, he has addressed international seminars both in Central Europe and UK.

Michael's additional activities include appointments as a Chief Examiner for Professional institutions, External Examiner for Universities, Moderator for the UK Business and Technical Education Council and he is a member of the Chartered Institute of Purchasing & Supply's Professional Standards Board.

Michael is a registered purchasing and supply management specialist with the United Nations and has been published widely in appropriate professional journals.

Logistics:
an Integrated Approach

Michael R. Quayle

TUDOR

© Michael Quayle 1993

First published in Great Britain by Tudor Business
Publishing Limited. Sole distributors worldwide,
Hodder and Stoughton (Publishers) Ltd, Mill Road,
Dunton Green, Sevenoaks, Kent, TN13 2XX.

British Library Cataloguing in Publication Data

Quayle Michael
    Logistics:Integrated Approach
    I. Title
    658.7

ISBN 1–872807–60–7

Graphics by K. Doughty

Typeset by Deltatype Ltd, Ellesmere Port, Cheshire
Printed and Bound in Great Britain by
Athenaeum Press Ltd, Newcastle upon Tyne.

Contents

Equipment: degrees of automation; applications of robotics; static and mobile equipment.

Surplus, scrap and obsolescent stocks; treatment and disposal.

Modes; alternative methods of transportation; performance variables.

Road, rail, air and sea transport: optimisation; roll on/roll off arrangements.

Import/Export documentation and procedures.

Management considerations: procurement of transport services; purchase, lease and hire options; licensing; traffic regulation; transport laws; scheduling and planning and utilisation, containerisation; control and monitoring of costs; personnel; health and safety; COSHH regulations.

Despatch and delivery; resource planning; distribution channels; distribution audits; budgetary control; co-ordination.

Corporate planning; purchasing planning and strategies; corporate and environmental factors; SWOT; Gap Analysis; flexibility.

Structure; definition and purpose; centralisation and decentralisation in complex organisations; purchasing consortia; policy issues.

Directing the function; staff; resources; job description, motivation, professional and supervisory staff.

Management and implementation of change; impact of change on people and jobs; effect on performance; scope for more creative work and decision making.

Introduction

This book is about decision making and actions which determine whether an enterprise excels, survives, or dies. This process is called "logistics management". The job of logistics managers is to make the best use of an organisations resources in a changing environment.

Because this book focuses on top-level decisions, you may have a problem with the relevance of the subject matter for your short-term career interests. But several reasons can be given for why the knowledge you can gain in the study of logistics management is practical and useful for your early career stages:

You are likely to perform better in your function, regardless of your level in the organisation if you know the direction in which the organisation is going. As the manager of a sub-unit, you would like to know how what you do fits into the broader picture. If you know how your function contributes, you should be able to do a better job of helping the organisation reach its objectives. If your unit is successful and higher level managers realise how you contributed to this success, this will reflect positively on you. Furthermore, lower-level units often interpret strategies and policies set at higher levels. If you understand why those were established, you can implement them more effectively. Finally, if you understand how your job relates to others in the organisation, you will be in a better position to effectively work with peers when co-operation is called for and compete for resources when the time comes.

In your study of the logistics management process you will begin to identify factors which may lead to significant changes in the organisation. Some of these strategic changes could be positive or negative to you personally. For instance, a major divestiture could eliminate your unit! Or a new market thrust or product development could make your unit more critical for organisational performance. If you understand what factors may be pushing the organisation in certain directions and how your job fits in, you might decide to change or keep your job. Foresight about critical organisation changes can be a real asset to your career.

If you are aware of the strategies, values, and objectives of higher-level managers, you are in a better position to assess the likelihood of acceptance of proposals you might make. As you consider offering your suggestions, tying the reasons to your assessment of the interest of higher-level managers is likely to enhance their acceptance and your visibility.

Thus I believe that an understanding of how and why logistics decisions are made can be helpful to you in terms of securing resources beneficial to your sub-unit, improving your job performance, and enhancing your career development. This book's purpose is to help you make sense of the logistics management process while you are a first-line manager or a middle manager. It is also designed to help prepare you become a successful top manager. Its goal is to show you that if you understand the business policy and logistics management process before you get to the top, you become a more effective manager.

The book also is designed to fulfill a teaching function in schools of business management, and administration. The material is designed to help you integrate the functional tools you have learned. These include the analytical tools of physical distribution, marketing research, logistics, and purchasing management. All these provide help in analysing business problems. This book and the materials in it provide you with an opportunity to learn when to use which tools and how to deal with trade-offs when you cannot maximise the results or preferences of all the functional areas simultaneously.

More importantly – enjoy it!

I would like to acknowledge the invaluable assistance of my many colleagues in the logistics field and Sharon Scott for her priceless secretarial support.

MRQ. 1993

Chapter 1

Developments in Logistics

Logistics into the Future

Logistics is changing at a rapid and accelerating rate. It is changing for two sets of reasons.

The first set is the pressure for change arising from managerial and technical development from within the logistics system itself. These include:

- The increased speed and intelligence of computing systems for the control of the information flows in logistics. This has given rise to what is called "Time Compression" in logistics. High speed computing and data transmission can transmit and react to user demand almost instantaneously over any distance.

  Distributed data terminals coupled with "Real Time" data processing makes logistics planning and control both more flexible and more accurate. When this is the case "Intelligence" can replace "Investment", for example, a computer system which can effectively plan inventory needs will reduce the necessity for holding contingency inventory levels. "Just-in-Time" logistics is also dependent on fast data handling systems so that assets deployment outcomes can be improved.

- The availability of flexible computer facilities enables logistics companies to engage in "Dynamic Simulation" of problems. There are many variables in the majority of logistics problems. Real time interactive computer systems enable logistics undertakings to explore a variety of inventory level, transport mode warehouse location and other problems. This increases the accuracy of logistics decisions.

- Lastly, the realisation of the systems nature of logistics and of the potential importance of "Trade offs" within the total system. These trade offs require an awareness of total cost measurement and sophisticated management accounting.

However, all these pressures for change will only take root with a sophisticated management process and, in particular, a willingness to manage across functional barriers in the organisation to meet particular organisational goals. This is sometimes described as a "Missions" approach. The key to the introduction of this managerial culture in organisations lies in a strategic management informed on logistics issues.

The second set of pressures for change comes from the wider economy. Again, these include three factors:

- Trends in the economy suggest a future uncertainty in the growth of consumer markets. This will require manufacturing and retail organisations to deal with markets which may vary in size at fairly shortening notice. The basis of effective strategies in this context must be effective flexible logistics.
- Market structures are also changing. There is increasing fragmentation and specialisation in markets and a growth in specialising retailing. This puts pressure both on the marketing and, in turn, the logistics functions.
- Life cycles for products are also shorting with more selective and critical customers. As a result, logistics systems are necessary to promote shorter product lead-times and faster and more flexible distribution provisions.
- In the production function, a move is occurring away from mass production towards flexible manufacturing systems (FMS). These systems enable a company to switch production quickly from one product to another. In the marketing function a variety of changes in distribution channels, for example, the growth in large out of town supermarkets has led to a concentration of buying power and an emphasis on improved distribution services levels, especially "Just-in-Time" delivery. Producers and retailers are sharing information systems to promote "Just-in-Time" delivery.
- Competitive pressures in markets are also growing. In static markets competition becomes more aggressive. The growth in international marketing has made such aggression more acute. This, in turn, places pressure on logistics systems to support

production and marketing initiatives. It is especially true since so much competition, in both consumer and industrial goods is now fought on dimensions of customer service.

Logistics Education

Logistics has been an important feature of industrial and economic life for many years, but it is only in the relatively recent past that it has been recognised as a major function in its own right. Distribution and logistics activities make extensive use of the human and natural resources which affect a national economy. Recent studies have attempted to estimate the impact of distribution and logistics on economic life.

One such study indicated that about 30 per cent of the working population in the UK is associated with work related to physical distribution. Another study estimated that up to 40 per cent of the UK gross domestic product was spent on distribution and logistics activities. A further study has indicated that, using a fairly broad definition of distribution, the associated costs in the UK were approximately 17 per cent of company sales revenue.

Need for Education and Training

It is now accepted by both the academic and the business world that there is a need to adopt a more formal and global view of the many different logistics and distribution-related functions. The appreciation of the scope and importance of distribution, especially with respect to new technology, has led to a more scientific approach being adopted toward the subject and to a recognition of the importance of managing the new technology and the changes that it can bring about. This approach is aimed at the individual sub-systems but especially at the overall concepts of the distribution and logistics function.

One of the major features of logistics in recent years has been the speed with which the industry has advanced. Technology has developed, demanding a good knowledge of both physical and information technology, and the jobs span a much greater area of responsibility, requiring a good overall logistics perspective together with the traditional demands for management and communication skills.

Logistics is therefore now recognised as being a vital part of the business and economy of a country. In recent years in the UK, for example, the industry has set out to develop a distinct professionalism to reflect this new found importance. In doing this, the industry has recognised the need for established career structures and good education and training programmes.

Lately there has been a number of initiatives to provide education and training opportunities for those seeking to develop their career in distribution and logistics. These opportunities include:

- Correspondence courses
- Diploma and first degree courses
- HND in Distribution
- Higher degrees – most notably Masters degrees

A New Concept in Logistics Education

How does the busy distribution manager keep up-to-date with new ideas in a rapidly changing environment? How can he/she learn about new techniques and how to apply them? How can he/she do this whilst also obtaining a recognised educational qualification? One way is to embark on an advanced course of study which provides relevant education and training without significant periods away from the workplace. It is for this purpose that the Executive Masters Degrees which have programmes in Distribution and Logistics have been set up.

Relevance of Part-Time Study

The programmes are designed to cater for distribution managers and executives, enabling them to continue in a full-time job whilst participating in postgraduate education. For young graduates who are just beginning their careers, the course provides an opportunity to receive a solid grounding in all major aspects concerning Distribution and Logistics. For more mature staff who have already spent some years in industry or commerce, the course allows them to consolidate their existing knowledge, update themselves in the latest concepts and techniques in a more formal environment and broaden their experience.

This initiative is aimed at enabling companies to pursue an active management training programme in Distribution and Logistics which also provides an internationally recognised postgraduate qualification.

There are opportunities for companies to attract and keep high quality distribution staff by using the Executive Masters Degrees to enhance their own management training course.

Companies will also be attracted by the work-based content of the programme. In the second year the major input to the course is a company-based thesis, which will be of immediate relevance to the company.

Programme Outline

The courses are based on the core elements of Distribution and Logistics, covering logistics strategy, distribution system design, the planning and management of transport and warehousing operations and the design of appropriate operational systems. Emphasis is given to the impact of information technology and the development and use of distribution information systems and planning tools.

Relevant analytical and management techniques and methods are covered, such as modelling techniques, statistics, operational research, management accounting, materials and inventory management, human resource management and the interface between law and business activity. Time is also given to developing personal effectiveness and communication skills.

A selection of options and electives are available to allow participants to study particular aspects in greater depth, or to broaden their scope by selecting new topics.

Typical areas of specialisation include:

- Distribution Strategy and Planning
- Distribution and Transport Management
- Warehousing and Materials Handling Systems
- Distribution Information Systems
- Information Technology and Logistics
- Logistics System Design
- Materials Management
- Advanced Warehouse Design
- Supply Chain Management

The course programme has been structured to fit within a full-time working environment. Attendance in the first year consists of long weekends, single days and a summer school. Of necessity the teaching programme is intense and requires a full and active commitment. A certain amount of reading and support work will be undertaken on a homestudy basis.

Year two, which is concentrated on a company-based thesis, requires some work days as well as sessions held at the individual's work place with a tutor for the planning, discussion and review of the individual project.

What sort of manager from what type of organisation typically participates in a course of this nature? Some useful facts are summarised below, based on those who are currently undertaking the course:

- Ages range from 23 to 48 years, with the average at 34.
- Qualifications vary from those with some type of diploma (plus many years of relevant management experience) to others with a First at degree level.
- Positions vary from Distribution Analyst to Distribution Director, and include a number of different job titles – Distribution Development Manager, European Logistics Manager, Distribution Consultant, General Manager – Quality Control, Distribution Information Systems Manager, Distribution Services Director.
- Different industrial sectors and interests are well represented; there are manufacturers, retailers and third party companies. Industries represented include brewery, clothing, pharmaceuticals, leisure, telecommunications and food.

The foregoing demonstrates the importance of logistics education and its overdue recognition in the academic world.

Professional Competence – Food For Thought!

It is a sad fact that the level of understanding in the field of materials management is often low or not well balanced across the whole purchasing, production control spectrum. It is more worrying that we do not have a complete common yardstick by which to recognise the limited numbers of professional practitioners.

The concept of effective materials management is vitally important. Without effective materials management a business which markets final products and which is supported by excellent manufacturing facilities and purchasing skills cannot survive. The impact of materials management on business performance and cost controls is well understood. How can we expect professional performance if we don't measure capability and provide the help to obtain it?

We have internationally recognised professional and technical standards to declare the ability and potential of accountants, engineers, metallurgists and even our shop floor workers. Until now, materials management staff have been handicapped, only half equipped as it were. Admittedly the purchasing side of their professional responsibilities has been well supported by the long established and readily accessible Chartered Institute of Purchasing and Supply (CIPS) Foundation and Professional level education programmes, taught in so many locations in the UK and overseas.

Undeniably however, Materials Directors and other senior management are so right when they bemoan the absence of equally sound teaching for the other key aspect of materials management – Production and Inventory Control.

The need has long existed for education of similar standing, a well structured modern syllabus, accompanied by recognised levels of accreditation of successful students. Unfortunately, most practitioners are trained by "sitting with Nellie" or by reading the manuals provided with the new computer system. It doesn't help having the best tools if the understanding is weak. Indeed it can be positively dangerous.

Chapter 2

Definitions and Concepts of Logistics

The Role of Logistics in Profitable Companies

With major changes occurring in industry, the perception of logistics in executive offices has failed to evolve in concert, principally due to continual changes in logistics terminology. Nevertheless, business executives are increasingly questioning the logistics potential for contributing to overall profitability. These questions are typified by the following comment from a chief executive of a leading company:

> . . . I now know what logistics can do to save money. Tell me what it can do to improve my profits, to increase my share of the market, to improve my cash flow, to open new territories, to introduce new products, and to get the stockholders and board of directors off my back . . .

Notice that the chief executive asks if logistics can do anything important for profitability, and if so, what? Logistics must make this profitability contribution if it is to expand its role in the company.

Expenditure on purchasing goods and services in a company may account for between 30–75% of total costs. Expenditure on storing and distributing materials may absorb a further 10–20% of total costs.

Using some very different benchmarks, stock as a proportion of total funds employed can account for anything between 30% and 50%. Total distribution costs expressed as a % of sales, range from 9% (Industrial Manufacturing) to 34% (Wholesale Consumer Goods).

The effective sourcing of material (embracing raw materials, components, assemblies and finished goods), and the subsequent management of that material through a production or value-adding process and on to the end customer, is therefore critical to the success of most businesses. Moreover, these activities have a major impact on some of the main strategic problems facing many businesses today. Such problems will often include:–

- How to reduce costs and best add value to products and services.
- How to sustain the highest quality standards.
- How to improve customer service.
- How to adapt to ever increasing environmental pressures.

Logistics management is a powerful means of resolving these problems. Understanding and management of the logistics supply chain is critical to any company's drive to improve productivity and profitability.

What is Logistics?

The underlying philosophy of logistics management is straightforward and can be defined alternatively as:

- Logistics is the process which seeks to provide for the management and co-ordination of all activities within the supply chain from sourcing and acquisition, through production where appropriate, and through distribution channels to the customer. The goal of logistics is the creation of competitive advantage through the simultaneous achievement of high customer service levels, optimum investment and value for money.
- The detailed organisation and implementation of a plan or operation.
- A term that was originally used in the military sphere to describe the organising and moving of troops and equipment. It is now applied to any detailed planning process in an organisation which entails the distribution or redistribution of resources.

Logistics concepts invoke a strategic view of thinking which seeks to account for all links in the flow of materials and related information in a flexible but integrated manner so that they perform in unison to achieve an overall optimum result for the business. Such a view is shown in diagrammatic form in **Fig. 1**.

Logistics is not simply a vogue word for Supply Chain Management, which evolved as an ideal rather than a management function, or Materials Management which is often narrower in scope. Logistics does indeed embrace these management philosophies; and does so without difficulty. Just as Marketing grew in the 1960's to encompass

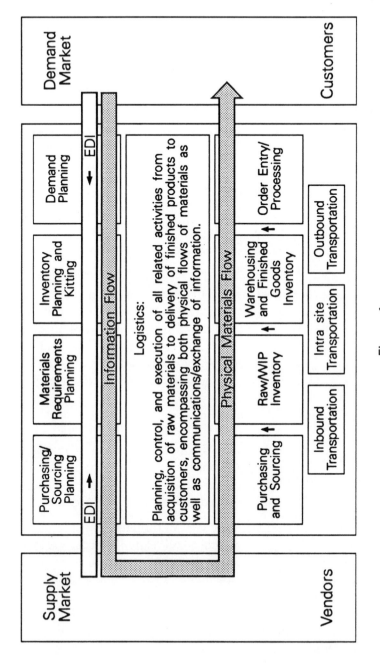

Figure 1.
View of Logistics
(Source: C. D. Wareham)

sales, retailing, advertising, customer relations, product design, market research and in so doing encouraged an overview which then revolutionised the approach to serving the customer so logistics has evolved to encourage a similar integration of materials-related functions. Moreover, what is perhaps more important, the logistics approach recognises the importance of those functions both individually and collectively and the need to manage then in totality.

Logistics management co-ordinates and integrates all of the materials-based functions inherent in planning and forecasting, manufacturing or servicing and processing a product, and its distribution:–

- The aim is to enable businesses to keep ahead of market changes where quality, price, response time and service are crucial factors.
- The goal is to link the market place and its distribution channels to the procurement and manufacturing operations in such a way that competitive advantage can be achieved and maintained.
- The benefits accrue in cost reduction, sales generation, much improved service levels, and increased profitability.

The Logistics Mix

The business functions which fall within the scope of logistics management are included in what is commonly known as the logistics mix:–

Planning and Marketing Strategy – the major influences of design and marketing on materials requirements and distribution requirements.

Purchasing – source research and selection, negotiation, building supplier partnership programmes.

Production Planning – plant capacity, location and layout, scheduling, manufacturing resource planning, and the control and support of work in progress.

Storage and Materials Handling – the handling and storage of goods, utilisation and packaging.

Inventory Management – control over inventories, sustaining minimum practical stock levels, minimising holding costs, wastage and obsolescence.

Warehouses and Stores – location, capacity, mix and operation.

Transport – mode decisions, scheduling, routing and operation.

Customer Service – demand forecasting, service levels, order processing, parts/service support, and aftermarket operations.

Technical Support – the provision and management of the systems needed to support these activities.

Not all of the elements in this mix will necessarily coincide with all business interests. The logistics concept however, actively concentrates on those elements which do. Again, as examples – for the retailer or FMCG (Fast Moving Consumer Goods) distribution, Sourcing and Distribution are likely to be the key elements. For the manufacturer, Purchasing and Production Planning are naturally more dominant.

Rarely will all of these elements be of equal importance to a business, but depending on its characteristics a number may be identified as having a major impact on the bottom-line, as well as having a critical inter-relationship which requires skilful management to secure the most profitable results:–

Market strategy and product design:– in combination determine the nature, volume and timing of demand to be met by the purchasing operation. Additionally Marketing and Engineering functions can greatly influence the extent to which the product to be procured or manufactured is "logistically friendly".

Materials management:– embraces all aspects of materials flow from determination of requirements and capacity planning through purchasing, source search and selection, and scheduling – the latter including the planning and control of production processes, applicable most commonly when manufacturing is central to the business. Tools employed to achieve effective planning and execution may include Manufacturing Resource Planning (MRPII), Just in Time (JIT – ie, the elimination of waste) and Optimised Production Technology (OPT), as appropriate to the individual needs of the business.

Inventory Management:– (often seen as part of material management in manufacturing enterprises) – determination of stocking policy to ensure continuity of suppliers with minimum investment costs – including the effective control and execution of that policy.

Storage and Materials Handling:– covers the safe, secure and disciplined handling of materials as initial receipts, as parts awaiting processing, as Work in Progress during manufacture, and subsequently as finished product. Embraces packaging design, unitisation and the full range of simple to sophisticated aids to storage.

Distribution:– includes warehousing and both inbound and out-bound transportation: all strongly influenced by demands for higher levels of customer service, JIT requirements and the evolution of Contract

Distribution. With an estimated 500,000 vehicles dedicated to freight movement in the UK alone, Distribution is under increasing pressure for greater control on environmental grounds.

The Scope of Logistics

The basic nature of business is that it procures or buys something, whether goods or information: changes its form in some way which adds value; and then sells a product or service onto someone else. In manufacturing industries in particular, this sequence may occur a number of times:

Inbound Logistics		*Core Business*		*Outbound Logistics*
Raw materials	–	process or refine	–	supply others
Refined materials	–	manufacture	–	components/ assemblies
Components	–	assemble	–	finished product
Finished goods	–	distribute	–	customer

At a similar, albeit oversimplified level, within a manufacturing or processing organisation we can identify three basic operations:

- Change of form – Production or Process
- Change of ownership – Marketing or internal transfer
- Change of time and place – Logistics

But these three operations are not clear cut and do not stand alone. Taking over-packaging as an example of a process. It does not strictly change either the form of the product or its time and place, but rather its outward appearance. Packaging must, of course, be designed with a change of ownership in mind – ie unitisation to suit an industrial customer's needs, or display packaging for marketing. It must also be designed for movement – ie protection against damage, ease of handling or for security in transit. However, which requirements takes priority not only has a major influence on the costs of the packaging but also distribution costs. There are therefore, some apparently discrete, activities which can be influenced by a number of individual functions or management areas. The logistics concept aims to capture and to analyse such activities.[1]

Logistics an Integrative Process?

The organisational emphasis of traditional business is normally on vertical line management within individual functions. Such a framework actively promotes sub-optimisation as many of the trade off opportunities outlined above are not visible. It is essential to highlight the pattern of materials and information flows and their interdependence. An example of the process of integration is shown in Figure 2.

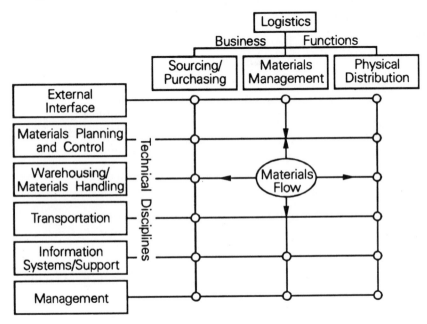

Figure 2.
The Process of Integration

Each of these business functions is discussed in later Chapters of this book with an emphasis on the need for integration as part of the logistics process.

The role of logistics in today's and tomorrow's profitable companies will change as the value of products changes, and also as the value that buyers or customers ascribe to product changes. This statement represents a new concept for many logistics managers, who were trained in transportation, warehousing, and other such functions to conduct their activities based on least-cost or other hard measure priorities. Modern logistics managers must find innovative ways to help their companies improve profits, increase market share, improve cash flow, open new territories and introduce new products. However, logistics neither creates demand nor product. Logistics is the organisation that responds to demands, and creates a bridge between that demand and those who supply it. A professional and integrative approach is clearly needed!

Notes and References

1. Pagnosis, W.E., *Moving Mountains: Lessons in Leadership and Logistics from the Gulf War*, Harvard Business School, 1982.

The author acknowledges the kind permission granted by Mr C. D. Wareham for the use of material from his publication, *Competitive Logistics*, IPS, 1991.

Chapter 3

Provisioning and Inventory Control

Provisioning

A necessary pre-requisite to deciding upon provisioning and stock replenishment policies, is to encode and classify stock.

Some 20% of stock items account for 80% of the value of stock held, therefore if you strictly control stocks of these items, you are controlling the greater part of stock values. Classification enables these items and the remaining 80% of stock to be easily identified.

A system of reduction and the standardisation of stock items will reduce the number of individual items carried in stock, and enable stock control to be more effective.

First consider what the term provisioning means, so that you have a clear definition in your mind. It is the determination of when to order and how much to order so that stockholding may be kept in line with Management Policy.

The responsibility for provisioning will fall on different departments, depending on the size of organisation and the class of stock. In small organisations provisioning will be carried out by the storekeeper who will raise requisitions against minimum or re-order levels, any items not stocked being requisitioned by the user's department. As size increases so the responsibility moves to Stock Control, Production Control or Planning Departments, until you find separate provisioning sections in the largest organisations.

It is impossible to generalise on where the provisioning function will fall in the overall structure. However, in one class of stock, it will certainly be the responsibility of the Stock Controller, this class being those items shown on a General Stock List. A General Stock List shows those items which will be held in stock for common use and not for specific contracts. Based on a policy of this nature, the responsibility for provisioning must be with the Stores Manager, through his Stock control and Provisioning staff.

General Stock Items

The two main points relating to provisioning are – "when to order" and "how much to order."
　　When to order:

- When stocks fall to re-order levels.
- When an additional forward load has been advised.

　　How much to order:

Ordering Quantities

There are five main considerations to remember when arriving at an order quantity and these are the basis of any formulae.

The Accuracy of Forecasts

This will be of prime importance and every effort should be made to check as the period of a forecast passes, to compare actual usage with the estimated usage. Where differences occur some action is required to adjust forecasts in order to increase the accuracy of these. An important point to keep in mind is that as the period of the forecast increases, so does the probability of error, a point which is obvious but often forgotten. Where long term contracts are placed, close attention must be given to the rate of call-off as alterations are not always easy to arrange, particularly in the short term. Therefore, if the rate is insufficient it may well be two or three months before an increased rate can be obtained or longer if further production equipment is necessary.

Storage Space

It is essential that all items provisioned have suitable storage facilities on receipt, bearing in mind that overflow may have to be housed by an outside warehouse, for which, rent will be payable. The main point to bear in mind is that any such extra facilities should be known in advance from careful consideration of the intake, and not be discovered when goods are left outside because there is no room in the storehouse.

Cost of Storage

The cost of storage is calculated over a year and averaged to give a nominal value as a percentage of value of each item. It does not necessarily represent the true cost of stocking a particular item.

Cost of Ordering

The cost of ordering is calculated over a year and averaged to give a nominal value of ordering each item; the cost encompasses enquiry, proposal, evaluation and order placement.

Acquisition Cost

The acquisition cost is the cost of storage plus the cost of ordering, and, if you consider this statement, you will appreciate that there is a balance between frequent ordering and high stockholding. The following examples show both this, and the relevance of the value of the item.

Commodity X

Purchase Price	–	10p each
Rate of Use	–	4 per week
Cost of Storage	–	15%
Cost of Placing Orders	–	£1 each

	Ordering every week	*Ordering one year's stock*
Purchase price	£20.80	£20.80
Cost of Storage	NIL	£ 3.12
Cost of Ordering	£52.00	£ 1.00
Total	£72.80	£24.92
= Price Each	35p	12p

Commodity Y

Purchase Price	–	£20
Rate of Use	–	4 per week
Cost of Storage	–	15%
Cost of Placing Orders	–	£1 each

Purchase price	£4160.00	£4160.00
Cost of Storage	NIL	£ 624.00
Cost of Ordering	£ 52.00	£ 1.00
Total	£4212.00	£4785.00
= Price Each	£20.25	£23.00

These examples demonstrate that the higher the unit purchase price becomes, the lower the relevance of the ordering cost. They also demonstrate that there is a relationship between the cost of storage and the cost of ordering.

Items not contained in the General Stock List

There are still two questions which provide the key, how much to buy and when. Consider these two problems separately.

- The quantity of stock to be purchased must be governed by the programme laid down for production of the finished items, usually a function of top management.
- The time at which the purchase should be made must be governed by the laid down programme, but, there is room here for local initiative to decide when to purchase, ensuring that the material arrives by the required date.

Responsibility for Provisioning

In considering items not on the General Stock List the responsibility cannot rest with the Stores Manager. The opening paragraphs of this chapter provide some ideas as to where the responsibility may fall.

Methods of Provisioning

The Provisioning Department, or user if the item required is not a production material, raises a Purchase Requisition for the requirement. This requisition may take several forms. It will, however, contain the following information:

- Code number (where these are used.)
- Quantity – in standard unit of issue or accounting.

- Description – where this is not supported by a code number it must contain all the information necessary for purchase. It may be dispensed with when code numbers are in use and the description inserted at a later date.
- Standard Price – where these are in use, again this may be inserted at a later date.
- Suggest Suppliers – this may be left blank or completed for special items to assist the Purchasing Department.
- Job or Contact Number – showing which Works Order the material is for.
- Date required.
- Delivery address – this will be within the organisation and indicates where the goods should be routed after inspection.
- An authorised signature.

There may be other information required, depending on the needs of a particular organisation.

The completed requisition is then sent to the Stores Manager so that he or she can check that this item is not held in Stores, he or she may also keep a record of recurring items with the object of putting them on General Stock or offer an alternative. After this check it is passed to the Purchasing Department for action.

The Provisioning Department makes out planning sheets for each assembly, giving details of material requirements. These will show the quantity of an item per unit, which has to be extended for a total requirement. In many instances Parts Lists are used for this purpose. These provisioning sheets are sent to Stock Control, who action those items which are held in Stores and forward the remaining items to the Purchasing Department for action. It may well be that you will find a situation where the Stores Provisioning Section do not pass on the planning sheets, but forward a purchase requisition for action. There is a great disadvantage to this system where one item is used in more than one sub-assembly, as all the requirements will not appear on one sheet.

The Provisioning Department issues a complete list of parts, or Bill of Materials, to Stores who action this in the same manner as a planning sheet. This gets around the problem of parts appearing in different sub-assemblies.

A computer issues a Purchase Requisition for those items not on General Stock and a Stores Requisition for items on General Stock. This is a very fast operation and has the advantage of being able to present the information in the most useful manner, for example presenting items in Part Number, Supplier or Unit Order.

An important point to keep in mind is the fact that although the responsibility for provisioning does not rest with Stores, all the items may require storage prior to use and therefore all Purchase Regulation activities may be carried out by this Department.

There are several classes of goods which will be provisioned directly from the User Department to Purchasing, Stores being advised of their future receipt by a copy of the Purchase Order. The following are typical:

- Plant and Machinery
- Office equipment and furniture
- Special items for the Maintenance Department
- Vehicles

A great deal of the information on which provisioning is based, relies on forecasting. Because of this it is desirable to consider some aspects of the foregoing techniques used. An outline of the main foregoing techniques is given below however, bear in mind that they are relevant to many aspects of Management and not only to Stores and Inventory Control.

- *Graphs* – You will find many examples of graphs used to illustrate situations where there are two variables. It is of course possible to present the historical data graphically and then project the future trend by draughting. This is useful to predict future trends in a general manner but not satisfactory for details forecasting. As an example the forecasting of next year's financial needs could not be arrived at by this method, but the trend of future capital requirements in the succeeding years could be.
- *Exponential Smoothing* – This is a technique where a weighting factor is incorporated in the average demand. The weighting factor is known as alpha, written α, with a value between 0 and 1. The basic equation arrived at is:–

New Average Demand = D + $(1 - \alpha)$ Old Average Demand

D = the actual demand for the most recent period

The use of this equation gives emphasis to the latest actual demand figures.

- *Forecast Error* – Extending the principle in paragraph 2 the following equation is used:–

$$\text{New Average Forecast Error} = \frac{\text{Current Error} + (1 - \alpha)}{\text{Old Average Forecast Error}}$$

This Forecast error is important when using statistical methods for determining future requirements, because it will influence the setting of minimum stock levels. The higher the forecast error, the higher the minimum stock will be for safety reasons.

- *Critical Path Analysis* – This technique is also known by various other terms such as PERT and is used to forecast accurately time scales for large projects, usually in the construction industry. The following are the basic principles.
  – The whole project is listed as a series of events.
  – Each event is then examined to ascertain the exact time required to arrive at that event. These are known as Activities.
  – All the events are then placed in an order of happening that appears to be the optimum solution.
  – The events are then connected by the activities giving an overall time for completion.
  – Include as many of the activities that can be performed at the same time. Only those which have to follow a sequence form the critical path. Alternatively those activities which have the longest time requirements may form the critical path leaving those which do not require the full time available with a "float".
  – The activities can then be shown graphically with duration shown for each activity.

  Although used largely for construction projects this technique can be used in storehouses to analyse activities such as stocktaking or issues against schedules.

- *Bar Charts or Gantt Charts* – This is the pictorial display of a Critical Path Analysis in chart form. Taking the example above the chart would show the following.

  This type of display can provide a more useful means of showing the layout of activities and can be readily used as a progress chart by the use of markers showing work complete.[2]

The success of CPA relies on accurately laying down the activities and the appropriate times: it will be no more accurate than these.

All of these techniques have one feature in common, that is: Control!

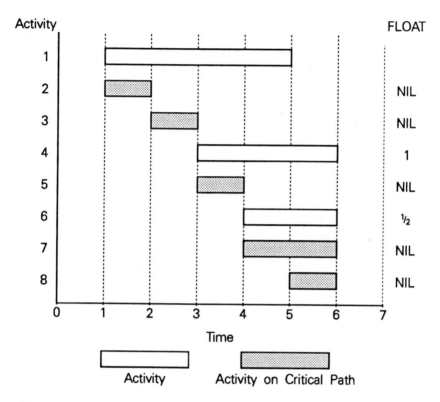

Figure 4.3
Bar or Gantt Chart incorporating Critical Path Analysis

Cyclical Provisioning

There is one method of ascertaining "when to order", which has not yet been covered, namely Cyclical Provisioning. Where items of a similar nature are in constant use. There is likely to be a constant flow of Purchase Requisitions resulting, for many instances, in uneconomic purchasing. This can be overcome by provisioning the whole group of items at the same time at regular intervals such as one week, one month, every six months or possibly once a-year.

The following classes of items are typical examples of those suitable for this type of exercise:

- Small tools – drills, tool bits, soldering iron bits.
- Fastenings – nuts, bolts, screws and washers.
- Toilet items – soap, towels, toilet paper, disinfectant; items which can often be purchased from one source to advantage.

Although provisioning of this nature is performed regularly, there must be protection against Stock running out. To do this minimum levels are set and urgent action taken if stocks fall to this level, there must also be a maximum to prevent overstocking.

The Provisioning of Matching Items

In varying the principle of Cyclical Provisioning there is one aspect that is often neglected, an appreciation of the need for a matching part, for example, the provisioning of a bolt without a matching nut or washer. Although this is not an easy problem to solve, attention can be given to lessen the likelihood of a stock imbalance, marking Stock Records to bring matching items to the notice of the Provisioning Clerk. This will also lessen the danger of an item being deleted from the General Stock List without actioning the mating item.

There is one danger in this approach that you may recognise, namely that a matching part may be used for several different functions. Going back to the example of a nut and bolt, the nut will almost certainly be used on several bolts of varying length.

The use of computers can greatly facilitate the provisioning activity, particularly where mathematical formulae are used. This is an operation which is carried out at great speed. A computer also has a good memory and can rapidly assemble and compare data, a useful asset when provisioning matching parts.

Automatic Replenishment

This is an adaptation of the old "two bin" method of provisioning, when the storekeeper had two bins for an item. When both were full, it represented maximum stock, when one was empty this represented re-order level.

Today under automatic replenishment methods, figures represent-ing these levels are indicated on the stock record, and when they are reached the correct action is automatically set in operation. In practice this would be built into the computer programme, and the computer will print out a recommendation for action, or a purchase order if it is a routine item. Appropriate purchasing information is also programmed.

The Use of Computers

The use of advanced electronic equipment is becoming widespread in many fields. The use of computers is leading, and is particularly prevalent in the accounting function coupled with Management Statistics. Gradually the use of computers is extending into many activities – airline bookings, railway timetables and stock control are typical examples that make use of a special quality possessed by this equipment.

That special quality is memory, from which the machine can draw information and make decisions. Any decisions made will only be as accurate as the information and instructions given to the machine but they will maintain this accuracy when repeated. Remember, a computer can make decisions!

The Objectives of an Inventory Control System

Whatever decisions have been made on stockholding it is essential that there is enough capital to back up policy. Because this capital will be tied up in stores, management will want this money to provide the maximum return or use. Consider the following points which can affect efficiency:

Efficient Control by Stores

- There is no need to stock large quantities of goods which are available at short notice. It may be possible to avoid any stockholding if stocks are under review constantly.
- Stores can ensure that any supplies received are directed to the location required and not routed for use on another project. You should note, however, that Stores cannot ensure that an item is used for a particular job and that Stores should forward items as directed by a responsible authority in the user department.

- Any materials which are lost because of their perishable or fragile nature or through theft, represent capital which has been expended to no purpose.
- A close watch on the rate of turnover can ensure that the minimum of working capital is required to finance stockholding.

How Controls are Exercised

- The basis of control is the setting of standards in stock levels, receipts, issues and rates of turnover. These standards are set in relation to a known programme. By regularly reviewing actual performance against the present standards, the success of the laid-down programme can be assessed. The system for setting standards must be flexible to allow for correction after each check.

- Various classes of items should be treated separately showing any variations that indicate that the inventory is out of balance. For example, the value of sheet steel held in stock has increased by 20%, but the value of paint used for finishing it has dropped 10%. This is worth investigation.

- Often, when studying the standards for various classes of goods, it will be found that certain of them account for the bulk of the money held in stock. These should be given special attention to ensure that they have a regular rate of turnover. This does not mean that other classes should be neglected, however.

There is one important point to be remembered: constant checks should produce some action when a departure from the plan is found. Remember, the ability of the organisation to control such activities can be a measurement of the success of the original budget or plan. For this reason the budget must be flexible.

Why Have Controls?

Stock values have to be ascertained for the purposes of budgetary control, financial accounting and confirmation that items are priced correctly when issued.

This is done from stock records or a physical check of stock or, more probably, from a combination of the two. You must remember that those materials which have not been charged out, but which have been physically issued, should be included in the evaluation. Typical examples are materials which have been sent to a site and free issue materials sent to suppliers. These are sometimes missed.

When a stock valuation has been arrived at for the various classes of stock, possibly covering different storehouses, the Inventory Control Account is checked to see if the balances agree. However, discrepancies arise, even in the best of organisations, for any of the following reasons:–

- Goods received notes and issue notes have been incorrectly priced and consequently entered at an incorrect value on stores or accounts records.
- Prices for issues have been made against standard costs.
- Prices for issues have been approximated to the nearest selected monetary unit, e.g. two decimal places. This often occurs where items are purchased at a price per 100 or 1,000 and the price of each unit does not coincide with a unit of money.
- Through an incorrect posting on a stock record (which will cause two errors) e.g. through a posting not being entered on any stock record; through incorrect reading of code numbers.
- When variations found during stock checks are not entered on records.
- Incorrect arithmetic causing the balances to be entered wrongly.
- Errors made during any copying of the reports.

When you consider the above points, discrepancies are bound to occur. If this is so, why bother to check them? You should think about this before going on.

When discrepancies occur the Inventory Control Account has to be adjusted. This is done by a stock valuation adjustment entry, and a debit or credit note made to the balance. This entry has, of course, to be verified and agreed by the accounts department who will usually keep a separate subsidiary account for these entries.

The Physical Aspect of Inventory Control

Since we are considering the physical aspect of inventory control it will be useful to restate the main purpose of this, which is, to provide user departments with materials as and when they are required whilst making the most economic use of working capital and minimising storage costs.

The first problem to be considered when engaging in inventory control is deciding what items should be stocked. The following are some of the factors affecting this choice:–

- Delivery – rate of usage
- Delivery – uncertainty
- Bulk purchasing
- Bulk manufacturing
- Market price fluctuations
- Insurance
- Work in progress
- Finished units

The following are some of the factors influencing the extent of stockholding:–

- Operational needs
- Lead times
- Capital
- Cost of storage
- Insurance

There are two means by which the consequent inventory levels can be maintained. These are:–

Regulating Input

Input can be regulated by advice to Purchasing who can then contract outside suppliers to increase supplies. If supplies are obtained through internal sources similar action can be taken by liaison with the Production Control Department.

Time is an important aspect of this control for the measures regulating output are seldom instantaneous. This means that control levels must make allowances for changes in input to have effect.

Regulating Issue

This is not an easy exercise to carry out because the main function of Stores is to provide a service: issues must be made to the requirements of the users. Regulating input usually takes time to have effect and the same is true of issues, although some regulation of daily issues is desirable. Some control of issue can be made by consultation with Production Control and any issues against schedules should be reviewed.

Method of Inventory Control

Visual

Here stock levels are controlled by physically separating stock so that a remainder may be isolated. This can be done by:–

- Partitioning a bin
- Tying a quantity of stock with tape
- Keeping a separate bin

When a storekeeper has to break into this separated stock he or she knows that a new order must be placed.

Visual methods aid the control of stock by quantity and, as you will realise, are limited in use. They can be employed successfully only on items for which demand is regular or for which supplies are available at short notice. With predictable items for which there is regular demand and easy supply, it is possible to carry on without any stock records other than the bin card. This requires periodic checks to ensure that supplies are satisfactory.

Control of inventory by quantity

When controlling inventory it is essential that every item receives attention. Records are therefore essential. To run a stores function efficiently detailed information on past history and present policy is necessary. Records provide this information and should give a 'case history' for every item which can be used to forecast future trends.

The following factors have a marked effect on quantity control:

- *The Unit of Issue* – This may be in terms of quantity, weight or numbers and is the smallest unit that is issued. Once this unit has been set for each item, all documents must be made out using that unit. One exception to this may be the purchasing requisition which must be understandable to suppliers. If any alterations are necessary it is up to the individual firm to decide whether they should be done by the purchasing department or before sending the purchase requisition.
- *Probable Requirements* – of necessity this must be an estimate and to be effective needs close liaison with other departments. Future trends have to be adjusted against requirements ascertained from past records.

- *Lead Times and Availability* – As with probable requirements past knowledge must be supplemented by close liaison with the purchasing department.
- *Quantity Prices and Discounts* – Saving of this nature must be compared with storage costs to arrive at a true saving.
- *Cost of Ordering* – Since the necessary paperwork and labour are expensive the frequency of ordering must be considered, particularly on items of low value.
- *Rate of Issue* – It is necessary to consider what batches of economic loads will have to be made.
- *High Value Items* – Attention must be given to items of high value.
- *Frequency of Deliveries* – Two factors affect this aspect of supply, the size and nature of the item and the distance the goods have to travel. As you will realise, frequent deliveries over long distances are not very practical and are to be avoided as much as possible.
- *Seasonal Fluctuations* – These occur for several reasons which are related to changes in demand, supply or labour available. These fluctuations occur on a regular basis and cannot always be explained by the obvious such as the Christmas period or the harvesting period for crops. It is necessary to review historical data to keep in touch with these fluctuations.
- *Stock Allocation* – When calculating stock quantities, allowances must be made for any stock allocated for particular uses.
- *Standard Ordering Quantities* – You should not confuse this with the unit of issue, although the two may be identical. A standard ordering quantity is one which is set by usual trade conditions. A typical example is the sale of wood screws, bolts and other small items which are sold in multiples of 100 or a gross.
- *Obsolescence* – Constant checks must be made to minimise the risk of over-stocking items which may become obsolescent.

Control of Inventory by value

When an inventory policy is formulated, attention must be given to the amount of finance available for use in storing materials. It is vital that the capital allowed for this purpose is not exceeded.

The first step is to set a limit against which the main stock account can be compared, this monitors the overall performance. Where the stock value is shown to be excessive, action must be taken to lower the total value, the problem being to know which class of material has caused the error. This can be overcome by splitting the financial limit between the classes of materials or storehouses and running separate account for each.

It is most important that a commitment record is kept, showing the value of outstanding orders. This can then be compared with the average level of issues to forecast future stock values. Action can then be taken to ensure that the financial limit is not exceeded by deferring future deliveries.

Accurate value control requires regular information, in detail, of the following:–

- Current balance
- Committing costs
- Current rate of issue

All these figures being in monetary terms.

Control by value is exercised on groups of items in monetary terms. Any detail required must be obtained from the stock records.

Minimum Stock Level

This level is most important because it indicates the amount of stock which is essential for the continued running of the organisation for the period of the lead time for new supplies. As an insurance it normally will include a margin of safety to allow for extended lead times which may occur due to unforeseen circumstances. For example, it may be the case that the rate of use of an item is 1,000 per month with a lead time of two months. The minimum stock level would be 2,000 plus 750 safety margin, making a total of 2,750. You will realise that the setting of these levels demands careful consideration and will have a marked effect on the smooth running of the organisation.

The Maximum Stock Level

This level is set to limit the quantity held in stock to a figure that is within the financial limits laid down as a policy. Consideration must be given to items which are likely to become obsolete and maximum levels may well be lowered to avoid excessive redundancy.

The Re-Order Level

This level is set at a quantity which normally should bring in further supplies before stock falls below the minimum level. Occasionally the re-order level is incorporated in the minimum level particularly where the items have a steady supply and demand.

There may be a further level set between the re-order and minimum levels known as the *hastening level*. This indicates that supplies are approaching the minimum and that action should be taken to check that further supplies have been ordered and will be supplied in time.

Stock control by quantity then becomes a matter of checking stock records whenever a posting is made, comparing balances with stock levels and taking action accordingly.

- *Stock Balance at Minimum Level*
  Ensure that further supplies are ordered and progress outstanding quantity.
- *Stock Balance at Re-Order Level*
  Take action to provide further supplies.
- *Stock Balance at hastening level*
  Ensure that further supplies are ordered and progress outstanding quantity.
- *Stock Balance at Maximum Level*
  Check for any outstanding orders and advise Purchasing to delay deliveries.

To make stock control by quantity effective there must be a regular review of stock levels, adjusting those which are ineffective. This does not mean that levels should not be altered between reviews, should this prove necessary. It is also essential that personnel operating these records are trained adequately and made aware of the importance of accurancy in posting and acting on stock levels when balances are made. This inventory model can be illustrated diagramatically in Figure 4.1.

Order Level Systems

Order level systems are based on the premise that the two relevent variables remain constant. These two variables are:

- Lead Times
- Demand

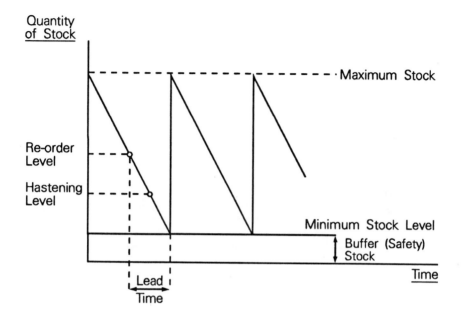

Figure 4.1
Re-order Level System

In reality lead times can vary and the assumption that inventory is issued at a constant rate is generally unrealistic. Consequently the theoritical model in Figure 4.1 above is not representitive of what happens in reality. Figure 4.2 below illustrates what is more likely to happen in reality.

As can be seen in the diagram sudden variation in lead times and demand result in periodic over and under stocking with the possibility of stock-outs. For this reason it becomes necessary to hold buffer stocks with the subsequent implication for costs.

The disadvantages of order level systems can be summarised as follows:

- They use historical data which may or may not be relevant to the present.
- They can become unrealistic and result in under and over stocking.
- They do not relate directly to actual demand.
- They assume that demand is at a constant rate i.e. 'smooth'.

Material Requirements Planning (M.R.P.). systems are related to

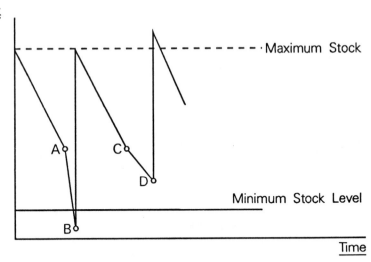

A - B   Indicates Increased rate of usage
C - D   Indicates Reduced rate of usage

Figure 4.2

Re-order Levels with Fluctuations in Usage

actual current demand and cope better with demand which is not smooth, or is 'lumpy' (see later).

Economic Order (or Batch) Quantity

Purchasing in large quantities can give lower prices but leads to higher levels of inventory.

Long production runs spread set-up costs and increase efficiency. However, they can result in stock levels that are too high. Meanwhile, other finished stocks are available, while they await their turn to be produced.

A balance must be struck. Economic Order (or Batch) Quantity theory (EOQ or EBQ) tells us that when total stock holding costs are the same as total stock ordering (or set-up) costs, this balance is achieved.

The graph in Figure 4.3. illustrates this. The vertical axis represents the costs per period of time, usually one year.

This theory has shortcomings. It may be difficult to arrive at ordering or set-up costs. The formula assumes linearity. Fortunately,

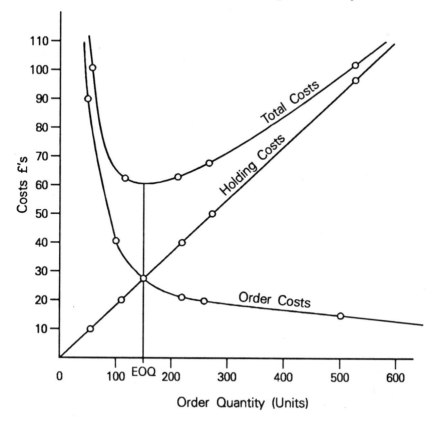

Figure 4.3.
Economic Order Quantity (or EOQ)

the overall result is not affected too much by errors in arriving at these figures. A 10% error, in for instance the set-up costs, only changes the EOQ by 5%.

EOQ theory tends to institutionalise set-up costs. The greater the set-up cost, the greater the economic batch. So we must strive to reduce these costs. Assumptions must be challenged. Methods to study techniques can simplify and speed up changeovers. Spare change parts can allow cleaning to be carried out within the cycle time. "Just in Time" thinking looks at all ways to eliminate or reduce these costs.

On a positive note however, EOQ can, and does, work. For example an engineering company purchased castings in batches of 25. After carrying out EOQ analysis it found that the economic order quantity was 40. The purchasing department, armed with this information, negotiated a better price. The new price was fed back into the EOQ equation and a new EOQ of 48 was indicated. The buyer then renegotiated a second price improvement.

Cost of Inventory Investment

There are three costs involved.

- Cost of carrying inventory
- Cost of ordering
- The inventory records show allocated stock. What are the costs of these items?

Cost of Carrying Inventories

These comprise of stores operating costs (eg. labour costs, rent, rates etc), loss of interest on capital, deterioration and obsolescence, insurance and cost of Inventory Control.

Ordering Costs

These comprise of the cost of placing the order (eg. typing, stationary), progress costs and receipt and inspection costs.

Cost of running out of stock

This comprises of the cost of production 'down time', cost of arranging special orders and delivery and the loss of goodwill through lost customers.

Inventory Control and Accounting Methods

Inventory Control Accounts

These accounts are necessary:–

- To provide figures for the Final Accounts.
- To provide the information necessary to run a costing system for materials.
- To provide a means of operating Inventory Control within the financial limits laid down by the Management Policy.

- To give detailed figures for the various classes of goods and for different storehouses or stockyards.

The Main Inventory Account

This account should be kept by the Finance Department and shows the total value of stock currently held, this figure being used, after adjustment, for Balance Sheet purposes. To maintain this figure all receipts are debited to the account and all issues are credited.

You may be confused over the use of the terms 'debit' and 'credit' when talking about receipts and issues in the Main Stock Account. To understand this clearly you must remember that items in stock, although an asset on the Balance Sheet, are a liability in the Stores Account. Another point that you should be clear about is the method of entry. Receipts are added to the existing balance and issues are subtracted.

For example:–

TABLE 1

Date	Receipts	Issues	Goods receipt or requisition no	Balance (stock in hand)
1.1.70	£100		0020	£100
3.1.70	£250		0021	£350
4.1.70		£150	3412	£200
5.1.70		£70	3413	£130
5.1.70	£300		0022	£430

Subsidiary Accounts

The main Inventory Account gives only a general picture of the financial situation and therefore has to be supported by more detailed accounts kept by the Stores Organisation.

These subsidiary accounts are separated into classifications in the same way as the inventory, giving a means of controlling specific areas of expenditure. An alternative method of control can be obtained by separating the subsidiary accounts according to storehouses. In large concerns this may well be done in addition to classification accounts.

There are therefore, three methods of separating subsidiary accounts:–

- By classification of inventory – using code numbers where these exist.
- By storehouse – where several are in use.
- By both of the above methods.

Remember that the Main Inventory Account is run separately from the subsidiary accounts, thereby providing a means of checking both, since the stock values shown in subsidiary records should equal the total value in the Main Account.

Inventory Records

To support the subsidiary accounts which are kept in monetary terms, detailed records showing physical inventory quantities are necessary. The Inventory Records provide these details and are kept in three forms.

- Those showing quantity only;
- Those showing quantity and unit price and;
- Those showing quantity, unit price and values of all entries, such as receipts, issues and balance.

The system used depends entirely on the particular requirements of an organisation and the following points should be considered when deciding.

- The simpler the system the lower the risk of errors.
- Where a minimum of information is used, reference has to be made to other documents to extend physical balances in monetary terms.
- When prices are shown on the Inventory Record this can be used as a price list and special attention can be given to expensive items when provisioning.
- Where a full record is made checks can be readily performed on all major transactions, avoiding the necessity of checking entries that represent minor values.

Coding of Accounts

All subsidiary accounts will bear a code number to identify the class of material and user department or storehouse, which enables immediate identification to be made on any particular class or location of expense.
  For example:

Material Code	002	=	Steel
Material Code	003	=	Brass
Material Code	004	=	Copper
Storehouse Code	100	=	Storehouse No A
Storehouse Code	101	=	Storehouse No B
Storehouse Code	102	=	Storehouse No C
Account Code 100/002		=	Value of Steel in Storehouse A
Account Code 101/002		=	Value of Steel in Storehouse B

The whole purpose of having detailed accounts is, therefore, to provide information from which *control* can be exercised, and, to be able to provide the earliest possible warning of excess expenditure.

The Integration of Accounts and Material Codes

It is possible to combine the Account Number with Material Codes. This is particularly useful where computers are used and can print an analysis of a particular class of goods.

Pricing Issues

It is most important for the successful running of an organisation that material costs are accurately computed, for the following reasons:–

- To ensure that all material expense is recovered during the course of a period, usually twelve months.
- To ensure that jobs that are costed for the purpose of quotation to customers and do not bear unrealistic material costs that make them either below a reasonable profit margin or high enough to be uncompetitive when selling the finished products.

Before considering pricing methods you must be quite clear on one point: the purchase price is the net cost incurred to obtain the material delivered to the required location.

Starting with the basic price quoted, adjustments have to be made for the following factors:–

Discounts

These are allowances made by suppliers to members of a particular trade, or given because large quantities are ordered. The "Trade" discounts may vary according to quantity. Discounts are usually quoted as a percentage which has to be deducted from the price list.

Transport

Where the cost of transport is not included in the supplier's price it must be added on to the supplier's net price; this may have to include movement within the organisation.

Packaging

Care must be taken to ensure that where a supplier's price does not include packaging, an addition to the price must be made.

No allowance need be made for returnable packaging, unless the full cost is NOT refunded, but accurate records and quick return of packaging is *essential*.

Insurance

Where "Ex Works" prices are quoted and goods are insured in transit at a separate charge, an addition to the basic price *must* be made.

Duties and Taxes

When Duties or Taxes are payable on goods, these must be included in the total purchase price. Particular care must be taken on Import Duties and other levies which may be refundable under certain conditions.

Methods of Pricing Issues

Cost Price

Issues are made using the actual purchase price, in one of two ways:–

- First-in-first-out referred to as "FIFO". As the name implies each consignment is priced out at the purchase price of that quantity, the price changing when issues are made from a batch having a different purchase price.

- Last-in-first-out referred to as LIFO. This works in the same way as FIFO but uses the purchase price of the latest consignment as a base. It is rather awkward to work and is very seldom used.

Advantages:–

- Very simple to operate as no calculations are necessary, with the exception of balance totals.
- Balances are related to fact therefore no difficulty will be found in reconciliation of accounts.
- It is very simple to find the total value of goods in stock, by the addition of balances.

Disadvantages:–

- Where prices change frequently, it requires a great deal of clerical effort to keep stock records and price issues.
- The comparison of job costing is difficult when prices vary on different issues.
- When prices rise or fall there is an equal over-valuation or under-validation of stock. This may be particularly undesirable when stocks are over-valued as it becomes necessary to "write off" the excess value.

Standard Price

Issues are made at a fixed price irrespective of actual purchase price or quantity. This standard price is determined by analysis of market prices, future requirements and *must* be set for a specific period, usually six or twelve months. When consignments are received the difference between the purchase price and standard price is credited or debited to a "Variance Account". The balance of this account at the end of the financial period is reflected in the Profit and Loss Account as an overhead.

Advantages:–

- This is an easy method for pricing issues.
- The possibility of error due to changing prices is reduced.
- Issues and receipts are priced at a constant rate and it is not

necessary to extend financial balances. When such a balance is required it can be readily obtained by multiplying the physical balance by the standard cost.

- There is less clerical effort in posting entries on stock records.
- Job comparison, in terms of material use and manufacturing efficiency, is easier.

Disadvantages:–

- When material prices rise or fall there is an equivalent under or over-validation of stocks.
- Unless the standard price is set with a close degree of accuracy, there will be a danger of losing the profit necessary for the successful running of the business. It is possible that material costs are being over-recovered, but this may well make the organisation unprofitable due to quotations being uncompetitive.
- Very careful recording must be carried out to ascertain why differences between standard and actual costs occur, so that future standards may become more accurate.

Average Price

An issue price is arrived at by dividing the total purchase price by the total quantity in stock, giving an average price for each item. When a further delivery is received the total purchase price and quantity must be added to the existing stock balance and value (at average cost), and a new average calculated. This exercise must, of course, be repeated for every new receipt.

Advantages:–

- Each item bears an equal proportion of the total purchase price.
- Pricing issues are easier.
- Easy to operate when machine accounting is used.
- Stock balances when calculated into monetary terms are at cost.
- Large or frequent price changes are levelled out.

Disadvantages:–

- Calculations are necessary after every receipt.
- Goods returned to stores may be difficult to price.
- The difficulty in comparison of job costs due to varying material costs.

- The balancing of accounts becomes more difficult.

Market Price (or Replacement Price)

All issues are charged at the current market price at the time of issue.
   Advantages:–

- It provides a good basis for quotations to customers, because the material content is priced at current rates.
- Variations in material costs, with the resulting profit or loss, are shown up in the Stores Accounts rather than the Works Account.

   Disadvantages:–

- A great deal of work is necessary to maintain a record of current prices.
- Stocks are likely to be over or under valued.

Selling Price

Issues are priced out at a rate which includes a profit margin, calculated to recover stores costs.
   Advantages:–

- Stores units become self-supporting because the stores costs are recovered directly from issues and not through overheads.
- Profits or losses that occur tend to be standard throughout the organisation, and this often results in discrepancies being noticed more frequently. This is very often the case where different divisions of a large organisation are critical of the prices charged on stock transfers.
- The balancing of individual Storehouse Accounts is made easier.

   Disadvantages:–

- Due to profit being included in stock values, the true value of the stock held requires detailed examination of Stock Records to arrive at the correct figure.
- For Balance Sheet or Tax purposes the cost price is necessary, and this requires calculation.

General Comments

The choice of pricing method is dependent on the nature of the business and the class of material, many organisations using several systems. The following are typical examples of those in use:–

Cost Price

Used for short run jobs that are typical in jobbing shops. Commonly used for pricing main equipment, machines or high value items and bought out items which require no processing before despatch to a customer.

Standard Price

Used where there are large-scale issues regularly made as in the mass production industries or large supply organisations such as County Council Stores or the Armed Services.

Market Price

Used mainly for raw materials where prices fluctuate, particularly in mercantile organisations dealing in such commodities.

Average Price

This is a variation on cost price and selection of this would be a matter of choice in a particular situation.

Selling Price

Used by supply organisations primarily, to simplify the recovery of stores costs.

When selecting which system to use, one fact *must* be kept in mind. Inventory values for Balance Sheet and tax purposes are required to be at cost or market price, whichever is the *LOWER*. This requirement is necessary to eliminate any possible inflation of figures, giving an unrealistic appraisal of inventory in the Balance Sheet.[3]

Inventory in the Final Accounts

It is necessary at least once a year to arrive at a figure, which represents the value of inventory in hand, for entry in the Profit and Loss Account, this figure being subsequently entered in the final Balance Sheet.

The accuracy of Inventory Valuation is important for the following reasons:

- For taxation purposes the figure is required to be at cost or market price, whichever is the lower.
- Where inventory has appreciated, (that is, increased in value) care must be taken when adding a provision to the cost value. In many instances this is considered unwise, due to the possibility that the situation may change and the value fall. In addition, appreciating inventory is, in effect, claiming profit which will not be obtained until a sale is made.
- Under or over-valuation of inventory does not show the true percentage of working capital that is employed for stockholding purposes.

Calculation of Net Value

Starting with the balance figure shown in the Main Inventory Account the following adjustments are necessary:–

Price Adjustment. Depending on the method of pricing issues, with the exception of the cost price method, there will be a difference between the inventory stock account figure and the actual cost, this difference being shown in the Variance Account. If the cost price method is used it is necessary to calculate the difference between the cost or market price.

Using the figures obtained above, a decision can be made on what provision should be made for price adjustment. This figure will usually cover the variance that has occurred during the past year and the anticipated variance for the coming year.

In nearly every case this provision will result in a deduction from the Inventory Account figure, as it is inadvisable to appreciate inventory values. Should be inventory value appreciate, no provision adjustment to the Main Inventory Account figure is necessary.

Obsolescence. Obsolescence is the period when the *future* use of an item is limited, but there is still a demand for it. When the item is no longer required it becomes obsolete. A typical example is the spares holding for machinery in present use, which is due to be replaced in one year's time, or the phasing out of certain piece parts.

Although every effort must be made to keep the level of inventory down on obsolescent items, until they finally become obsolete, some stocks must be kept to maintain the necessary service to users.

It will be possible to ascertain from the previous years' records the value of obsolete items that occurred, which can be related to the present year's situation, making due allowance for any known changes in requirements. This information can then be used to arrive at a figure, usually expressed as a percentage of the total inventory figure for the year, which can be deducted from the main inventory balance.

Obsolescence is not confined to any one class of inventory, but the most difficult to make allowance for, is that caused by a design change or production programme amendment and the provision for this requires careful consideration.

Deterioration. This can be considered in the same manner as obsolescence and is dealt with in the same way. "Shelf Life" is one of the factors affecting the setting of levels, but however carefully these are controlled some deterioration is often inevitable.

Inventory Appreciation. Where value has increased with the passage of time, it may be necessary to add provision to the main inventory account figure, although this must be done with extreme care.

Uninvoiced Goods. Where goods have been received and entered on the Inventory Accounts, but no invoices have been received, those items must be shown in detail in the Final Accounts. If these goods are not shown as a separate item, the Main Inventory Account figure will show an asset that has not yet been debited to the Purchase Ledger.

The value of inventory for Balance Sheet purposes, put in a simple form, is the following:–

- Main Inventory Account Balance
- Plus or minus Price Adjustment Provision
- Minus Obsolescence Provision
- Minus Deterioration Provision

You may well find that the last two are grouped together as one provision for obsolescence and deterioration, known under another name, such as wastage. This provision is often used to cover another aspect of loss that occurs, namely, pilfering. This is a point to consider with great care, particularly when any discussion takes place, because it has personal implications. It is, however, a significant factor in some organisations, particularly large retail stores which have to make fairly large provision for it. Remember, the question of pilfering is a very sensitive subject and you should choose your words carefully when it arises.

Identification and Coding of Materials

The Importance of Identification

The wide variety of materials and components moving in and around an enterprise is constantly being referred to, for one purpose or another, by one of the following departments:–

- Design and Development
- Process Planning
- Production Control
- Material Control
- Production
- Stores and Inventory Control
- Invoice Section
- Cost Accounting

In some cases other departments may be involved, but it should be fairly clear that, if every department uses a different language in describing or identifying an item, considerable confusion will occur.

This kind of confusion can lead to a number of inefficiencies in a company and result in financial losses and unnecessarily high costs. It is vital, therefore, that a common means of identifying material supplies is devised and implemented firmly throughout the company.[4]

Methods of Identification

We normally refer to, or identify most things, by a name or description, and in some cases this method is quite satisfactory. Provided that all interested parties use the same name or description, and provided that it is clearly understood how records should be maintained for the items in question, no confusion need arise.

Example: 3″ × ½″ Bolts and Nuts may also be called
3″ × ½″ Nuts and Bolts, or
½″ × 3″ Bolts and Nuts, or

½" × 3" Nuts and Bolts, or
3" × ½" Hex, Rd, Hex. Bolts & Nuts, etc. or
3" × ½" Pins and Nuts, etc. or
3" × ½" Screws and Nuts, etc.

This is a relatively simple example of differences in terminology, which can result in the same item being referred to be a score of different names, so that several Stock Cards are in being filed under the different descriptions. This in turn may result in several batches of the same items being ordered or manufactured, so duplicating requirements many times.

Multiply this simple problem by the thousands of items in the inventory and you can see the difficulties which may result from "Identification by Description". Furthermore, the administrative operations of classification, filing or analysis, are complicated by the many items which, though different in themselves, have very similar descriptions. Another problem is that clerical activities become unnecessarily prolonged where there is a continual need to reproduce long descriptive titles.

Only where there are relatively few items involved, where the descriptions are short and cannot be misused or confused, and the point of reference for filing purposes is quite clear, is "Identification by Description" likely to be satisfactory. In other cases an alternative method must be devised, and the usual approach is to use alphabetical numerical or alpha-numerical *coding*.

It is clear that some form of coding will be essential in firms where a wide variety of materials is in use. This need would be even greater where sophisticated forms of classification, analysis, or data processing were to be used.

Coding could simply involve allocating a number to each item as it arises, but this method makes the identification of items from their codes more and more difficult as the number of items involved increases. This difficulty is reduced by grouping like items together and devise a coding system to indicate the groups into which items are classified, as well as identifying the individual items within each group.

The first stage, therefore, in any coding exercise is "Classification". This involves grouping items into types or classes. It will be necessary to *identify* and *specify* each of the items and then categorise them within the group or sub-group to which they belong.

Having classified all the items into groups, we can devise a coding system which will be much more helpful in readily identifying items from their codes and which will provide a better basis for analysis of information.

The complete sequence of operations therefore would be:–

- IDENTIFY – What the items is, what it does;
- SPECIFY – Its description, dimensions, tolerances, etc.
- CLASSIFY – To its correct group and sub-group;
- CODE – By allocating group, sub-group and item designations.

Benefits of a Coding System of Identification

Having decided that, in the majority of cases, coding is likely to provide the most effective method of identifictation, we can study this technique in more detail.

In the first place, we should consider the major benefits which may arise through the use of this technique, so that our subsequent planning of the system will achieve the most advantageous results. The application of a coding system may achieve the following benefits:

- It will identify each item accurately;
- It will become a common means of reference by all functions throughout the organisation;
- It will obviate the need for the repeated use of descriptive titles;
- It will assist in the simplification or rationalisation and subsequent standardisation or materials.
- It provides a better means of recording and analysis;
- It provides a better means of physically controlling stocks;
- It will help to prevent unnecessary duplication of stocks;
- It will provide a better basis for instruction and training of personnel throughout the company;
- It may be used as a stock location reference.

Coding therefore eliminates many of the problems that may occur when "Identification by Description" is in use.

Methods of Coding

Before deciding which method of coding is to be used, it is important that we consider the main purposes being served and the principal functions that are going to be affected. Frequently, there will be a conflict of interests between the management functions that will use or be affected by the coding system; it is essential that the method we ultimately decide upon gives the greatest overall benefit to the company.

The main purposes and the principal functions interested may be:

- better identification of the physical materials in the factory – this will be of the greatest interest to the Stores, Inspection and Productions;
- easier reference for recording and analysis purposes – this will obviously be of concern to the administrative and clerical functions;
- better means of identifying and classifying for charging the value to jobs – this will be an objective of the accounting functions;
- an aid to all activities of materials management and control – this will be of significant importance to top management;
- an aid to applying mechanical or electronic methods of recording and control – this will be the aim of data processing personnel.

Some systems of coding will be more suitable than others in achieving one or other of the above purposes. We must decide which of the objectives is the most important, in the particular company with which we are concerned. The method of coding must be "tailor made" for that company.

When we have decided the main objectives of our coding system and have obtained agreement from all the functions affected, we must then determine the basis on which materials shall be classified and coded.

Methods available include:–

- *Identification by the Nature of the Material* – this is the method most commonly used because of its flexibility. Materials are classified into groups and sub-groups by virtue of what they are, e.g.

Main Group	Sub Group	Item
Steel	Bar	½" Rd Mild
Steel	Strip	4" × ¼" 18/23 Carbon
Fixings & Fastenings	Bolts & Nuts	3" × ½" Hex Rd Hex
Fixings & Fastenings	Rivets	1" × ¼" Pop rivet
Oils & Greases	Lubricant	20/50 Engine oil
Oils & Greases	Coolant	Transformer oil

From the examples above it can be seen that, however wide the variety of materials in use, classification *by the nature of the item* is flexible enough to cope. This factor is extremely important if we wish ultimately to use a Digital Significance Coding, such as the Brisch system.

Identification by End Use of the Material – this is the method of classification which works back from a finished product and all materials are ultimately coded according to the finished product, of which they form a part, e.g.

Model	Main Assembly	Item
Escort	Engine	Cylinder Block
Escort	Engine	Cylinder Head
Escort	Steering	Steering Arm
Escort	Steering	Column
Escort	Transmission	Universal Joint
Escort	Transmission	Drive Shaft

It can be seen from the above examples that this system of classification is less flexible because materials are used on more than one finished product. Provision must also be made for items common to the range of products such as oil seals and bearings, thus, a coding system will be required for such "common" items.

Consumable items and spares will also require separate coding systems.

There are other bases for the classification of materials which may be used in rather special circumstances, such as:–

- Identification by sources of supply;
- Identification by customer;
- Identification by the location of the item;
- Identification by the handling characteristics of the item.

These methods are very limited in their application and are usually inflexible once they have been implemented.

The next consideration in devising our coding system is to determine the whole range of information that the system must be designed to cover, so that every item is individually recognisable from its code number. We may want the code to indicate the following items of information:

- Main group classification;
- Sub-group classification;
- Item within sub-group;
- Sizes or shape of item;
- Colour of item;
- Chemical composition of item;
- Differences in use of item;
- Units of quantity (e.g. pairs, sets, dozens, rolls, gallons);
- Variations from standard;
- Accounting significance.

Many systems go no further than coding by group and sub-group and then merely allocating a number of each item within each sub-group; but where there are many items within sub-groups, quick identification becomes virtually impossible.

Finally, we must decide whether we are going to use alphabetical, numerical or alpha-numerical coding. Many companies use letters of the alphabet as initial letters for main groups of items but this practice usually results in confusion, as the number of groups increases and initial letters are duplicated for several groups. Furthermore, if it ultimately becomes necessary to mechanise the accounting, recording or control system, it is much more difficult to cater for letters than figures. In general, therefore, it is usually preferable to use numerical coding throughout.

Development of the Coding System

Having decided the main objectives our coding system is required to achieve and, having determined the most suitable method of classifying the materials, we must now look at the type of code to apply. First we must consider the main principles to follow in the development of any system of coding. They are:–

- the system must be capable of covering all items likely to be used, both at present and in the foreseeable future.
- it must be designed to suit the particular organisation;
- it must allow for expansion *without* duplication;
- each item must appear only once in the vocabulary;
- it must be easily understood by all those using it;
- there must be a constant number of symbols or digits in all code references;

- each group of symbols or digits must signify only one object;
- descriptions and specifications, upon which coding is based, should be as brief as possible, without affecting accuracy.

Any system of coding should be founded on these fundamental principles, whether it be a system of Group Coding or a system of Digital Significance, such as Brisch.

Group Coding

This method is one in which major commodity groups are given specific code references; for instance:

Example 1   01 = Steel
                  02 = Oils, greases and fluids
                  03 = Fixings and fastenings *etc*

The sub-group within each major group is then allotted a sub-group code, so that:–

Within Group 01 Steel –
                  01 = Bar
                  02 = Strip
                  03 = Sheet
                  04 = Coil *etc*

Finally, we must code each item within the sub-group. This may be done by allocating numbers, in sequence, as the item arises, or, the item number may be designed to indicate the qualities inherent in the item, such as size or quality, by retaining certain series of numbers for certain item classes; for instance:–

Within Group 01 Steel, and Sub-group 01 **Bar**
    0001–0199 reserved for Mild Steel
    0200–0399 reserved for 05/08
    0400–0599 reserved for 08/13 Carbon Steel *etc*

Based on this coding system, 05/08 Carbon Steel Bar would have a code number:–

    between 01/01/0200 and 01/01/0399

depending upon the particular item number allocated to the size and length of the material in question.

If the items number 0273 has been allocated to ½" Round in Random lengths then:–

01/01/0373 – ½" Round 05/08 Carbon Steel Bar, Random length.

Example 2

Similarly, within the next major group "Oils, Greases and Fluids", the following code may arise:–

02/01/0071 = 20/50 Lubricating Oil,

because 01 has been allocated to the "Lubricant" sub-group, and within that sub-group 0071 has been allotted to 20/50 Oil.

Example 3

Within our third group, "Fixings and Fastenings", we may get a code number –

03/16/1729 – 4 × ³⁄₁₆ Hex Rd Hex Bolts & Nuts

because within main group 03, Fixings and Fastening, 16 has been allocated to Bolts and Nuts, and within that sub-group 1729 has been allocated to 4" × ³⁄₁₆" Hex Rd Hex Bolts and Nuts.

As can be seen from the previous examples, Group Coding has the following advantages:–

- Simple to understand;
- Can be applied quickly;
- Can be implemented at a low cost.

Its major disadvantages, however, are as follows:–

- Immediate identification from the code is difficult because the item codes do not represent specific features of the item concerned, they are merely allocated as the item arises;
- Group coding is less flexible than codes using "Digital Significance" and is more likely to break down when the varieties of groups, sub-groups and items become too great;
- Group coding is of less assistance in the maintenance of standardisation.

Digital Significance Coding

This type of coding system is used where it is considered important that the description and specification of an item should be clearly represented by digits or symbols making up the code number. Each digit has a particular significance and describes a particular factor of the description or specification.

The best known method of digital significance coding is the Brisch system. In this system the code number is made up of a "Surname", which broadly classifies the item concerned, and a "Christian" name, which provides the detailed description of the item.

Example 1   "*Surname*"   –   "*Christian Name*"

          112   –   0120   which,
                                                  interpreted,
                                                  means

1st figure – 1   = main classification = raw materials
2nd figure – 1   = secondary classification = steel
3rd figure – 2   = type of steel = bar
4th figure – 0   = specification of Steel Bar = Mild Steel
5th figure – 1 ⎫
6th figure – 2 ⎬   = diameter of bar in $\frac{1}{16}$ths of an inch = ¾"
7th figure – 0   =   lengths   of   material   =   Random
                    lengths.

Therefore: 112–0120 = ¾" Mild Steel Bar, Random lengths.

Example 2   "*Surname*"   –   "*Christian Name*"

          347   –   4036   which,
                                                  interpreted,
                                                  means

1st figure – 3   = main classification = piece parts
2nd figure – 4   =   secondary   classification   =   fixings   &
3rd figure – 7   fastenings
4th figure – 4   = type of fastening = bolts & nuts
5th figure – 0 ⎫   = length in inches = 4 inches
6th figure – 3 ⎬
7th figure – 6   = diameter in $\frac{1}{16}$ths of an inch = ³⁄₁₆"

                    = finish of product = galvanised.

The foregoing examples simply indicate the way in which the digits in a Brisch code number may be interpreted to give a description or specification. When designing a coding system of this type it will be necessary first to decide how all items to be included in the system can be divided into ten or less main classifications, so that this factor can be covered by using figures 0– 9 in the first column.

Then *each* of the Main Classification must be divided into ten or less sub-classifications – obviously the sub-classes under a "Raw Materials" Main classification will be different from the sub-classes under a "Piece Parts" or "Consumable Materials" main classification. With ten main classifications and ten sub-classes under each, we can get as many as 100 sub-classes.

The third figure of the 'surname' will be used to indicate type of item within each sub-class, and, with a possible ten types of item within each of 100 sub-classes, we can describe 1,000 types of item by just using the 'surname'.

Should we require to identify more than 1,000 *types* of material we may need to increase the 'surname' to four figures.

The 'Christian name' can then be used quite differently for each *type* of material described by the 'surname' to provide detailed specifications of the item. The figures may be used individually or in pairs to represent some important factor of the description.

The major advantages of the Brisch system are:–

- Direct identification of any item from its code number;
- Much more flexible for expansion;
- As the code must be directly related to the description, it can be used to maintain a standardised range (code numbers not included in the standard range are not ordered or manufactured) – this advantage brings others, namely reductions in design costs, reductions in storage costs and reductions in tooling costs.
- Assists in location of equivalent or alternative materials, when out of stock;
- Is ideal when mechanising data processing.

The one disadvantage is that it takes a good deal of planning to devise a Brisch system, and, the personnel who do that planning need to be more than usually skilled in the planning process and knowledgeable about the materials, their descriptions and specifications.

The Stores Vocabulary

When materials have been coded, it is necessary to prepare a Code Book or Manual, showing material descriptions and the codes which will represent these descriptions; this is called a Stores Vocabulary. The Vocabulary has four main purposes.

- It provides the means by which all people, departments or functions are initially notified of the new codes;
- It provides a permanent record, against which additions or amendments to the materials-range are decided;
- It is a ready-reference book for day-to-day working for all departments;
- It provides a sound basis for future training of people concerned with materials;

To be of any permanent use the Stores Vocabulary must be properly prepared, designed and presented so that the people using it have confidence in its accuracy and validity.

Stages in Preparing a Stores Vocabulary

Earlier we determined that the stages leading to the development of an effective coding system were:

Identify → Specify → Classify → Code

These same stages are inherent in the preparation of a Stores Vocabulary, but we shall look in more detail at the practical situations in which this work is carried out.

It will be seen from the following that several departments or functions will be involved in the various stages of development and preparation of the Vocabulary that follows.

Preparing Library of Information

As comprehensive a knowledge as possible will be required of all materials, components and supplies in use, or likely to be used in the foreseeable future. This will mean *identifying* potential material needs and filing each piece of information for use in later stages.

The department given the responsibility for this task (usually a Vocabulary or Standards section, or, Stock Control) can make a major contribution to the ultimate effectiveness of the system, if the collection of the information is done with care, and if the filing of the information is done efficiently.

The information may be obtained from Design, Production, Stores, Inspection, Maintenance, and Purchasing Departments, from Outside Suppliers, Customers, Trade or Research Associations or from the British Standards Institute.

At this very important stage it will also be necessary to prepare specifications for each item or range of items so that each is filed in an orderly fashion in readiness for subsequent classification and coding. In preparing the specifications it will be helpful if we adhere, as far as practicable, to the following basic rules:

- Try to make descriptions or specifications simple, clear and specific;
- Develop accurate physical descriptions;
- Determine accurate performance requirements;
- Determine inspections or tests that must be met for acceptability;
- Determine any special marks to be used on materials for identification;
- Indicate where specification will meet several alternative needs.

Consideration of Present Coding Systems

In some cases several attempts may have been made in the past to codify individual classes of materials; or Supplier or Customer codes may have been used. We must understand the nature and purpose of these past systems, and how they were used, so that adequate consideration is given to such requirements in our new classification and coding.

Consultation to Determine Coding System

When all the information has been collected, meetings should be held, at which all interested departments are consulted, to determine the coding system most likely to meet the most important requirements. Another purpose of these meetings will be to programme the work to be done and determine the contribution any department may have to make within the programme.

Preparation of "Originating Sheets"

The next stage is the actual Classification and Coding exercise. It will have been made very much easier if the first stage has been done well. In fact, if an excellent job has been made of "Preparing the Library of Information", the preparation of Originating Sheets will virtually be a clerical task, as very few difficulties or queries of classification will arise.

An "Originating Sheet" is simply a record of all items in a particular classification of material. All the items are recorded in a logical sequence and ultimately a code recorded against each, to provide to the Stores Vocabulary.

The first originating sheet will show only the main classifications.

ORIGINATING SHEET 1	*Main Classification*
Material Group	*Code*
Raw materials	0
Piece parts	1
Oils, Greases, Fluids	2
Consumable Stores	3
Tools, Jigs, Fixtures	4
Building Materials	5

etc.

An originating Sheet will then be prepared for each of the above material groups. For example:

ORIGINATING SHEET 2	*Raw Materials – Code 0*
Material Group	*Code*
Steel	0
Cast Iron	1
Copper	2
Brass	3
White Metal	4
Wood	5

etc.

This process of preparing Originating Sheets will be continued in more and more detail as the classifications are broken down further. In the more detailed Originating Sheets, where descriptions become more extended, drawings may be used to help in showing specification. For instance:–

ORIGINATING SHEET 346

Salt Glazed Drainage pipes – Tees – Code 573–4 . . .

Diameter A	Diameter B	Measurement C	Code No.
10cm	10cm	1 Metre	573–4441
10cm	10cm	2 Metres	573–4442
10cm	15cm	1 Metre	573–4461
10cm	15cm	2 Metres	573–4462

Finalising the Stores Vocabulary

The preparation of the "Originating Sheets" is the process of Classification, and when the codes are allocated we have a Stores Vocabulary. In some cases, however, it may be necessary to show conversions from old code numbers, in old code number sequence, as an appendix to the new Stores Vocabulary. In other circumstances it may be only necessary to issue certain parts of the total classification to certain parts of the organisation, with one or two departments getting a complete copy. It is this preparation of the Classification and Coding, for general use throughout the company, which demands the finalisation of the "Stores Vocabulary" in a suitable format and using terminology that is readily understood in the explanatory sections.

Bar Coding.

Bar Coding is a form of Automatic Identification which has been widely adopted in the retail sector, however it has a much wider range of applications and is being increasingly applied in the field of inventory control, production and operations management, warehousing, distribution, and quality control.

Automatic Identification systems such as Bar Coding allows information to be coded so that it can be read by a machine and processed by a computer without the risk of human error.

There are two main categories of Bar Code:

1. European Article Number (E.A.N.).

A numeric only symbology which has four fixed length symbol types: EAN 13 encoding 13 digits and EAN 8 encoding 8 digits. EAN 13 is widely used in the retail sector. The EAN numbering system ensures that no two retail products in the world have the same number.

2. Code 39.

Code 39 can contain up to 32 digits including alphabetic and special features. The size of the symbol can be increased or decreased to suit the capabilities of the chosen printing methods.

Code 39 is the most widely used Bar Code for industrial application. It has the advantage of having the capability of being printed by less precise printing methods and can therefore be printed in-house, for example by dot matrix printer.

Bar codes can be read by either hand held readers or fixed scanners.

Bar Coding and Logistics

Bar Codes can be of major assistance in the management of the logistics function. Typical applications include:

- Receiving.
- Stores.
- Production.
- Quality Control.
- Packing.
- Warehousing.
- Despatch.

Automatic Identification systems such as Bar Coding make possible the accurate tracking of virtually every transaction from receipt to despatch, and can therefore be considered as a management information system, consequently the following advantages and benefits result.

Advantages

- Accurate raw materials stock control.
- Reduced down – time due to non availability of materials.
- Measurement of work-in-progress throughout the factory.
- Fast access to production statistics.
- More economical use of labour.
- Accurate recording of rework.
- Accurate recording of finished goods which have been warehoused or despatch

Benefits

- Reduced material stocks.

- Improved production efficiency.
- Improved quality control.
- Minimised warehouse stocks.
- More accurate despatch.

The improved management control should result in improved management control and increased profitability.

Standardisation, Rationalisation and Variety Reduction

In most organisations and particularly if the organisation has been in existence for some time, a large number of parts, components and materials will be held in stock. A critical examination of these items will reveal that

- A number of items, carried as different items, may in fact be the same.
- many items are similar to other items and one may be used in place of two or more different items.
- Some items carried as "company specials" will be found to be similar to items covered by National Specifications.

The advantages to be gained from a policy of standardisation and rationalisation, are:

- A reduction in stocks carried;
- Reduced inventory costs;
- Costs of carrying stock lowered;
- More effective Purchasing and Stores procedures as they can concentrate on fewer items;
- Design department can reduce their range of products and adopt a more positive attitude to design;
- Quality control can be more effective;
- Production methods can be simplified and improved.

In order to prepare our Store Vocabulary it was necessary to prepare a Library of Information; we now need this information to assist in deciding those items which will become our standard range. We shall also need to examine carefully each item currently carried in stock, and to compare our range of stack items with actual requirements. The next steps are to:

- Identify each item and its purpose or use;

- Eliminate from the stock range those items not essentials or duplicated;
- Examine critically those items which have similar features – it may be possible to reduce the list even further;
- Make a list of items and components that are to be carried as a standard stock range;
- Decide size range, standard pack size, methods of packaging, and so forth for the standard stock range;
- Specifications can now be entered against each item in the standard range.
- Arrange for publication of the list of standard items, and its issue to all interested departments (for example Design, Production, Purchasing, Stores, Costing).

There will always be a need for certain items not in the standard range to be carried. However, these must be strictly controlled and only allowed in particular circumstances.

A written procedure for obtaining authority to purchase non-standard items should be issued, as part of the "standards list". Those persons authorised to allow the purchase of non-standard items should be named, so that the responsibility for carrying a non-standard item can be clearly seen.

In a similar manner, a written procedure must be laid down for amendments and changes to the standard list. This will obviously be necessary since lists will need up-dating to cater for new requirements and to delete items no longer required.

Again we cannot have just anyone altering standard lists, as this would make a nonsense of the system. The following must be clearly stated:–

- Those persons who may request an amendment to the standard range (named by their appointment);
- That all interested departments must be consulted on any proposed amendment and a system for ensuring this must be built into the procedure;
- It must be shown who has the final authority to permit any change in standards;
- That no change may be made in the standard list unless properly authorised.

The standards list when published has the following advantages:–

- There is available throughout the enterprise, as a handbook, a record of all standard stock items. This will assist all departments, particularly design, Production, Stock Control, Stores and Purchasing;
- It is a method of informing everyone of the enterprise's authorised standards;
- It is the means of ensuring that the Company's standards policy is carried out.

Specifications

The more widely accepted the specifications we use in adopting our standards, the easier will be our task in obtaining the items concerned. In fact, life is simpler if we can quote a specification, in the confidence that others will know exactly what is required. Consider the problems if there were not National Specifications for items such as bolts and nuts; every manufacturer would use a different thread form. It was to avoid such problems that organisations like the British Standard Institute were set up.

Among specifications in wide use are

- British Standards Institute (BSI)
- International Standards Organisation (ISO)
- British Pharmaceutical Commission (BPC)
- American Society for Testing Materials (ASTM)
- American Petroleum Institute

Wherever possible specifications such as those above should be used. The benefits are likely to include:–

- Lower costs, since the items will be manufactured on a large scale for several users;
- Easier availability of components and items, since they are not specially made;
- Avoidance of the need to draw up specifications on each occasion an item is required.

There are instances however where the company must issue its own specification; where, for instance, no specification is available. If a company wishes to ensure that it's designs and products are not copied, it may also decide to issue its own specifications.

All specifications and drawings must be entered on the Standards List against each item.

Inventory Reduction

When illustrating the principle of inventory reduction if a project involves a cost reduction, not only does this result in an ongoing cost saving but it will also be reflected in the fact that the book value of the components concerned will be reduced when standard costs are next revalued.

This means that any of the components being held as stock (including WIP) at the next annual stock check will have a lower asset value, resulting in the value of assets in the company's accounts being reduced. This reduction will be additional to any changes in asset value caused by changes in stock levels.

Although the aim of any cost reduction project is to increase profits, and the ongoing cost savings will do this, the reduction in book value caused by revaluation will appear in the accounts both as a reduction in assets and a corresponding reduction in profits. Although this reduction in book value does not itself represent a change in cash flow, the reduction in reported profits represents a reduction in tax liability which does provide a cash flow gain.

Taking an example of a component which used to have a book value of £100.00 and which has been reduced to £75.00, the effect will be:–

	Old Costs	New Costs
Material	£40.00	£30.00
Labour and variable cost	£20.00	£15.00
Manufacturing overhead	£40.00	£30.00
Book value	£100.00	£75.00
Reduction in asset value	£25.00	
Corresponding reduction in reported profit	£25.00	
Saving in tax liability (resulting from reduced reported profit) (£25.00 @ 35%)	£8.75	

Stock revaluation results from a change in the standard cost value of components, not from a reduction in stock levels. Thus, for a project which involves a reduction in both the value and quantity of stock, there are four elements to be considered:

- One-off cash flow saving from curtailing the supply process to reduce the quantity of stock;
- One-off reduction in tax liability resulting from having a lower quantity of stock at annual stock check;
- Ongoing cash flow savings resulting from the reduction in cost of manufacture or purchase;
- Reduction in tax liability as a result of stock having a lower book value at annual stock check.

However, if a project involves both a major cost reduction and a major reduction in stock levels, care must be taken in deciding how the reduction in stock levels is to be valued. It is necessary to decide whether the cash flow element (such as material, labour and expenses) in the saving from reducing stock quantities is to be valued on the basis of the old method of manufacture or the new method. Two different situations may exist.

- Little risk is perceived in the introduction of the new process, so stocks are allowed to run down before the new process is fully commissioned. In this case it is the old supply process which is curtailed and savings would be valued using the old costs.
- Where there is risk of uncertainty regarding the new process, it may be decided to have it fully commissioned before starting to run down stock levels. Full production would be achieved before in order to use up stocks. In this case the savings would be valued using the new stocks.

Because the saving comes from curtailing the supply process for both material purchase and manufacture rather than from the sale of the excess stock, the valuation of the cash flow element of inventory reduction must be based on whether it is the old or new process which will be curtailed.

Although this cash flow saving will occur at the time when the supply process is curtailed, such as by avoiding the purchase of raw material, the reduction in asset value in the company accounts may not be reported until the stock level check at the end of the financial year. By this time the inventory may have been revalued on the basis of the new cost of manufacture.

Two examples are taken to illustrate this, one where the inventory reductions are based on the old method of manufacture, with a subsequent revaluation to calculate the reduction in stock value; the other where the inventory reduction is costed on the basis of the new method of manufacture. The component costs are: old book value £100.00, new book value £75.00; stock levels are:–

Before change – 200 off
After change – 150 off

The first example is based on the reductions being made while the old method of manufacture is still being used and the savings are:

Cash flow savings (£60.00 × 50 off)	£3,000
Reduced tax liability (£40.00 × 50 off @ 35%)	£700
Initial saving from stock reduction	£3,700

150 components are revalued (from £100.00 to £75.00)

Reduced tax liability as result of revaluation (£25.00 × 150 off @ 35%)	£1,312.50
Total cash saving	£5,012.50

The second example assumes that the reductions are made after the new method of manufacture has been introduced, and the revaluation is done after the reduction in stock levels has been recorded. Savings are:

Cash flow savings (£45.00 × 50 off)	£2,250.00
Reduced tax liability (£55.00 × 50 off @ 35%)	£962.50
Initial saving from stock reduction	£3,212.50

150 components are revalued (from £100.00 to £75.00)

Reduced tax liability as result of revaluation (£25.00 × 150 off @ 35%)	£1,312.50
Total cash saving	£4,525.00

The reduction in stock levels (such as 50 off) is recorded in the accounts only at the end of year stock check. If the stock has not yet been revalued at that time, the reduction in assets recorded will be 50 off at £100.00 each. As this stock would have been produced using the new method, only £45 would have been already recorded as a change from stock to cash; the remaining £55.00 would now be reported as a reduction in assets.

In the second example above, it is assumed that the revaluation is done after the reduction in stock levels is recorded. If, however, the revaluation is carried out before the stock check, the total cash saving will not change. The values will be:

Cash flow savings	
£45.00 × 50 off	£2,250
Revaluation of 200 components	
£25.00 × 200 @ 35%	£1,750
Reduction in book value of 50 components	
£30.00 × 50 @ 35%	£525
Total cash saving	£4,525

The importance of inventory revaluation will be dependent on the magnitude of both the stock reduction and the cost reduction. The way any evaluation is done will depend on the nature of the project, the timing of the changes and the way the company records changes in inventory levels and book values.

For any project where a reduction in inventory levels or a change in the value of inventory is going to be a major factor, it is essential to investigate, in detail, how the changes will be costed and what effect any changes in the value of assets will have on the company's balance sheet.

Any reduction in inventory values in a company's accounts will not only produce a cash flow saving but also a change in asset values which will be reported as a reduction in profits. There is a paradox in that while inventory reduction is always portrayed as an ideal objective, achieving the reduction may appear to have had exactly the opposite result to that originally intended. Because of this, any project involving a planned change in inventory values must take into consideration the effect on the company's management of having to report to shareholders an apparent failure to meet profit forecasts.

Although high inventory levels are always portrayed as being a symptom of inefficiency, there is no such thing as a correct level of inventory. The optimum required level is something which is dependant on many different factors, such as market requirements, manufacturing facilities and product design.

High inventory levels themselves are not a basic problem, only a symptom of other problems. There is a danger that if the real reason why the inventory is there is not understood, the action taken to reduce stock may not be solving the correct problem. It is important to start by identifying and changing the basic reasons why inventory is there; only then should stock levels be reduced.

Carrying stock is an integral part of a company's manufacturing operation and stock is there to help iron out problems in both the supply process and the sales function. The supply problems may be due to the length and uncertainty of the process or the inflexibility and unreliability of the ordering and scheduling procedure, while the sales problems can be caused by fluctuations in sales volume and product mix. The combination of these problems can result in the production process being too long and inflexible to satisfy the market requirements for variations in product specification and delivery.

Holding stock at various stages in the manufacturing process is used to overcome these problems, and different types of inventory reasons. High WIP may be a result of long lead times and uncertainty of supply, such as can be caused by the problems of scheduling work in batch manufacturing environment where there is the possibility of scrap and rework if the manufacturing process is not completely reliable.

It is unrealistic to expect marketing to forecast short term order input with any accuracy so that manufacturing can plan a uniform through-put. Therefore, to obtain orders, companies may either have to carry finished or semi-finished stocks or change their manufacturing process to provide the flexibility quickly to change output in response to customers' needs.

Changing the manufacturing process to reduce the need for stock, such as WIP, will not in itself bring about a change in stock levels; making a permanent change in stock levels requires a change in the way that the stock is ordered in the material control system. While large sophisticated Material Requirements Planning (MRP) packages may contain a number of different sets of ordering rules which can be used simultaneously for different components, some MRP packages may have little flexibility for rule changing.

If the change in manufacturing required to reduce stock levels is such that the ordering rules within an MRP package need to be altered, there is a danger that unless there will be a major saving in inventory value, it may not be worthwhile making the change. For example, inventory reduction is often portrayed as an objective for investing in CNC machining centres because the number of operations can be reduced. However, the introduction of a single machine may only affect a relatively small percentage of components and without a change in ordering rules, all that will happen is that some lead time is lost and the components put into finished part stores at an earlier date, in effect increasing the value of inventory.

In evaluating the benefits of inventory reduction it is important to identify the way in which the supply process will be curtailed to bring about the stock reduction. In reducing brought-in components and the raw material content of WIP, it is likely that material purchases will be reduced for a short time to use up existing stocks. However, in order to reduce WIP the manufacturing process will be restricted only for a short period of time. As a result, there is a danger that the labour element will not be curtailed because unlike material purchases, labour cannot easily be turned off and then turned back on again.

It is unlikely that operators' wages will be stopped so that unless specific plans are made which identify how the labour savings are going to be implemented, it is possible that Parkinson's Law will operate, with work expanding to use the labour available. As a result there will be no cash flow saving in labour costs at all. If the planned labour saving does not occur, the forecast cash flow element will be reduced while both the reduction in asset valued and corresponding profit reduction will be increased.

A commonly-suggested method of reducing inventory is to have smaller batch sizes by reducing ordering quantities. This will only be economical if changes can be made which will reduce ordering costs, such as batch set-up times, thereby reducing the cost penalties of smaller batch sizes. However, consideration must also be give to other problems which can arise from an increase in the number of batches.

Review of Recent Concepts

Arising from issues such as sourcing and how to control stock will be less standardised approaches requiring less rigid purchasing methods including more thinking about strategy and less fire fighting? In order to examine the strategy and draw a considered conclusion it is necessary to establish typical views with regard to sourcing policy and examine some recent concepts.

Of major concern to managers at the present time is the perceived challenge to the West from Japanese manufacturing industry. Kanban, Just-in-Time, F.M.S., robotics, CAD/CAM: a whole new vocabulary has been devised to describe differing aspects of the changes that are taking place. It is necessary therefore to focus attention on the implications for the Purchasing function of these developments, impact on Buyer behaviour, collaboration and the actual effect on industrial sourcing policy in Europe.

Russell Syson (Pro Dean of the East Midlands Regional Management Centre, Derby, UK) argued the Kanban Opportunity at a Purchasing and Logistics Conference in 1986 in Brussels.

Kanban, (as illustrated below) means card and is the Toyota Company's much advocated version of just-in-time production control system. Honda uses a DOPS (daily overhead and perfect supply) system.

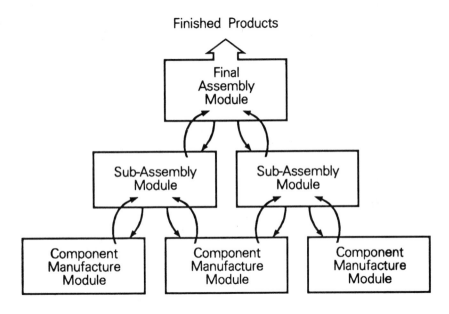

Figure 5.
Kanban

Just in Time is clearly publicised as a Japanese system although some would argue that the system originated in USA after the 1939/45 War. Similarly there are many stories of successfully implementing the system. Equally Syson argued that Just in Time is relevant to the whole industrial spectrum. I, however, can see little evidence of this for the following reasons:

Looked at from the purchasing viewpoint Just in Time has the following objectives:

- Reductions of raw material stocks;
- Improvement of input quality;
- Achievement of greater schedule flexibility;
- Reduction of bought-in costs through long term cooperative contracts with suppliers.

These objectives require a number of changes in purchasing practise:

- Highly reliable material planning;
- Vastly improved supplier quality performance;
- Reduced delivery lead times;
- Smaller delivery quantities;
- Greater increased delivery frequency;
- Creation of long term contracts with Suppliers;
- A shift from competitive price reduction to long term competitive cost reduction programmes with Suppliers;
- An increase in the level of single sourcing.

Crticism of Just in Time (JIT) has focused in the UK on its reliance on a policy of single sourcing.

Such a policy is essential to the implementation of JIT because the technique requires suppliers to make a number of significant changes to their operating procedures. They must, for example, change from a batch to a smooth continuous form of production to match the change in the buyer's demand pattern. They must achieve enormous improvements in quality control and implement major changes in transport operation. Few suppliers are likely to be willing to contemplate making such fundamental and expensive changes without the stability and certainty that long-term, single-sourced contracts provide. Single-sourcing is an essential pre-condition for the successful implementation of JIT. Awareness of this fact has stimulated warnings about the effects of single-sourcing on continuity of supply.

However, as the UK's Austin Rover have pointed out: "Dire warnings from critics when Austin Rover first embraced single-sourcing about the danger of relying on a sole supplier have not so far materialised, due to an improved industrial relations climate".

Moreover, the cost benefits of single-sourcing are undeniable. On the face of it, the car industry would appear to have confounded doubters and critics. Appearances can be deceptive however, and I suspect that the truth may be different. Companies adopting JIT may well be storing up a uniquely devastating kind of trouble for the future.

The source of this threat is to be found in the combination of JIT's requirement of single-sourcing with its objective of stock-minimisation. Not only does JIT seek to reduce finished goods, work in progress, and bought-in stocks within the organisation itself, it also demands similar reductions from the organisation's suppliers. The effect of failure to achieve this goal has been spelled out by Fortune magazine commenting on the experience of American companies that have tried to implement JIT: ". . . the auto companies are forcing suppliers to 'eat inventory'" – in other words, much of the inventory still exists, but instead of being in the manufacturers' warehouses it has been pushed out to the suppliers. A mere shifting of inventory, of course, will largely defeat the goals of just-in-time. Over the long run, the suppliers will find a way to get manufacturers to pay for it.

With very little, or (ideally) no safety stock in the system, companies using JIT become extraordinarily vulnerable to supply stoppages certainly much more vulnerable than companies running a single-sourcing policy in conjunction with conventional control policies. The longer the system is in operation, the lower the total stock levels become, the smaller the total number of suppliers, the larger the amount of investment the remaining suppliers are persuaded to make, the more difficult and time-consuming it becomes to re-source, and therefore the more vulnerable to collapse the system becomes. It can be seen that the nearer an organisation approaches to the JIT ideal, the more exposed it becomes to the effects of stoppages down its own supply chain.

There must be good reason for the Japanese to have devised and embraced such a potentially unstable system. As we all know, their success in the field of manufacturing is unrivalled. The mystery deepens if we consider the conventional responses to the kind of high supply risk situations that JIT creates. In the West, companies typically follow one of two courses of action. Firstly multi-sourcing and secondly vertical integration. Multi-sourcing is clearly not a Japanese favourite and the evidence on vertical integration appears at first sight to be equally unpromising: "Many operations which, in Britain, would be undertaken by enterprise employees, are performed in Japan by sub-contractors outside the factory gates . . . Each major Japanese enterprise swims in the economy like a shark with its cloud of pilot fish, surrounded by voluminous sub-contractors . . .".

This description looks like the very antithesis of vertical integration in which organisations acquire their suppliers and in this way secure their sources of supply. The truth is more complex. The Japanese industrial scene is not what it appears to be. "The principal stock-holders of Japanese companies are normally other companies. Individuals hold less than 10 per cent of the stock in 97 per cent of the companies listed in the first section of the Tokyo Stock Exchange, which includes the 1005 largest publicly traded companies in Japan. It seems plausible that in many markets these patterns of inter-locking directorships improve the allocation of resources. In some respects companies with inter-locking directorships can mimic the resource allocation decisions of vertically integrated companies".

We can now see that although the large Japanese corporations are devotees of subscontracting, they have also developed a method of obtaining the benefits of security and supply certainty that accompany Western-style vertical integration without resorting to outright acquisition of their suppliers. This begins to explain the Japanese enthusiasm for single-sourcing and their willingness to abolish safety stocks. It is perfectly safe and rational to become dependent on a small number of suppliers if you are directly represented on the boards of those companies and have some control over the way they are run.

The second relevant major difference between Japan and the UK is frequently dismissed by JIT supporters as being old news and therefore worn out and of no significance.

It is true that we have known for some considerable time that Japanese Industrial relations are positively tranquil compared to the UK, but the age of that knowledge does not dilute its relevance. Japanese companies face significantly lower risks of supply stoppages caused by strikes than do their UK competitors. It is also true that the current levels of unemployment have had a pronounced emasculating effect on Trade Union activity in the UK. However, it is difficult to predict whether this state of affairs will persist.

Another factor that is considered negative towards JIT is to achieve management effectively and a JIT network, the Japanese tend to focus production of smiliar items in small factory units of under 300 each. This is fine in Japan where two thirds of the 240,000 manufacturing corporations have fewer than 30 employees and where indeed the culture is far different from UK.

The Author's view is that the combination of minimal safety stocks and single-sourcing is perfectly rational and desirable for Japanese purchasing techniques, however, without first creating conditions in the European economies comparable to those in Japan may be foolhardy. Single-sourcing per se is not the problem. The European car industry has already convincingly demonstrated the cost advantages of volume concentration on a small number of suppliers, but single sourcing plus a just-in-time stock-holding policy could be a recipe for disaster.

Within the European industry the supply sources of the often highly specialised materials and components needed are not numerous. Aerospace for example is to some extent unusually vulnerable to supply disruption and the costs effects of a fairly narrow field of market competition. It seems that a sensible policy of dual sourcing together with good order and market intelligence, is an essential part of overall purchasing strategy.[5]

Materials Requirements Planning (MRP)

It is rarely the case that the demand for an item is smooth and at a constant rate. In manufacturing it is more likely that the demand for an item will occur in large increments at varying points in time, a characteristic referred to as "lumpy" demand. In such situations the MRP approach has been developed as a means of managing inventory. The MRP system is for controlling inventories of raw materials, work-in-progress, component parts and sub-assemblies. A further characteristic is that production takes place only for, as far as it is possible, actual sales. It has proved to be a very powerful tool in the planning and control of manufacturing industries.

MRP could be defined as "a system for supplying the number of components required to produce a known quantity of finished assemblies."

The three ingredients of an MRP system are the Bill of Materials (BOM), the Inventory Status File and the Master Production Schedule. These ingredients are fed into a computer system.

The system begins with a production plan and schedule and ends with orders being placed on suppliers and the receipt of those materials.

In comparison to traditional systems, MRP seeks to control inventory by what is occurring or is going to occur, rather than by what has occurred. Thus, the order sizes are linked to needs and the delivery becomes paramount. There may be a tendency to over-emphasise expediting incoming deliveries from suppliers. Obviously, any halt to production calls the cost-effectiveness of the system into question.

However, production plans have been known to change!

In the context of supplier relationships, it is quite possible for customer and supplier organisations to be computer-linked giving access to production schedules, which allows suppliers to increase their own effectiveness by being able to plan and schedule their work.

MRP pushes organisations into the realisation of a Materials Management function, whereby the overall responsibility for the control of materials from the point of leaving the supplier, passing through the organisation and finally reaching the customers, resides in the hands of one person. This is often cited as a crucial stage in the progression of an organisation towards realising its full performance potential, particularly in manufacturing industry.

Take, for example, a product which has a few components, none of which are manufactured, but are all bought from various suppliers. The organisation only assembles the components to make the product, and there is also only one product. (In such a situation in real life, a traditional control system would probably prove quite effective).

The first item is the Bill of Materials, which is a schematic listing of all the components that go into making the product in the sequential order of production, or build. The product is "exploded" or "cascaded" into its various assembles, sub-assemblies and components at various levels. Some items such as a nut and bolt, could appear at various different levels. If this were the case, it could be allowed to filter through these levels and accumulate at the bottom. It may be a cheap item, but it could well be crucial to production and therefore it might be subject to a separate traditional system of control, such as re-order level.

Suppose the Master Production Schedules calls for 150 of Product A to be ready for delivery in week 17. Then an MRP plan can be developed. The plan is constructed by combining the information contained in the Master Production schedule, the Bill of Materials, and the Inventory Status File. This latter file, shows what materials, components, sub-assemblies and such like are already held in stock together with their lead time.

This simple example indicates the large number of combinations and calculations facing the computer, where a large number of complex products are produced to meet continually changing demand.

MRP appears quite complex but to assist you a summary list of the stages is given below.

● Sales Forecast – updated with latest actual sales information.

- Sales Forecast, customer orders and production policy used to produce Master Production Schedule (MPS).
- MRP programme computes how many of each component and raw material are needed by "exploding" end product requirement into successively lower levels in the product structure.
- Net requirements calculated utilising Inventory Status File for instance, Stocks and current orders deducted to give Net Requirements.
- Net requirements adjusted by lead times.
- Purchasing place order.
- Goods received.

The process is illustrated in the flowchart below:

Reported benefits from MRP include the following:

- Reduction in inventory;
- Improved customer service;
- Quicker responses to changes in demand;
- Greater productivity;
- Better machine utilisation;
- Reduced set-up times and changeover costs.

MRP is therefore a useful technique in manfuacturing industry for overcoming the problems of inventory management for components which are in dependent and lumpy demand.

Manufacturing Resource Planning (MRPII)

MRPII is an extension of MRP. The first stage in the conversion of MRP into MRPII is the development of a "closed loop" MRP system. Closed-loop means that the various functions in production planning and control (capacity planning, inventory management and shop floor control) have all been integrated into a single system. This represents an improvement over MRP because it provides a number of additional features such as:–

- Priority Planning – "rush" jobs, can be brought forward in time and others put back in time and the necessary adjustments made to material delivery schedules.
- Integration of related functions into the system allows feed-back from them, making sure that the production plan is constantly kept

up to date. In particular capacity planning, inventory management and shop floor control.

• There is feedback from vendors, the production shop, stores, and so forth when a problem arises in implementing the production plan which enables adjustments to be made to overcome these problems immediately, that is, before they become insurmountable.

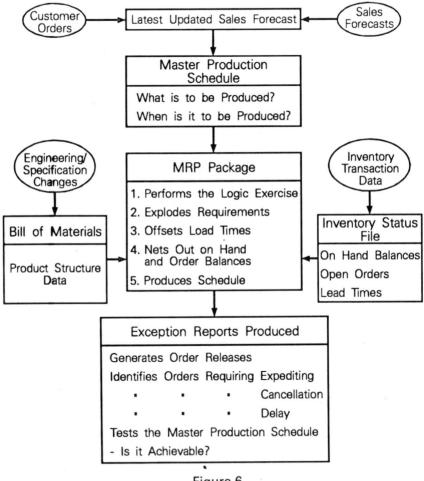

Figure 6.
Materials Requirements Planning[6]

The tying together of these various functions as a closed loop MRP system represents a considerable improvement over the basic MRP system. However, it is the final step which is the essential one. This converts the closed loop MRP system into a full MRPII system, linking the closed loop MRP system with the financial systems of the organisation.

Hence a closed loop MRP system plus financial system produces MRPII. The inclusion of the financial systems in the operation of MRPII gives it two invaluable characteristics which represent a significant improvement over closed-loop MRP.

- It is an operational and financial system and;
- It can be used for simulations.

MRPII is in fact a company-wide system which is concerned with all aspects of the business and includes purchasing, inventories, production, sales engineering and cash flows. All departments operate with the same data for a common database. This recognised the interaction of all business activities; what happens in one area has direct effects elsewhere and these affects are captured by the system which adjusts throughout each area. In all areas the data is reduced to the common denominator of financial data which provide management with the information it needs to manage the business successfully; for example the values of inventories, work-in-progress and finished goods, are known at all times. MRPII is a total management control system.

Another benefit which can be derived from an MRPII system is that it can be used for simulation purposes. This can be done by taking a "cut" or section across the database and posing "what if" questions. For example, we may wish to bring forward a production date so we pose the question "what if we work an extra shift?". The system will stimulate the consequences for order releases, current order schedules, inventories, work-in-progress, finished product, labour costs and cost flow. If this is not a viable proposition then an alternative can be tested, and once this is found the necessary adjustments can be made throughout the system. The same approach can be used with financial plans, production plant, inventory levels and so on. It is of course vital that the data within the system is completely accurate otherwise the results will not be as reliable.

MRPII is obviously a computer based system and the ultilisation of Visual Display Units in simulations can be a most helpful aid in planning, since the alternative "scenarios" can be tested during management meetings.

The objective of systems such as MRP and MRPII is really quite basic – it is to give greater control and accountability, but, also to reduce inventories to a minimum and reduce the length of time between identifying a need and fulfilling it for the customer with the ultimate aim of improved cash flow and increased profitability.

Notes and References

2. Lock, D., *Project Management*, Gower, 1989
3. Rook, A., *Transfer Pricing*, BIM, 1972
4. Little, D. and Barclay, I., *Materials Management: The Technologist's Role in Controlling Material Costs*, IPS, 1986
5. *Just in Time: the Purchasing Viewpoint*, IPS, 1990.
6. Cox, J., *Contemporary Stockless Systems*, Purchasing and Supply Management, May 1988

Chapter 4

Stores Management

Stores Management Objectives

The stores function is concerned with holding appropriate levels of stocks of the required quality, under the correct storage conditions, for use by other departments.

To realise these objectives stores management has a number of duties including:

- Receiving, storing and issuing stock;
- Controlling the movement of stock;
- Control of all storage units;
- Material handling procedures;
- Quality and quantity control;
- Staff training;
- Clerical administration duties.

The Store's Function

The stores have a wide range of functions. These must be carried out efficiently and logically to ensure the smooth running of the department. These functions are:–

- Receive and maintain the quality of all incoming materials;
- Supply materials to user departments in order to ensure continuation of production;
- Store, control and issue all items in stock quickly and efficiently;
- Issue any tools or spare parts that may be required by the departments;
- Ensure that all health and safety regulations are followed;
- Undertake training of all stores staff and;

- Comply with the Control of Substances hazardous to Health Regulations 1989.

The stores provide a service to the company as a whole and to individual user departments. Obligations to particular departments include:

- PRODUCTION DEPARTMENT – To ensure that materials are available as and when they are required;
- DISTRIBUTION DEPARTMENT – To ensure that all finished products are marshalled ready for dispatch;
- SALES DEPARTMENT – To ensure that stocks for sale are stored and issued correctly;
- ACCOUNTS DEPARTMENT – To ensure that information on the value of stock, goods received and invoice queries is provided promptly.

In turn, the stores rely on other departments. For example, the purchasing department must ensure that all goods required by the organisation are purchased – of the correct quality and at the right price – for timely delivery to the stores.

For any stores management system to function efficiently, considerable time and attention needs to be given to:

- Siting of stores;
- Construction of buildings;
- Stockyards;
- Internal layout of stores;
- Types of stores and;
- Storage equipment.

This Chapter deals in turn with each of these critical matters.

The Siting of Stores Buildings and Stockyards

It is usually necessary to settle for a site that is less than ideal but it should be one which, as far as possible meets the following requirements:–

- Clear, level, well drained land capable of providing foundations suitable for the building or stockyard required;
- Of a size sufficient to accommodate stores buildings, stock-yards, access roads, car and lorry parks and possible future expansion;

- Convenient for main services, (drainage, water, electricity and gas);
- Convenient for transport facilities, (motorways, rail points, airports and docks);
- Away from congested urban areas, where traffic may have difficulties collecting or delivering;
- Close to user departments, or, centrally situated to serve a number of units. Planning permission will be required and buildings must conform to local authority specifications.

The site will also have to be within the limits of finance available for purchase, or obtainable on a satisfactory leasing agreement.

The purpose of the building of a stockyard must be borne in mind and the following matters taken into account:

- The size, weight and handling characteristics of goods and materials. Nature of the goods are very important since this will determine the structure of buildings and the site. Consider particularly explosives, petroleum spirit, deep frozen food;
- The location of the user departments and depots to be served from the stores building. Quantities of goods likely to be stored and the rate of turnover;
- Methods of transporting goods to and from the building, (palletisation, containerisation);
- Loading and unloading facilities required, with special regard to maximum weights to be handled, and maximum size of containers;
- The traffic volume anticipated. (This will influence the type of handling equipment for which provision will have to be made);
- Storage methods and equipment that will be required;
- Any security system that will be needed;
- The number of staff that must be provided for in operating the building.

Construction of the Buildings and Stockyards

When deciding upon the construction of the building and stock-yard, certain basic matters require consideration, these are:–

Type of building: single or multi-storey

Single storey buildings are cheaper, a lighter shell is possible, ventilation and lighting easier, materials handling presents fewer problems.

Multi-storey buildings make the best use of a restricted site, and may be necessary when an existing site must be re-developed.

Type of Structure

Steel frame or brick pillars; the type of infill must be decided. Here the load bearing of the framework is the main factor, based on suitable foundations. In a store it may be necessary to support additional floors, overhead cranes and other equipment.

The stacking height and free movement of materials are the factors that effect internal construction.

Load Bearing of Floors

This must be carefully considered, so that it is suitable for the goods to be stocked. Floors will also need to be dust free and non-slip.

Receiving Bags and Loading Docks

These will need to be of correct size, type and height to suit vehicles using the stores.

External Doors and Windows

These will need to meet security requirements. At the same time doors must provide an adequate means of entry and exit, for this reason power driven roller doors, with a wicket gate are suitable. The larger doors can be risen for vehicles and the wicket gate for the entry of personnel.

Draught proof screens of polythene or other plastic strips help to conserve heat. Internal rubber doors provide the same facility and allow movement of fork lift trucks. There must also be doors and screens adequate to prevent the spread of fire. Internal partitions should be of a type that can be easily moved around to give the greatest flexibility in the use of space.

Heating, Lighting and Ventilation

In a stores building much planning should go into these aspects. Some form of heating will nearly always be required, the problem being to provide a source of heat that is sufficient, economical without interfering with the storing of materials. Many buildings use fan-heaters for this purpose.

Adequate ventilation must be provided. Air conditioning may well be required in many situations since it is important that stock is kept in the best condition. A specialist should be consulted if this is the case.

Natural lighting is the best form of illumination and should be provided if possible. Roof lights are a convenient method of doing this. Fluorescent lighting is effective and cheaper than tungsten lighting.

Welfare Facilities

It is essential to provide for facilities such as a canteen, first aid post, toilets and garages. Suitable welfare facilities will be required and provision must be made for them.

Stockyards

These provide a means of storing certain classes of materials more cheaply in an enclosed building. Those materials include such items as bricks, sand, gravel and timber. In fact any materials which do not deteriorate in the open. A firm surface area will be required for vehicles, and handling equipment, such as cranes and fork lift trucks. These areas are usually concrete or tarmac. Stacking areas may be of ash or shale.

Adequate lighting will be required, particularly if work is to be carried out in the hours of darkness. There are several types of tower floodlighting available.

Security fencing and goods gates will be required for stockyards.

Internal Layout

Before planning the layout of any store with any degree of certainty so as to provide the most satisfactory base for efficient operations, we must determine all our storage needs very carefully and then decide:—

- The best that can be done in terms of grouping stocks;
- What can be provided in the way of a building or site for each group;
- Exactly what type of service the store will provide;
- What kind of supporting facilities a particular stores area will require.

Disjointed planning of stores layouts, where each section does not form part of an overall plan, is likely to result in poor service, inadequate control, costly administration, unnecessary duplication of equipment and facilities and frequent emergency rearrangements to meet unforeseen circumstances.

The factors which will form the basis of our overall planning of storage facilities throughout the company are, therefore vitally important and must be carefully considered. The main factors for consideration are as follows.

- What types of service can the organisation reasonably afford?
- What materials must be handled at each location?
- What facilities will be required at each location?
- How will they be constructed?
- What kinds of equipment will be needed at each location?
- What provisions, if any, must be made for overall "work flow" throughout the company?

Detailed Planning of Layouts

Now we should have a clear picture of our overall requirements in mind, and we can begin to plan the facilities at each of the designated locations, and then the layout of those facilities to give the greatest possible efficiency.

Whilst satisfying the needs of our overall plan for stores, the layout at each location must be dictated by the particular requirements of individual stores areas. These requirements will be influenced by the following characteristics:–

- Determination of material needs;
- Receipt and inspection of incoming materials and supplies;
- Storage, safekeeping and issue of materials and supplies;
- Centralised or decentralised storage of materials and supplies;
- Recording and administration of stocks;

- Handling and transportation of materials;
- The need for "work flow" to be considered in the particular location;
- The working space required by each of the functions involved and;
- The type of materials involved in the "mix" of materials in the particular location such as raw materials, piece parts, bought-out parts, work-in-progress, tools and patterns, jigs and fixtures, equipment and spares, general stores, packaging materials and finished products.

The nature of certain materials which require special consideration:–

- Those which are valuable or attractive to pilferers.
- Whether it is fast-moving or slow-moving.
- If it requires special means of storage (eg liquids) and the type of freight containers used such as those shown in Figure 7.

- Whether bulky or awkwardly shaped.
- If the material is in any way dangerous.
- Whether there are identical components which must be stored in two separate areas for different purposes, such as production supplies and supplies of spares.
- The gangways, corridors or free areas necessary for the "lift" or travel of overhead cranes or the movement of other materials handing equipment.
- Areas for the receipt or dispatch of internal or external transport.
- The need to assist administration and supervision to maintain control efficiently.
- The need for flexibility, so that the facilities can be adjusted to meet changing circumstances.

Types of Stores

It may well be that, in a small company, all stores facilities must be provided in a single building, and if an efficient service is to be provided, all the above factors must be considered when planning the layout of the building. The larger the company one is dealing with, however, the more fragmented the stores facilities become, and the more specialised become the activities of each stores location. Whilst this may simplify the layout of individual stores locations, it demands a more detailed consideration of the function or purpose of each.

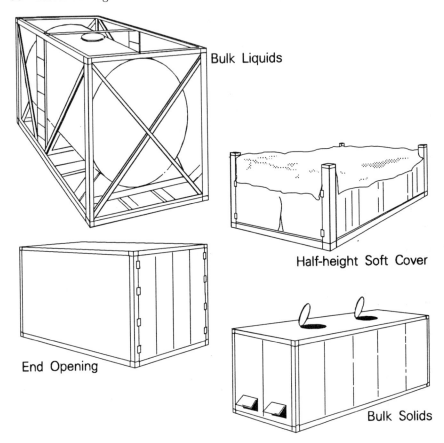

Bulk Liquids

Half-height Soft Cover

End Opening

Bulk Solids

Figure 7.
Typical Freight Containers

Some of the more specialised applications which justify individual considerations are:–

- Centralised goods receiving;
- Centralised storage;
- Special storage facilities;
- Popularity storage.

In considering these we can examine specific needs as far as layout is concerned.

Centralised Goods Receiving

Firstly, it is essential to recognise that control over the material assets of any organisation is very difficult to achieve or maintain unless it can take control of the material as soon as it arrives on the premises. If that initial control is lacking there is a considerable danger that materials will be lost or misused and their cost may eventually prove an insupportable burden on the company. The first step in the application of this control is to limit the number of points at which materials may be received, if possible, restricting receiving points to one.

It is necessary to consider the "Nature of the Function being Performed", and the activities involved at such a point:–

- Receipt of transport of various kinds;
- Unloading and subsequent re-loading of materials of various classes;
- Initial checking of goods for damage in transit;
- Recording and documenting goods received;
- Provision of facilities for the "technical" inspection of those goods requiring it;
- Provisions for goods awaiting distribution to user departments or storehouses;
- Provisions for goods awaiting return to suppliers.

The "Nature of the Function being Performed" will tend to decide the general location and pattern of layout, which will then be varied by certain other factors, such as:–

- The need for "work flow";
- The volumes of work being handled;
- The types of materials;
- The nature of certain materials;
- The working areas needed;
- The need for flexibility.

Bearing in mind the importance of goods receiving, and recognising its purpose in the overall scheme, we can design the department's internal layout in order to achieve its purpose in the most efficient and economical manner.

If the centralised goods receiving department occupies part of a building, the remainder of which is a storehouse, this is a further factor to be considered in our layout.

Centralised Storage

There are four quite different interpretations to the term "Central Stores", and it is most important that we appreciate the meaning and significance of each before we consider their application or their overall effect on the layout of storage facilities.

- *Central Stores only.* This type of central stores will exist where only one storage point is justified in a factory, and all supplies are provided from that one point. In addition, all other storage activities will probably be carried out at that one location.
- *Central Stores supported by Sub-stores.* Where stores facilities are organised in this way, all requirements are controlled and ordered by the central stores where the materials are received and stored. Normally, the sub-stores are located adjacent to the operating departments they are designed to serve, and the stocks held in them are limited to reasonable operating levels. Stocks in the sub-stores are replenished at intervals from the central stores: for example as in Figure 8.

    This type of central stores organisation may be used in a large company where there are many departments to be served within the one premises, and where many of the materials used are common to all departments.
- *Central Stores in addition to Departmental Stores.* When stores are organised in this way the departmental stores operate independently, ordering, receiving and storing those materials which are used only by the department served by that departmental stores. The central stores is responsible only for providing supplies of those items which are common to more than one department.

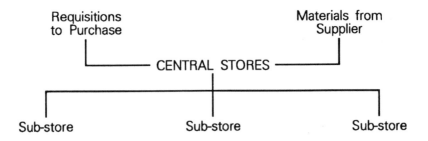

Figure 8.
Central Stores supported by Sub-stores

The central stores will order, receive and store common items and departmental stores will replenish their stocks of such items by requisitioning their requirements for central stores. This type of central stores organisation may be used where the factory departments are widely dispersed geographically, and transportation costs only make it worthwhile to centralise those items common to all departments, and which can be bought and stored in bulk. Another justification may be that the work of the various departments is so diversified that it would be unreasonable to bring highly specialised materials into a central point merely for them to be distributed to one department.

- *Central Stores (Main Distribution Warehouse) and Depots.* Sometimes the term "central stores" is applied to a main warehouse in which the finished products of a company are held prior to distribution. From such a stores the products may be distributed to sub-stores or depots which are located at strategic geographic points from which the best service can be provided to customers. Such depots may operate with or without the control of the central warehouse but, as with all centralisation, a central stores does tend to ensure *closer* management control over distributional priorities whilst a depot reduces the transportation problem within its own area, in addition to providing quicker service.

Advantages and Disadvantages of Centralised Stores

Both centralisation and decentralisation have their advantages, and there is an unfortunate tendency to rush to obtain the advantages claimed for centralisation without giving any consideration to it's disasvantages or the equally strong claims of decentralisation in certain circumstances.

Advantages of Centralised Stores

- Allows *closer* management control;
- Justifies the use of more advanced control methods and techniques;
- Creates economies in storage space (because quantities held in stock can be proportionately smaller – e.g. five separate stores may need to hold twenty each of a particular item: if centralised it would not necessarily mean that a hundred of the item need be held);

- May justify the use of better storage, handling and transportation facilities;
- Better facilities may be provided for receipt, inspection and testing of materials;
- Stocks will be "turned over" with greater regularity, thus avoiding depreciation or obsolescence;
- Allows for more specialisation by stores personnel;
- Reduces the number of orders placed for the purchase of particular materials thus facilitating quantity buying.

Disadvantages of Centralised Stores

- Involves extra handling and transportation costs;
- Requires a much stronger organisation or inefficiencies may arise;
- Will involve more documentation if it involves distribution through sub-stores;
- Greater dangers of shortages and loss arise if the central store is badly managed;
- Bad management of any kind will have more serious repercussions and be more costly;
- Central stores personnel may be less concerned with local need in the factory and so deal less efficiently with them.

If one is considering the claims of decentralisation the advantages and disadvantages tend to be the reverse of those for centralisation.

Special Storage Facilities

In listing the factors to be considered in the detailed planning of layouts the following factors were mentioned:

- The nature of the functions being performed;
- The need for "work flow";
- The volumes of materials to be handled;
- The working areas necessary for each function being performed and for the volumes of materials.

These factors are considered again when considering the requirements for effective layout in a central goods receiving department. The factor listed earlier which has *special relevance* when considering the layout of the facilities specifically for the storage of supplies was:–

- The nature of the materials.

Whether a company or it's stores function is large or small, whether or not it justifies central goods receiving, and whether it uses a centralised or decentralised stores organisation, there will invariably be some materials which require special consideration as far as storage is concerned.

There will be those materials which may be better controlled if held in different storehouses, such as:–

- *Raw Materials* (such as ferrous or non-ferrous metals, whether in bars, strips, coils or sheets);
- *Component Parts* (for example piece parts or bought-out parts stored for final use);
- *Engineering Supplies* (such as tools, jugs, fixtures patterns, equipment and spares);
- *General Stores* (for instance consumable materials, small hand tools, protective clothing, packaging);
- *Finished Goods*

There will also be those materials which may be stored more suitably in stockyards, such as:–

- *Raw Materials* (ingots, billets and slabs of ferrous metals, timber, etc.)
- *Solid Fuels* (coal, coke, etc.)
- *Building Materials* (bricks, sand, gravel, stoneware, etc.)

Then there will be those materials which require special consideration either because they are dangerous, or because there must be special means of dispensing or controlling them, e.g.:–

- *Oils*. Fuel oils may need to be stored in containers, above or near to the boilers or furnaces using them. Lubricating oils may be stored in reservoirs above or below special purpose or automatic machinery.
- *Petrol*. This may be stored in underground tanks in or near to a company garage or maintenance shop, but in an accessible position for all vehicles requiring supplies.
- *Dangerous goods*. Goods such as explosives or highly inflammable materials, which may have to be located at safe distances from normal working areas, need specially-constructed buildings with protective earth mounds or baffle walls.

- *Solid Fuels.* Some of these may weather badly or may be subject to spontaneous combustion so that protective measures may be necessary to avoid physical or chemical changes taking place.
- *Valuable or attractive goods.* These are especially prone to pilferage and require special protection.
- *"Clean" goods.* These must be stored in a manner which prevents their becoming contaminated with other materials.
- *Specially "Bonded" materials.* This category covers a wide range of materials which must be segregated from other similar materials because they are "Free issue" materials which are a customer's property; approved or tested materials which must be segregated from non-approved materials; materials which are subject to a tax or duty which has not yet been paid; components designated as spares for customers and which must be held separately from production supplies.

Finally there are those materials requiring special consideration in order that they may be made immediately available to user departments to avoid unnecessary handling. This may occur in:–

- *Work-in-Progress Stores*
  It may be necessary to provide work-in-progress quarantine areas in appropriate locations in the factory if it is impossible to maintain a balanced flow of production from machine to machine or department to department in the factory; similarly, it is advisable or impossible to allow the work-in-progress to remain scattered around production departments, but where it is undesirable to bring large volumes of materials back into stores for short periods of time. These "stores" will provide control and safekeeping of materials and components, but may not be the responsibility of the Stores Manager. However, they will influence the planning of storage facilities throughout the company.
- *Open Access Stores*
  Where items of relatively low value are being used on a continuous basis at a rapid rate, and where the handling and control costs are disproportionate to their value we may decide to make them freely available to the user departments from an open access store within that department. Similarly where sets of components have been kitmarshalled for subsequent assembly departments, the sets may be transferred to open access stores ahead of the assembly production programme.

- *Popularity Storage*

  The final factor to be considered under the general heading of "Nature of the Material" is the rate of usage. Some materials are "fast moving", that is, they are used quickly and regularly; other materials are "slow moving", that is, whilst their usage may be regular or intermittent they tend to stay in stores for long periods of time.

  This "popularity" of certain materials will affect not only the ordering policies or stack levels, but also will need to be considered when planning the layout and location of supplies.

Fast moving materials are less likely to deteriorate, but they should be as near to the issue point as possible to reduce the distance travelling by personnel responsible for issue.

Slow moving materials can be stored further from the point of issue but are likely to be more prone to deterioration.

These points must be taken into account in stores layout.

Planning Storage Equipment

There are a number of basic principles which should be considered whenever planning storage equipment. These are:–

- Is the equipment making most economical use of the space available?
- Are the greatest overall benefits for the storage costs incurred being achieved?
- Are the most economical prices for the most suitable equipment being paid?
- Will the equipment help to provide the most efficient service?
- Will the equipment assist in the handling and controlling of stocks?
- Will the equipment help to provide the right conditions in which to hold stock?
- Will the equipment present any dangers to premises or personnel?
- Will the equipment provide the right degree of security for the stocks?
- Does the equipment provide flexibility in use?

Consideration of the general principles above would enable an organisation to arrive at a general policy for selection of Stores Equipment but this does not mean that we can then proceed to purchase a standard range of equipment to meet all needs effectively.

A very wide range of storage equipment is already available, and is being continually expanded, and, in most cases, it has been designed to meet the widest range of "standard" needs without necessarily meeting any particular need with complete satisfaction. One danger of such standard equipment is that it appears to be less expensive in the short term, while in the long term it may turn out to be more costly and probably involve some insurmountable space, flexibility or manoeuvrability problems.

This does not mean that all storage equipment must be special purpose or custom-built; what it does mean, however, is that we give the fullest consideration to our equipment needs if we are to get the best possible results at the most economic cost. Firstly we must look at the materials that have to be stored, and the locations at which they will be held, to determine the *types of equipment* necessary, based on factors such as:–

- The nature of the material (size, weight, shape);
- The volume of material to be held;
- The degree of protection required from pilfering, from dirt and from atmospheric conditions;
- The problems of handling the material;
- The needs for physical or administrative control over quantities and flow;
- The nature of the building being used;
- The location of the stocks in relation to their point of use, and the space available;
- The handling methods or facilities available or necessary;
- Whether materials are received, stored and issued in unit quantities;
- Rapidity of turnover of stocks of individual materials.

Consideration of these factors will outline certain requirements which must be met in selecting the equipment which will satisfy our needs, requirements such as:–

- Strength – to support weight;
- Durability – to withstand constant wear;
- Ease of operation – to assist efficiency;
- Flexibility – suitability for a variety of uses;
- Protection provided – against, for example, dirt or misappropriation;

- Adaptability – for different locations;
- Safety – for premises, materials and personnel;
- Manoeuvrability – for swift re-arrangement of storage areas where necessary;
- Cost – giving the greatest value for money spent;
- Dimensions – to fit the space or headroom available, or to contain the volume required;
- Suitability – to the method of handling or type of material held.

Careful consideration of the basic principles of effective storage, together with clear recognition of the practical requirements to be satisfied, will enable us to determine the best methods to adopt, and most suitable equipment to use. Any efforts we exert in this direction will help to provide maximum flexibility, and fullest utilisation, both now and in the future, within the economic and space limitations imposed upon us, avoiding:–

- Uneconomic use of space;
- Unnecessarily high storage costs;
- Unnecessarily high costs of equipment;
- Inefficiency in providing a service;
- Difficulty in controlling stocks;
- Detrimental effects on the condition of stocks;
- Dangers to premises and personnel;
- Lack of security for stocks and;
- Lack of flexibility in use.

Handling Equipment

Goods Movement Theory

The first thing one must remember about the movement, handling or transportation of materials is that it adds to the cost of the material without adding in any way to the value.

It is important to bear in mind that basic principle when planning the primary activities involved, so that unnecessary movement is eliminated.

Even then we cannot assume that, whichever handling methods are used, it is important to achieve the best results at the lowest cost. It is important to plan handling methods carefully considering the following principles:–

- Major handling or movement should be *restricted* as far as possible by siting incoming and outgoing materials correctly prior to any operation, and using the most helpful methods for 'holding' the materials at any point.
- Work should be planned on a *'flow'* principle which will involve correct routing of materials; correct movement of personnel involved in the activities; proper designation of working areas and working groups; suitable arrangements being made for obtaining and disposing of containers; proper routing of documentation.

Frequently these factors are determined prior to considering materials handling, and unnecessarily expensive handling methods have to be adopted as a result, whereas if they had been considered with the handling problems in mind, the handling methods could have been much simpler and the whole operation much less expensive.

- Eliminate wasteful methods wherever possible by employing unit loads to eliminate handling and perhaps counting individual items; using pallets where frequent movement is involved; using the force of gravity wherever possible to aid movement.
- Where mechanised methods of handling are necessary, select the most *appropriate equipment*, carefully considering what degree of flexibility is required from the equipment purchased; can some form of standard equipment be used? Does the volume of work involved justify special purpose equipment? Can some conveyor system be employed in place of handling?
- It may be necessary to provide *alternative methods* of handling in the event that the 'first choice' equipment breaks down – if so, will the layout adopted allow the alternative methods to operate?
- The methods adopted should be designed in the interests of *safety*, firstly of personnel, then of property.
- Equipment should be designed and installed for safe and efficient operation, and, where operators are required, they should be properly trained for the job.
- The environment in which the materials will be handled will affect the choice of certain equipment (see Layout Considerations).
- It is necessary to compare the overall 'Benefits' of alternative methods with the 'Costs' of employing those methods.

Investment Justification

The Investment and Running Costs of different handling methods can easily be computed, and these costs must be set against potential benefits of each of the alternative methods. The potential benefits may include:–

- Savings in time and labour;
- Reductions in damage or breakage;
- Increases in output or turnover;
- More efficient use of space, and;
- Reductions in risk to life or property.

The majority of the above benefits can also be quantified in terms of money, and cost comparisons between a number of alternative methods will show the type of handling which will more readily justify investments and give the greatest 'profit'.

Example:

METHOD A	*Cost per Annum*
Depreciation on equipment	Nil
Labour cost	£6,000
Space cost	£1,000
Potential cost of damaged goods	£200
Potential 'profit' on turnover in this area before Handling costs	£18,000

METHOD B	
Depreciation on equipment	£1,000
Labour cost	£4,000
Space cost	£2,000
Potential cost of damaged goods	£500
Potential 'profit' on turnover in this area before Handling costs	£19,500

METHOD C	
Depreciation on equipment	£5,000
Labour costs	£2,000
Space costs	£3,000
Potential cost of damaged goods	£700
Potential 'profit' on turnover in this area before Handling costs	£20,500

Method B is the more 'profitable' one to employ, although it is not so highly mechanised as Method C, nor does it achieve the same level of output or turnover. However, Method B does maximise 'profit' on the operation.

Reduction in overall costs of operations is the same as 'profit' in circumstances where 'profit' cannot be measured as return in excess of costs on output or sales.

Layout Considerations

Layout, of course, is one of the fundamental principles to be considered in planning materials handling, but it is a factor which deserves more detailed consideration since space utilisation is an inherent problem in all materials movement.

The planning of the layout and the best use of space must be accomplished along with the determination of the best possible Handling Method and *not* after equipment has been purchased. The main considerations will be:–

- The use of the 'flow' principle as far as possible in the siting of 'incoming' materials, the 'holding' areas for materials, obtaining or disposing of containers, the routing of materials through the 'process', designation of working areas, correct 'movement' of the people involved, implementation of alternative methods in case of break-down, siting of 'outgoing' materials.
- Maximising the use of the space available in relation to the type of equipment under consideration by the 'holding' or storage of materials at the right levels to assist operations and avoiding unutilised space.
- The provision of adequate room to manoeuvre by the provision of gangways, providing sufficient headroom or clearance for conveyors or overhead handling, access to and from all points for equipment and personnel and the provision of suitable surfaces for 'floor operating' equipment.

It is worth repeating that these factors should be considered BEFORE methods or equipment are selected, otherwise the best possible choice cannot be made to give flexibility, adaptability and ultimately profitability in the handling of materials.

A recent example of layout flow problems can be found in former "Eastern block" countries although it may not be uncommon in Western nations. Inefficient manufacturing is one of the problems facing Russia and its former satellite countries, but perhaps an even bigger obstacle to their future prosperity is widespread ignorance of efficient warehousing and distribution methods.

One company which helped to solve this problem is Mieback Logistics, Oxford. Partner Michael Boos and his team designed a new multi-million pound warehouse for a distributor in Moscow which supplies goods to Western embassies in Russia and former East Block countries, as well as to their embassies in the West.

The existing manual warehousing system involved 50 people picking and 25 people keeping records of stock movements. Lead time to locate and pick some items could take up to six months.

What the Russian distributor needed was a reliable warehouse, built on a greenfield site to Western standards, which would double throughput and achieve at least 95% order fulfilment at the outset. They also needed room for expansion.

Another key requirement was for a flexible warehousing system, owing to the enormous diversity of products to be stocked. These range from washers and light bulbs to construction materials and 10-tonne steel coils, and included such items as office furniture, safes, carpets and washing machines.

Miebach's concept study, involved storing the stock items on one-ton single and two-ton double Europallets in a 24 metre high-bay store.

Compared with an earlier Russian concept, the floor area used has been reduced to 15,000 sq meters, incorporating an additional 2500 sq meters for handling, leaving enough space on the site to expand the warehouse by 60 per cent.

Robustness and simplicity in operation was a further requirement. Although the system normally runs under computer control, it is

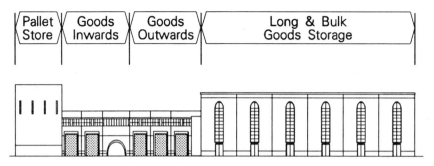

Figure 9.
The Warehouse Design

designed to be operated manually in the event of computer failure. Every item has been specified primarily for it's reliability. For example, manual stacker cranes are used instead of fork lift trucks. The job of any piece of equipment can be taken over by another in case of breakdown.

Types of Handling Equipment

Apart from the normal methods of handling, such as lifting, carrying, pushing or shovelling, – all of which may be quite adequate in some circumstances –- there is a wide variety of mechanical methods which fall into four categories:–

- INDUSTRIAL TRUCKS
- CRANES AND HOISTS
- CONVEYORS
- PUMPS – PIPELINES – FEEDER SYSTEMS

Industrial Trucks (Manual)

This range of equipment is designed to provide simple mechanical assistance in the operations of lifting, moving or transporting loads which are too heavy to man-handle, or which can be handle, or which can be handled more economically in bulk lots. Into this category fall such equipment as:–

- Sack Trucks;
- Platform Trucks (Manually Operated);
- Platform Lift Trucks (Manually Operated);
- Drum Lifts;
- Cylinder Trucks;
- Pallet Trucks (Manually Operated);
- Carboy Tippers;
- Lifts or Mobile Ladders (Manually Operated);
- Special Purpose Trucks and Trolleys.

Industrial Trucks (Power-Driven)

Power-driven trucks have been designed for a wide variety of applications. Basically their purpose is to handle loads which cannot be man-handled even with the assistance of the simple mechanical aids, or to transport loads over longer distances at greater speed. Into this category fall such equipment as:–

- The fixed platform power-driven truck;
- Power-driven platform lift trucks such as a 4-Directional Truck shown in Figure 10;
- Tractors and trailers.

As the volume of materials to be handled has increased, the problems of double-handling have demanded new methods of storage which, in

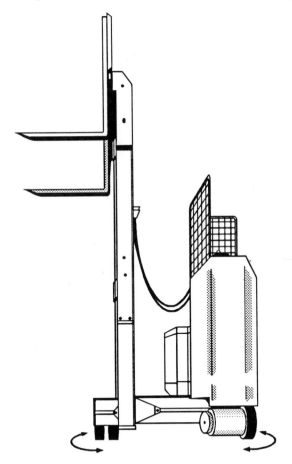

Figure 10.
Four-directional Truck

turn, have led to the need for new ways of handling. As a result we have the various types of pallet and stillage, and a wide range of fork-lift trucks to handle them.

Before dealing with the applications of such trucks we must consider the following factors:–

- Pedestrian or Driver operated: This will depend upon the loads to be carried, the space available and the distances to be travelled. A typical example is shown in Figure 11.

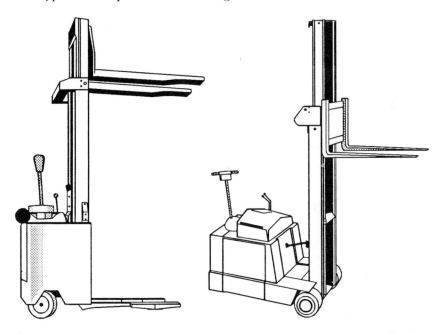

Pedestrian Pallet Stacker   Pedestrian Counterbalanced Truck

Figure 11.
Pedestrian Stackers

- Petrol, L.P. Gas, Diesel or Electric driven: consider here whether the equipment is for internal or external use. Consider also the economy of running, economy of maintenance, capital cost, and mechanical reliability and availability.
- Solid or Cushion tyres: this will depend upon the loads to be carried, the nature of the application and the surfaces upon which it is required to operate.

Standard or special fork-lift trucks designed to cope with a wide variety of applications are:

- Normal or High Lift;
- Reach trucks – with forward movement of the forks as shown in Figure 12.

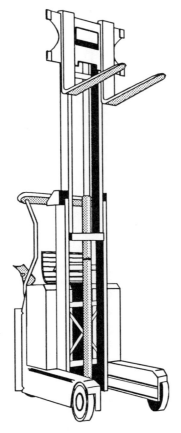

Figure 12.
Reach Truck

- Straddle trucks;
- Lifting attachments for special purposes eg Ram – for coils, clamps – for drums;
- Side loading trucks as shown in Figure 13.

Another development in the field of power-driven industrial trucks is

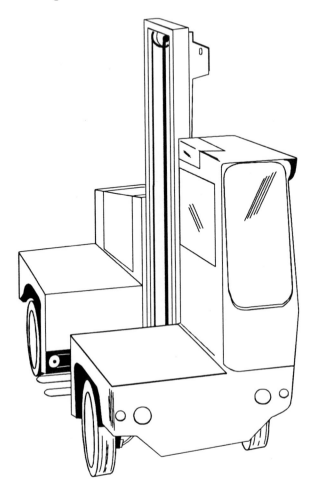

Figure 13.
Side Loading Truck

the automatic or 'robot' system, the main purpose of which has been to reduce the manpower requirements in warehouses or stores, for collecting or distributing large volumes of many items of stock.

The robot trucks are loaded at and controlled from a central point and are directed electrically along pre-wired gangways to the points within the warehouse where the goods are to be unloaded and stored. Similarly, goods from stock can be loaded on the trucks which are automatically directed to a central point for issue, packing or despatch.

Such a system is expensive to install and demands extremely careful planning of storage locations for fast and slow moving items and the balance between them; "traffic jams" of robot trucks would cancel out the benefits that the system was installed to obtain.

Cranes and Hoists

There are certain circumstances in which cranes or hoists are preferable to other forms of materials handling equipment. These include such situations as:–

- Where heavy materials must be lifted for loading on to trucks or other vehicles for transportation;
- Where heavy materials need to be lifted and moved only a short distance for further processing;
- Where awkward loads are involved which cannot be handled or industrial trucks;
- Where the movement involved is between two or more constant points or;
- Where insufficient space is available on the floor to allow materials movement.

The following are examples of the various types designed to meet the problem:–

- Pul-lifts – a hand operated chain-block at a fixed point to lift heavy materials for loading on to vehicles or machines;
- Electric Hoists – an electrically operated version of the Pul-lift for basically the same purpose;
- Monorail – a single overhead rail from which a Pul-lift or Electric Hoist is suspended on rollers, to allow loads to be moved to any point over which the monorail passes;
- Swinglift Jib – a swinging arm on which a Pul-lift or Electric Hoist is attached to allow loads to be moved to any point within the arc of the Jib;
- Mobile or Rolling Gantry – a steel structure which straddles the working area and is mounted on rollers and rails. A Pul-lift or Electric Hoist is suspended on rollers from the gantry which then allows manual movement from side to side, as well as along the length of the working area;
- Overhead Cranes – a power driven vehicle which is mounted on a fixed gantry running the whole length of the working area. The

lifting apparatus can be power-driven from side to side across the working area, as well as along the length of the gantry. The lifting is also electrically powered and can be controlled either from an overhead cabin attached to the vehicle, or from ground level by hanging controls;

- Jib Crane – a lifting arm which is fixed at one point; both the arm and the lifting apparatus are power driven and usually controlled from a cabin which rotates with the arm. It is usually used for lifting heavy loads to considerable heights;
- Mobile Crane – a jib crane mounted on a manually operated or motorised vehicle; usually used for lifting and transporting occasional awkward loads over reasonable distance, or where an overhead crane cannot be erected.

Conveyors

Where a continuous flow of goods or materials is passing between two or more fixed points, and the cost and utilisation of space can adequately be justified, a conveyor may be installed. Usually the expense that a firm is prepared to incur in installing conveyors will be in direct relation to the volume of goods or materials involved.

The type of conveyor selected must obviously depend upon the type of materials to be handled, but wherever possible one should use gravity to drive the conveyor and thus avoid the cost of power and driving plant.

Within the general classification of conveyors, therefore, we include the following:–

- slides and chutes – for parcels and cartons;
- gravity roller conveyors – used for many purposes from the movement of hot-rolled steel bar or strip, to the movement of packing cases.

Then there are the power-driven conveyors which are chain-driven by electric motors:–

- 'Live roller' conveyors – in which some of the rolls in each section of track are driven by chain – as with the wheel of a bicycle; or there is the *tow-line* principle in which cog-wheels, driven by electric motors, tow an endless length of conveyor;
- Overhead conveyors – for carrying materials or goods suspended

above the working areas in which they are to be used, or through process areas such as paint dipping or heat treatment;

- 'Sub-floor tow conveyor' – an endless chain below floor level onto which carts or trucks are hooked to tow them to the point at which the materials they contain are required.

Another conveyor system is the pulley-driven conveyor, an endless belt moved by power driven pulleys or rollers positioned at one or both ends of the conveyor system. Such a conveyor can be either:–

- A belt conveyor – mainly used for transporting small items which must be "contained" by the conveyor itself, such as small components, solid fuel, ashes, *or*
- A slat conveyor – where the "containing" ability of the belt conveyor is not necessary but where a flat surface is desirable.

Pumps, Pipelines and Feeder Systems

In circumstances where the materials to be supplied are in gaseous or liquid form, or are solids in powder or fine grain form, and where large quantities of such materials are involved, it may be advantageous to handle or 'transport' them via pipelines or feeder systems.

In this way the materials are enclosed in pipes or ducts giving the following advantages:–

- Easier control of material movement;
- Less likelihood of waste;
- Protection from contamination is facilitated;
- Flow of materials is more easily regulated;
- Sometimes provides the easiest method of connecting the storage unit with the user location.

Where the storage unit can be located above the user unit it may be possible to use gravity feed, which saves the costs of providing power. Examples of this situation are:–

- Fuel oil from tanks above furnaces;
- Lubricating oil for reservoirs above machines;
- Grain from silos to road transport.

In other circumstances it may be necessary to introduce pumping units to 'push' materials along the pipelines, or vacuum units to 'suck' the materials along.

This method of handling is now being applied to moving solids which can suitably be suspended in a liquid 'transporter' (for example coal suspended in water or ore-bearing earth suspended in a suitable fluid).

Pipelines and feeder systems have a wide variety of uses which can prove more profitable or less costly than more conventional forms of handling, but the same "Benefit to Cost" analysis must be applied, and invariably the main factor justifying their use is the volume of materials to be handled.

Security

Stock is often a company's greatest asset. Bearing this in mind, compare the level of security afforded to the collection of one week's wages, with that usually devoted to safeguarding the Stores.

The Security of Stores Buildings and Stockyards is a natural base from which to start discussing security. Particular factors to consider are:–

- A strongly built store, with security fencing in cases where the store is not part of the main premises. In case of stockyards, adequate security fencing is an essential requisite. Security lighting may also be considered in some locations;
- Weak points are doors and windows, therefore doors should be kept to a minimum. Proper locks and bolts should be provided to all doors. In the case of large doors necessary for vehicle access it is good practice to have a small "wicket" door for everyday use. Windows should also have locks if they open and have wire mesh or bars, for protection against forced entry;
- Burglar alarms of various types are available and thought should be given to their installation;
- Security patrols should of course include stores on their irregular patrols. The local police will usually have a crime prevention officer who will advise on security matters.

Keys are a weak point in any security system, and should only be issued to authorised personnel. The keys should be numbered and when issued, the name of the authorised person receiving the key recorded. Duplicate or master keys should be kept in a secure place in the charge of a responsible person.

Access to Stores be limited to authorised personnel under the control of the Stores Officer. Particular care must be taken to see that people such as drivers, maintenance fitters and the like do not get into the stores.

Out of hours issues are a problem for security, since quite often stores staff are not available. The best solution is preparation through avoiding the need for out of hours issues, by planning and issuing in advance of requirements. If it is essential to make an emergency issue, a named official should be made responsible.

In any stores, there are items attractive to a potential thief. Secure areas within the stores should be provided for these items.

Scrap and redundant materials are often a security risk, since they are often segregated from the main stores. This also applies to returns, awaiting despatch to suppliers.

Fire is always a hazard and the installation of fire fighting equipment is a necessity. This must be maintained at regular intervals.

The local fire brigade should be consulted on fire precautions.

Safety and Safe Methods of Working

It makes good sense to have safe methods of working both in order to avoid personal injury and to safeguard the company's interests.

In cases where personnel are injured at work the Manager responsible may well face prosecution under the Health and Safety at Work legislation, if he or she has failed to ensure that safe working conditions and practices are maintained.

The particular points to which the Stores Manager must pay attention are:–

- Good layout of the Stores, providing for clearly designated gangways, marked with white lines or similar methods. These gangways must be kept free from obstructions at all times. Areas for receipt of goods, inspection, returns to stores, scrap and redundant stock, as well as storage areas should be properly designated.
- Stores must be kept clean and tidy; what is generally called good housekeeping is an essential element in providing safe conditions of work. Many accidents are caused by tripping and falling over obstacles. Piles of inflammable rubbish such as empty packaging are also a hazard.
- Cleanliness must be enforced by management. This can be aided by the sealing of concrete floors, the provision of sheets and dust covers where required. The Factory Act lays down minimum standards for cleaning down premises, and for paintwork.
- All rubbish and arisings must be segregated and proper facilities

provided for temporary storage until removal. This removal must be on a regular basis, since old containers, paper cardboard, wood wool and so forth soon accumulates in any stores.

- Storage equipment must be properly used and goods stored in it correctly. Particular care must be taken to ensure that the weight limits and capacity of all equipment is known, and not exceeded. In a similar way, the load bearing capacity of floors and maximum storage heights must be known.

- Lighting is an important factor in safety, all working areas must be adequately lit. The actual lighting required will depend upon particular circumstances, where, for example, selection of small items is carried out, very good lighting will be needed. All passages and alleyways must be well lit in order to prevent accidents.

- Provision of handrails is required where gangways are above ground level, or the worker may experience difficulty in walking.

- The Health and Safety at Work Act required the guarding of moving parts of equipment and machinery, and the Stores Manager must ensure that all equipment under his or her control is properly guarded. Fork lift trucks will need overhead guards to prevent loads injuring the driver in the case of accidents.

- Where there is a possibility of slipping, non-slip surfaces should be provided, such as on ramps or sloping paths.

- Areas of particular danger in a stores are loading and unloading docks and wells. Removable handrails will be required, as will curbs or stops to prevent fork lift trucks running over the edge of the dock.

- Warning and information notices are an essential aid to safe methods of working. Many will be familiar, such as "Petroleum Spirit", "No Smoking", "Exit", and so on. These are available as 'standards' from suppliers. Other signs to suit your own particular requirements are available and can be made to your specification. In some cases such signs *must* be displayed. Colour is a useful method of conveying warnings or information. Danger signs and fire equipment are red, yellow indicates caution, and, for this reason, fork lift trucks are normally this colour.

- Protective clothing and equipment must be provided in appropriate situations and *worn*. It is the responsibility of management to ensure that safety helmets, goggles, gloves, overalls, safety shoes and boots are provided. The difficult task that the management must carry out is to make sure that the equipment is used properly.

- The organisation will have a Safety Officer, that the Stores Manager must consult on safety matters and take his or her advice. Instructions regarding the safety of equipment and practices should be issued in writing by management to all personnel working in the stores. It is important that people such as crane drivers, fork lift truck operators and slingers are aware of safety regulations.

Remember, it is the responsibility of management to provide safe working conditions and that under the Health and Safety at Work Act the Manager is personally liable to prosecution for failure to take proper steps to ensure safety.

Chapter 5

Transport

Introduction

Shipping, transport and distribution can be grouped under one heading, Logistics. Logistics planning involves not only the transportation side of distribution but also provides the "place element" in the marketing mix by helping to ensure that products arrive in sufficient quantities in saleable condition at points where the consumer can most easily buy them. Thus logistics management includes forecasting demand and matching supply to meet that demand through procurement of materials, production scheduling, inventory management, order processing, warehousing and transportation.

In international systems the logistics planning function involves a number of sub-systems which have central points of reach territory. There is a further sub-system for the management of local logistics such as the transport and distribution systems used by the importer to move products to customers in the market concerned.

Logistics, as well as being essential for moving goods to their destinations, is also a key marketing activity and as such, it requires the marketing management's attention. Logistics contributes to a major portion of costs, particularly in international business. Logistics planning also plays a major role in creating a good relationship with customers, ensuring that sales opportunities are not lost because of stock outs (which allows competitors to eat away at the company's market share).

In assessing the real cost of transportation you should be concerned with factors relating to reliability, time and price. Therefore, your decisions in choosing methods of transport and distribution will be based on "trade-offs" between these factors.

Transportation costs are often peculiar in that they frequently bear little relation to distance. The key factors in cargo pricing are competition and volume. For example, goods going from the Far East to the East Coast of the USA pay less than 30% of the rate of goods going the other way. Costs from the USA to South America are frequently lower than among South American countries.

In planning transportation the problems can be enormous and considerable hidden costs can be concealed such as the costs of out-of-stock positions which lose you business, or delays over insurance claims which you have to finance.

Transport is clearly a critical function within the overall logistics discipline. This Chapter looks at the component parts of Transport consisting of:–

- Fleet Management
- Vehicle Replacement
- Vehicle Scheduling
- Maintenance and Security
- Containers
- Loading Equipment
- Road Vehicle Design
- Haulage
- Rail Freight
- Air Freight.

Fleet Management

The main duties of the Fleet Manager are comprised of the efficient operation of the fleet and, in addition, the attainment of any further objective laid down by top management. He or she will do this by first achieving maximum utilisation of the vehicles being operated and by setting and maintaining correct weight and distance standards. It is also essential to keep within budgets and make sure vehicles are properly maintained.

There are a great many Acts of Parliament and Statutory Regulations concerning road transport and this situation is now being further complicated by E.C. Regulations. The Fleet Manager will need to be aware of these, including, for example:–

- The Highways Acts;
- The Road Traffic Acts;
- The Transport Act;

- The Vehicles and Driving Licenses Act;
- The Heavy Commercial Vehicles (Control and Regulations) Act;
- Motor Vehicles (Construction and Use) Regulations and
- Goods Vehicles (Plating and Testing) Regulations.

Note that the foregoing is by no means exhaustive and the Fleet Manager must ensure he or she is aware of all present and relevant legislation.

A whole host of matters arise from this legislation which impose duties upon Fleet Managers. Among these matters, some of the more important are to ensure that:–

- Vehicles are not overloaded;
- Vehicles are not loaded in such a way that the load is unsafe;
- Vehicles are properly maintained to the standard required by law;
- Vehicles are correctly tested and plated as stated in the Regulations;
- Drivers do not exceed permitted hours of work;
- A record of work is kept by all drivers;
- Drivers must hold a current driving license of the appropriate class for the vehicle to be driven and;
- The licensing authority is advised of any change in company ownership.

An important aspect of every manager's job, is to control their function. This means setting standards, measuring actual performance and, combining the two, enabling them to correct any deviations. A convenient and effective method of control is Budgetary Control. This can, of course, be equally well applied to Fleet Management. It is these costs which provide the Fleet Manager with the information he or she needs to control their department.

Other information required will be mileage: average operated per day, and average mileage maintained per day; tonnage or volume equivalent carried. The following indicators will be needed to measure performance:–

- Total operating costs per period (usually one month);
- Cost per hour;
- Cost per mile;
- Cost per ton (or volume equivalent);
- Cost per day operated;
- Cost per day maintained;

- Cost per depot;
- Cost per vehicle and;
- Cost per vehicle class.

You will see from the above that the manager can establish the cost and efficiency of the department and its individual depots, where applicable. He or she can also check the performance of types of vehicles or even an individual vehicle, if required.

Vehicle Replacement

Any car owner will know how quickly vehicles need replacing and the problem of financing the purchase of a new model. This is, of course, a much greater problem for a Fleet Manager who has to maintain a definite number of vehicles on the road to keep the company's goods moving. The first necessity is to establish a clear company policy on replacement, based not only on the need to replace vehicles at the end of their economic life, but upon such factors as:–

- Long term strategic planning (e.g. what goods are to be transported in the future, and where shall they be sent?);
- Capital resources available;
- Any legal requirements at home or overseas, or any impending legal requirements;
- The Government's Transport Policy (e.g. programme of motorway building, or a decision not to build new roads);
- Economic loads, unionisation, containerisation;
- Design and construction of vehicles;
- Vehicle maintenance needs and;
- Vehicle depreciation.

Having decided that the fleet must be renewed according to a planned policy and having decided which vehicles we need for the replacement programme, the question of financing the purchase of new vehicles is raised? Among the methods available to companies are:–

- *Outright Purchase*. This is simple if the capital is available at a reasonable price (remember the price of borrowing money is the interest paid). Capital allowances are available which can be set against the purchase.
- *Hire Purchase*. This is often favoured since it avoids the need to find large capital sums. At the same time a tax allowance is given as if it

were an outright purchase. Hire purchase rates are the price of borrowing the money, and must be studied before entering into an agreement. It is also worth noting that the purchaser does not obtain ownership until the last instalment is paid.

- *Lease*. This method avoids the need to provide working capital, and since the vehicles are on lease, the operator does not have to worry about depreciation. However, there are problems to be considered. One important point is that the vehicles will never belong to you. Leases are usually for a fixed number of years, and you are obliged to have a vehicle for that period of time. Lease charges will need to be studied, and you will also have to take into account operating and repair charges, which are often additional to the basic charge.
- *Contract Hire*. Details of the contract must be studied carefully, to ensure exactly who is responsible for insurance, maintenance and supplying of replacement vehicles. The basis of charging and the rates of charge also require careful investigation.

Choosing the Right Policy

As has been indicated this is not a straightforward decision, many factors have to be taken into account.

A detailed analysis of quotation for each method will have to be made; remember that it is not only the immediate replacement cost that has to be taken into account, but also the cost of operating over a number of years. An analysis must also be made between the various methods of replacement, and such matters as tax allowances and inflation taken into account. This will give the true cost of each method, and taken together with the company's objectives, strategies and financial recourses, aid the selection of the best policy for the organization.

Vehicle Scheduling

The objective of scheduling is to achieve optimum vehicle utilisation by operating vehicles at maximum load and at minimum cost. In attaining this objective the Fleet Manager will wish to ensure that the fleet is used efficiently and Vehicles are available when required. Similarly the manager needs to ensure that the most suitable vehicle for particular loads and journeys are used.

Constraints

In scheduling and routing vehicles the Fleet Manager must have regard to a number of constraints imposed by the law, the company's resources and the needs of the customer. Among these are:–

- The legal permitted driving hours;
- The need for drivers to have days off;
- Speed restrictions;
- The maintenance and servicing requirements of vehicles, which involve vehicles being off the road;
- The number of vehicles he or she has at their disposal at any one time;
- The types of vehicles he or she has available, since this will govern capacity available;
- Where the company's depots are located, and the number of depots the manager operates;
- The types of traffic involved; parcel traffic will be different from heavy haulage, when schedules are prepared;
- The number of calls to be made and their distance from each other;
- The time involved in loading or unloading at each call;
- If an urban area or a rural area is involved;
- If there are any special requirements of the trade or of customers involved;
- Such matters as public holidays, customer's industrial holidays, and local holidays; not forgetting early closing days in the retail trade;
- The type of roads that are available (motorways, dual carriageways and so on);
- Temporary restrictions caused by road works, building operations and similar work and;
- Certain loads may require special routes, to avoid obstructions, or bridges with weight or height limits.

How to Choose the Route

This is a considerable problem since, as has been shown, there are many factors to consider, several ways of selecting vehicle routes and loads for vehicles on that route, have been used, these include:–

- *Pigeon Hole Method.* This is probably the simplest method and is widely used for this reason. Delivery points are grouped together into geographical areas that have been adopted on the loading deck, usually in special bays. Thus, one would see bays for London, West Midlands, South East and so forth. When the goods for each area are known, a detailed schedule is worked out, and a vehicle allocated. This method is most suitable where the number of areas and delivery points are limited.

- *String Diagrams.* Another simple method is the use of string diagrams to select the best routes. A good map is required, showing your transport depots, and customer delivery points, the map will of course be to a known scale enabling distance to be read easily. A pin is fastened to each depot location, and also at each delivery point. A piece of string is fastened to a depot and taken to each delivery point in the sequence that appears to be the best route. In this way it is possible to show a number of alternative routes, and the distance involved can be measured. The best route or routes can then be selected. In practice the maps will be mounted on board and coloured strings used to show alternative routes more clearly.

- *Distance Saving.* This means selection of the optimum routes by first selecting the worst route. This would normally be by making an individual call each time to one customer, then linking the two nearest delivery points together and seeing what the savings would be. The next nearest point would then be linked up, and this would continue until an acceptable route emerged.

- *Travelling Sales Representatives.* This is sometimes used, and means visiting each customer by the shortest route and returning to the depot. It has a limited use in practice.

- *Linear Programming.* This is an operational research technique developed to show how limited resources can be used to their optimum. As the title suggests linear is proportional, and assumes that if for instance there is more time then more goods can be produced. The basic method used in linear programming is to locate an extreme point of a feasible region; examine each boundary edge intersecting at this point to see if any overmen along any edge would increase the value of the objective function. If this is so, move along the edge to the adjacent extreme point. This is repeated until the value of the objective function no longer increases.

If, for example, we assume that a company has depots and stock as follows

Depots	Stock
Anytown	30
Hightown	32
Northborough	22
Westborough	26
	100

Customer orders are:–

Customer	Order Quanity
Smith	34
Brown	40
Jones	36

The transport costs from each depot to each customer will be assumed in this case to be:–

	Anytown	Hightown	Northborough	Westborough
Smith	16	18	12	6
Brown	12	22	10	20
Jones	6	16	14	18

It is now possible to select the best routes, for there are a number of alternative solutions available. One may be for stock to be allocated as below:–

Customer	Qty	Depot Route	Qty	Depot Route
Smith	8	Northborough (1)	26	Westborough (2)
Brown	26	Anytown	14	Northborough (4)
Jones	4	Anytown	32	Hightown (6)

The cost of doing it this way is:–

Delivery Route	Cost/Item	Qty	Cost
1	12	8	96
2	6	26	156
3	12	26	312
4	10	14	140
5	6	4	24
6	16	32	512
		TOTAL COST	1240

This, of course, only gives the cost of using one method. It is necessary to repeat this excercise for each possible method and so, by a process of elimination, discover the most economic route. This appears to present a system of "trial and error" but linear programming is a planned method of trying all alternatives until the best solution is found.

In our example the allocations and costs are

	Depots			
Customers	*Anytown*	*Hightown*	*Northborough*	*Westborough*
Smith	16	18	8 12	26 6
Brown	26 12	22	14 10	20
Jones	4 6	32 16	14	18

An alternative is for Smith to take one from the Anytown depot, however, if this is so it is necessary to re-allocate issues from other depots. The whole exercise must then be calculated to see what the difference in cost in the revised method is, against the original. In this case:–

	Depots			
Customers	*Anytown*	*Hightown*	*Northborough*	*Westborough*
Smith	+1 16	18	8–1 12	6
Brown	26–1 12	22	7=1 10	20
Jones	4 6	32 16	14	18

So, in cost terms, this gives:–

Cost of Anytown to Smith 16, less Smith to Northborough 12 – an increase of 4. Northborough to Brown 10, less Anytown to Brown 12 – a decrease of 2. In this case a net increase of 2 in cost. This is repeated for each unused route.

Maintenance and Security

Maintenance and security are two factors to which all transport managers must give considerable attention especially since road safety is constantly receiving attention in Parliament and the press. Road vehicles carry the majority of goods in transit and so naturally there are many attractive loads being moved about the country in this way. Therefore, security is a major function of transport management.

Facilities for Maintenance

A very high degree of maintenance is required to keep a modern transport fleet on the road, maintained properly and according to law. Accordingly any firm operating vehicles must consider how it is going to maintain and service its vehicles. Methods available are:–

- *Company Garage and Workshops.* This requires properly equipped premises with all necessary facilities to service and repair vehicles. It also means employing qualified fitters, vehicle electricians and other staff. This method is convenient as you have complete control over maintenance programmes. Repairs can be carried out to suit the operating schedules. It gives a great deal of flexibility. On the other hand, it is expensive to maintain these facilities, and is therefore uneconomic for many operators with small fleets.
- *Contact Maintenance.* This is the method which must be adopted if circumstances do not justify workshop facilities. Most commercial garages will be willing to enter into a contract for the servicing and maintenance of vehicle fleets. The types of contracts available are too numerous to be dealt with here and, in any case, need to be considered in detail. However, the contract may cover regular planned maintenance or simply servicing when required. Vehicle manufacturers often have schemes whereby contract maintenance and servicing is carried out through their agents. In the U.K., Ford and Bedford are among the manufacturers who offer this facility.

Quality Control

This is a major aspect of vehicle servicing and maintenance, since there is little point in arranging for maintenance to be carried out, whether in workshop facilities or under contract, if it is not to the required standard. The Department of Transport in their "Goods Vehicle Testers Manual", make the following points:–

- Positive checks should be made at pre-determined intervals of time or mileage on items that affect the safty of the vehicles;
- Staff carrying out servicing and repairing of vehicles must be aware of the significance of defects;
- Any vehicle inspector, or other staff, whose duty it is to inspect vehicles must have authority to have defects rectified and to take unsafe vehicles off the road;

- Written records must be kept showing when, and by whom, inspections are carried out, the results of the inspections, and when and by whom remedial work is carried out and details of the work;
- Under-vehicle inspection facilities should be provided;
- A system whereby drivers can report defects must be provided, and these reports must be in writing. The clearance of the defect should also be recorded;
- The mechanical condition of hired vehicles and trailers is the direct responsibility of the user. (That is, the employer of the driver). Documents that are required to ensure an effective system of maintenance are service sheets for the pre-determined time and mileage checks, inspection check lists, drivers defect report, vehicles history record, job cards and planning sheets.

Proper planning maintenance is essential if the vehicles are to be kept on the road and there are a number of aids to the planning that are required.

It is interesting to note that the Freight Transport Association have a quality control scheme, enforced by inspectors employed by them. They check vehicles on behalf of members, whether they are maintained by company workshops or on contract.

Security

One has only to think for a moment of the wide variety of goods moved by road to realise how desirable many of these loads are to thieves. Insurance companies as well as operators of fleets are concerned that security should be effective. In fact insurance companies often require certain precautions to be taken by the operator as a condition of providing insurance.

Security is an attitude of mind that must be cultivated to ensure that everyone is aware of the problem and the elementary safeguards necessary. The advice of the insurance companies is always available, and so is that of the police. The police have crime prevention officers whose job it is to advise companies on security matters. The Road Haulage Association is also concerned about vehicle and load security and has produced a guide for the use of its members. Among the points mentioned are:–

- Recruitment of Staff. References should be checked over the last 5 years and any gaps investigated. Beware of telephone numbers for references, it may be an accomplice. If a driver is engaged do not allow them to take out a vehicle until you have their P45 and other documents. They also advise using the Association's engagement Form.

- Alarms and immobilisers should be fitted; models which provide protection without the driver getting out of the vehicle are available. The devices should be checked frequently.
- If a driver has a valuable load he or she should be instructed not to get out of the cab if stopped. If the police stop drivers they should offer to go to the nearest police station. As an anti-hijack measure, bolts should be fitted to the inside of doors.
- Vehicles should not be left unattended, especially at night.
- Keys should never be left in the vehicle. Numbers should be removed from security locks, starter and ignition keys or switches. If a key is lost, change all locks and switches.
- Drivers should be asked to change their routine by not visiting the same cafes at regular times.
- When a vehicle is sold, remove the company name.
- A cash bonus is suggested, payable if the drivers observe security rules.

Security is also important for the long term future of the business, since if a company gets a reputation for bad security, customers may withdraw their trade.

Containers, Unitisation and Palletisation

It is an obvious advantage if a consignor can load goods in some way at their premises, such that they can be transported and delivered to the consignee without the necessity of unpacking and handling individual items in transit. The above mentioned aids enable this to be done, as they are all methods of providing a 'unit' from one mode of transport to another. There is, therefore, no interference with the load in transit.

Containers

A container is now a major piece of transport equipment, and since its purpose is to ensure that a load is transported without interference to the consignor, it is important that it can be moved across national boundaries. It would be a major problem if containers were of different sizes and aptness in various countries. Therefore the International Standards Organisation (ISO) have made recommendations for freight containers in Draft I.S.O. No. 1496. These recommendations are accepted generally by national standards bodies, and also by Lloyds Register of Shipping. Lloyds also operate a system of certifying containers that meet these requirements.

The I.S.O. say that general purpose freight containers are of a rectangular shape, weatherproof for transporting and storing a number of unit loads, packages or bulk materials; they confine and protect the contents from loss or damage and can be separated from the means of transport, handled as unit loads and transshipped without re-handling the contents.

The I.S.O. gives a detailed definition of what a container is, which is well worth remembering.

They state that a freight container is an article of transport equipment:–

- Of a permanent character and accordingly strong enough for repeated use;
- Specially designed to facilitate the carriage of goods by one or more modes of transport, without intermediate re-loading;
- Fitted with devices permitting its ready handling, particularly its transfer from one mode of transport to another;
- So designed as to be easy to fill and empty;
- Have an internal volume of 1 metre or more.

The freight container does not include vehicles or conventional packaging.

I.S.O. Standard Container Sizes are based upon a module of 2.4 m × 2.4 m (8 ft × 8 ft), and will take the following loads:–

- 10 ft long = 10 long tons
- 20 ft long = 20 long tons
- 30 ft long = 25 long tons
- 40 ft long = 30 long tons

Types of Container

It is important to remember that an ISO standard, while a valuable one, is not going to meet all requirements and many companies will wish to design their own containers to suit their needs. Floors may be required to be strong enough for fork lift trucks to enter when loading or unloading. Sides and posts may be required to be suitable for use with special lifting devices. Many types of containers are available, among them are:–

- High Capacity Box
- Demountable Tank (for bulk liquids)
- Ordinary box
- Insulated
- Curtain sided

The companies despatching by these methods may have their own containers, which will be painted in their colours, and have an advertising value. Alternatively, they may be hired.

Continental Operation

If companies are regularly sending goods across Europe, it will be an advantage to have Transport International Routier (T.I.R.) Registration, which enables containers to cross customs frontiers easily. A point worth noting is that for tax purposes, the container is not part of the unladen weight of the vehicle.

Unitisation

This means assembling a number of small packages into one large package, or 'unit load'. It will be appreciated that this makes handling much easier and when loading or unloading will:–

- Reduce the amount of labour required;
- Enable mechanical handling to be used;
- Reduce vehicle turn round time;
- Make loading and stowage easier;
- Allow safer working practice to be used;
- Reduce damage and pilferage and;
- Permit marking and labelling of consignments to be simplified.

All this means reducing handling and transportation costs.

In the case of air freight these advantages are very important, since speed is the main reason for using this method of transport. Unitisation means a much speedier method of loading is possible, as against handling loose items of cargo. The customer can share in the reduced costs, since air lines offer special rates for bulk unitisation cargos.

Standard Packaging

Many companies have a range of standard packs, taking certain quantities of each product. Therefore when an order is received it is known at once which standard "outer" pack will be suitable. This not only takes advantage of unitisation principles, but means that the air or shipping space can be booked right away.

Palletisation

We are not concerned here with the description of pallets and their construction but in palletisation to facilitate transport loading.

As with unitisation the advantages gained from palletisation can be summed up as the reduction in handling and transportation costs, and the particular advantages are also similar, namely:–

- Enables mechanical handling to be used;
- Reduces road vehicle turnaround time;
- Makes loading and stowage easier, and;
- Reduces damage and pilferage.

The savings possible by the use of pallets are considerable, since goods can be picked up by fork lift trucks, and taken aboard ships or into containers and stowed.

Many port authorities have published details of savings through palletisation, which you can be referred to (e.g. Rotterdam and Oslo).

At this point it is worthwhile defining exactly what a pallet is, and for this purpose the definition of the "European Convention of Customs Treatment of pallets used in International Transport" is used:–

"A device on the deck of which a quantity of goods can be assembled to form a unit load for the purpose of transporting it, or of handling or stacking it with the assistance of mechanical appliances. This device is made up of two decks separated by bearers, or of a single deck supported by feet; its overall height is reduced to a minimum compatible with handling by fork lift trucks and pallet trucks; it may or may not have a superstructure". Two variations of pallet are shown in Figure 14.

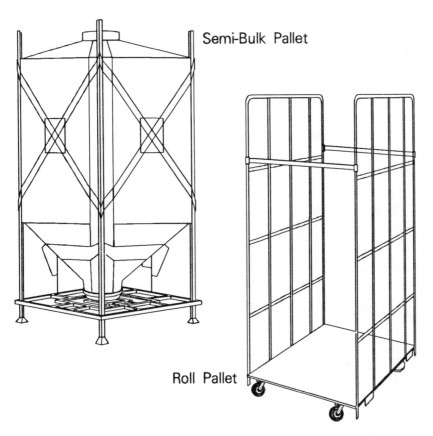

Semi-Bulk Pallet

Roll Pallet

Figure 14.
Typical Pallets

Ownership and Return of Pallets

This represents a considerable problem, since everyone using pallets has their own, and the cost of having them returned can be considerable.

One solution is to use "Low cost – non returnable pallets" known as LCNR pallets. The difficulty is to have it strong enough to support loads and either stand forklift trucks moving them, at a low cost. In practice they are usually re-enforced with plastic.

Another solution is to use a 'pallet pool', where all users contribute to the pool and use pallets accordingly, but this does not seem to have got off the ground. One exception is the one operated by the European Railways, but the U.K. is not a party to the scheme.

These schemes have not been taken up more widely and pallets not been universally adopted, as was once thought they would be. The reason is the drawbacks that pallets have when compared with containers. Among these are:–

- The pallet offers only limited protection to goods;
- It still requires a reasonable amount of labour, to handle pallets;
- The pallet loads cannot be transported under bond as they cannot be sealed and;
- A single pallet load is not an economic unit of transport.

In addition there has been a failure to agree among countries on a standard for pallets. The United States, the U.K. and Western Germany all have very different standards.

Mechanical Aids to Loading and Off-Loading

The time spent loading and unloading vehicles can be considerable and can therefore be costly in terms of vehicle time. Any aid to make this operation more efficient will reduce these costs, and speed vehicle turnaround.

There are types of equipment available which are suitable for most purposes and the problem is to select that equipment which is most suitable in particular circumstances. To decide on the correct equipment we must consider:–

- Weights of materials to be handled;
- Quantities of materials to be handled;
- Nature of goods involved;
- Handling characteristics of the goods;
- Frequency of loading, and
- Customer's needs.

We have to consider that while, in many cases, vehicles are unloaded or loaded by equipment mounted on the loading bays, circumstances often require the ability of the vehicle itself to load and off-load. Accordingly we shall look at equipment used in both circumstances.

Equipment for Loading and Unloading Bays

Automatic Dock levellers, or elevating platforms, are almost essential on loading bays, since vehicle platforms are of varying heights. These levellers enable fork lift trucks, barrows and the like to be driven from dock into the vehicle. These may be built into the bay or of the portable, power driven type.

Fork lift trucks are widely used and a wide range of models are available with an even wider range of fittings and adaptions. (e.g. fittings for handling drums, coils, clamps for certain loads, crane hooks, etc).

Pallet loads are of course intended for fork lift truck movement, and it is therefore an advantage if loads are palletised.

Cranes also have a wide range of uses in loading and unloading. They are particularly useful where large and heavy loads are involved, but are unable to deal with large volumes. The cost of installing cranes is high and the amount of goods traffic to be unloaded must justify the high capital cost involved. Cranes have freedom of movement within a certain area. There are several types of crane available, the main ones being:–

- *Fixed Jib*: This is a single mast in a fixed position, so naturally, the area where it can operate is limited.
- *Gantry Type*: This comprises load bearing girders supported at each end and running on rails which gives the gantry the means of movement. On the girders is a trolley housing the lifting mechanism which provides the traverse movement. Traverse is therefore possible in all direction. Control is by a suspended cabin or a remote control switch.
- *Wheeled Type*: When a crane is mounted on road wheels, it is a useful and mobile piece of apparatus. There are several types available for purchase or hire.
- *Rail Mounted Cranes*: are also used, but of course, are limited to areas where rails are laid.
- *Pully Blocks and Hoists*: In a sense these are a type of crane but are smaller, and can usually be fixed where required for a particular job. Awkward and cumbersome loads can be unloaded with these. There are many types available varying from traditional "rape-blocks", to the 'pul-lift' type using a roller chain.
- *Telphers*: These are another type of crane useful for particular operations. They are cub-operated and run over a certain area on a mono or single, overhead rail. Movement is, therefore, restricted to one direction only. When fitted with grabs they are often used for loading loose materials such as gravel or coal.

- *Pneumatic Tubes*: are another means of handling loose materials in powder form and are often used for. flour, sand and similar materials. The tubes are laid from the loading bay to where the material is produced and the material sucked along the tube.
- *Pipelines* are needed where liquids are involved.
- *Conveyors* are also widely used in loading and off-loading materials, since they are particularly suited to high volume loads as movement is continuous and comparatively cheap. Conveyors may be propelled by gravity or powered. They may also be fixed or moveable. A fixed conveyor takes up considerable space and for unloading purposes portable conveyors are often more useful. Care must be taken in handling conveyors as they are vulnerable to damage. There are many types of conveyors available to suit a wide range of materials, for example, flat belt, toughened belt, slatted, filler and so on.

In many circumstances, such as vehicles delivering to retail shops or scattered depots, handling aids are unlikely to be available at the site of unloading or loading. Therefore we have to consider aids that are available for use on vehicles.

Loading and Unloading Equipment Available on Vehicles

Tail Lifts are provided on a wide range of vehicles. Lifts are also available for the side of the vehicle, so loads can be transferred to the pavement easily. A tail-lift is the 'tail' of the vehicle which forms a platform on which goods can be lowered to ground level by power. The vehicle must have a chassis and framework strong enough to support the mechanism.

Rollers are provided in the floor of the vehicle allowing loads to be moved easily when actually inside the vehicle. Where they are provided they may be retractable below the floor to prevent the load moving.

Cranes are available for mounting onto vehicles. A specially strengthened floor and chassis is required. Various types are available to suit particular purposes.

Tankers are normally fitted with pumps permitting them to discharge their loads into the customers' tanks or wherever required.

Road Vehicle Design and Road Planning

As goods vehicles are costly to buy and maintain it is essential that the fleet is operated efficiently. This includes ensuring that the vehicles are those most suitable for their intended purposes.

In deciding the type of vehicle for our particular use, we must consider the following factors:–

- The goods or materials to be carried;
- The goods we may wish to transport in the future;
- The distribution area;
- The number of journeys made;
- Potential changes in distribution patterns;
- The expected life of vehicles;
- Any relevant government legislation;
- Any advantages offered in terms of cost, customer relations or turnround time in using special purpose vehicles, or particular design modifications and;
- What competitors or independent haulers are likely to do.

One of the first decisions to be taken is whether to use a standard vehicle available from vehicle manufacturer's or to have the vehicle, at least as far as the body is concerned, specially made.

Standard Vehicle Bodies

Manufacturers of road haulage vehicles have a large range of these available "off the shelf". Therefore a study of what is available will be well worthwhile, since a standard body will be much cheaper than a specially designed one. Indeed, in the light van class, (and most other vehicles up to about 6 tons), it is doubtful if its worth having a custom designed van body. Manufacturers also have available a number of engine sizes and various axle ratios.

Custom Built Vehicles

The main reasons for choosing to have a vehicle body built to the organisations specifications are:–

- To obtain more economic distribution because vehicles can be designed to carry greater loads;
- Vehicles can be designed to facilitate materials handling;
- Vehicles can be designed to suit specific routes and;
- A specially designed body may minimise damage to goods.

Disadvantages may be that a specialised vehicle has a lower re-sale value, flexibility of operations may be reduced and if the nature of a company's goods change, new vehicles may be needed.

Motor Vehicles (Construction and Use) Regulations

These regulations apply to commercial vehicles and trailers, and must be observed by all operators. Therefore anyone considering designing their own vehicle body, should understand them.

The items covered include such matters as:–

- Maximum weight in relation to wheelbase;
- Length and width of chassis;
- Brakes;
- Tyres;
- Lighting equipment and;
- Mirrors.

There is a choice of vehicle bodies available, and the most common types are:–

- *The bon van*, widely used where goods need protecting during transit, often used for clothing, foodstuffs and general parcels traffic.
- The main general purpose vehicle is the *platform truck* which comes in two basic forms. Firstly, the flat platform which has no sides, can carry most goods, which are protected by tarpaulin and ropes. Secondly a platform with sides – this is often used for loose material such as coal, sand, soil and the like. It may be fitted with tipping gear to facilitate unloading.
- *Swap or De-mountable Bodies* are an attempt to combine the advantages of the bon van, with the flexibility of the platform vehicle. The bon van in this case is a separate unit, which is lifted onto the platform vehicle, or off it, as required. This gives the effect of a dual purpose vehicle, for when the bon body is not mounted, a flat platform vehicle is available. The bodies can be built to suit the needs of the operator.
- *Articulated Vehicles* are now used extensively for the transport of goods, and the variety available is considerable. Basically, however, they are either flat platform or bon type. They consist of a separate towing unit and vehicle body. The towing or tractor unit,

comprises the cab and power unit, to which can be coupled various bodies. Therefore a towing unit can take a load to a customer, detach the body, couple up another body and return with it to its depot. This greatly assists loading and unloading, but, probably more important is the quicker turnround time that can be achieved by this method of operation.

- Many other types of vehicle are available and if money is no object almost anything can be built on a chassis. However, the most commonly used categories are special containers or skips used by scrap dealers for collecting swarf or similar materials, tankers for liquids (from milk to oil), special vehicles for ready mixed concrete, and refrigerated units.

Road Planning

The economic use of the vehicle is the ultimate objective of transport planning and this is likely to be better achieved if the vehicle is designed to suit particular needs. If it is decided to go ahead with custom built vehicles, to facilitate economic loading, the manufacturers of the vehicles should be consulted.

Factors considered in deciding size and type of body include:–

- The nature and weight of loads;
- The method of packing, size of pallets, unitisation and use of containers and;
- The nature of the goods and method of distribution.

A study of these factors will enable decisions to be made on such matters as:–

- The type of body and of chassis required;
- Which loads will require a bon van, or platform vehicle and;
- Methods of loading, e.g. rear loading, side loading etc.

Accessibility is an important feature when planning vehicles. Those delivering goods to High Street shops will have different requirements to the lorry delivering heavy machinery. Among matters to be taken into account are the platform height of vehicle and the need for rear doors, roller shutters, side doors or curtain sides.

Methods of Construction

A vehicle must be suitable for its purpose, but at the same time have durability, strength and lightness. A wide variety of materials are available in the construction of vehicle bodies, all with advantages and disadvantages. Among these are steel and its alloys, strong but liable to corrosion. Aluminium alloys are of course not liable to corrosion. All metal panels can be beaten out. Plastic which is durable, including glass fibre cannot be repaired so easily if damaged.

The purpose and use of the vehicle will enable the most suitable combination of materials for body construction to be decided. Often in large vans, roof lights are put in to assist loading.

Loading aids were mentioned earlier, and it is cheaper if these are fitted at the time of manufacture. In addition, other interior fittings may also be desirable and should be considered at the construction stage. Such items may include tie rails, shoving bars, rubbing rails and damage bags. The cab is an important part of any vehicle, but this is not strictly within the scope of body construction. However, the company will achieve it's objective more easily if strain on the driver is minimised. Therefore comfort and safety is important. Such items as seats, air conditioning, radio and so on must be considered. Good instrumentation and warning systems are also an essential aid to good driving.

Distribution and marshalling

The pattern of distribution must be studied and such factors as the following taken into account:–

- Urban and rural routes;
- Delivery of goods to a large number of individual customers;
- Bulk deliveries;
- Number of special loads (such as heavy machinery);
- Collections and;
- Vehicles needed for each load.

Suitable arrangements must be made for the marshalling of goods for distribution. This will usually mean:–

- The planning of loads according to geographical location, and the need to make up a full load;
- The planning of loading, so that goods are in order of delivery and;

- A separate marshalling area will be required with, perhaps, separate 'pens' for each route.

There will usually be part loads or parcels which will not justify sending a vehicle, in which case, it is usual to send by public haulers.

Road Haulage

The advantages of road transport are as follows:–

- Flexibility; HGV's can go almost anywhere and can carry almost anything;
- Door to door delivery from consignee to consignor;
- Speedy delivery;
- Capital investment in movement of goods can be low, as one vehicle can often carry a variety of goods over many routes and;
- Special or elaborate packing is not usually needed.

If a company decides to distribute goods by road, they may choose either to send them by a public hauler or to purchase or hire a fleet and operate it themselves. The advantages of using a *Public Hauler* include:–

- As the company does not operate any vehicle of its own, it has no responsibilities or problems in the area of transport when a load or consignment is available;
- A particular type of vehicle can be used to suit particular needs;
- All costs are known in advance (the rates charged), the most competitive charges selected, and plans made accordingly and;
- Transport facilities, such as garages, workshops and so on, do not have to be provided.

Charges

Charges for sending goods by the public hauler, are based upon the weight of consignments and the distance carried. Full loads and specials are also charged on a similar basis. The charge is based upon either a weight of one ton or, if the load is bulky, 80 cubic feet is taken to equal one ton.

General Parcels Traffice

Often called "smalls", most haulers issue a set scale of charges for small parcels. This scale of charges is made up of a set of country is divided for his purpose. There would, for instance, be a set of charges for parcels collected in, say, the Birmingham area and delivered in the London area, and a further list of charges for traffic between North Wales and Tyneside.

These scales are subject to various modifications according to particular circumstances. For example, there will be extras for collections and perhaps a reduction if parcels are delivered to a depot only. There are minimum charges levied by most carriers. Also, if vehicles are detained for a long time, extra charges may be incurred.

Where a company deals with large volumes of parcels, such as a mail order company, special contract arrangements can be made with the hauler. A typical contract agreement would be based on the number of parcels despatched over a period, the delivery areas, and the availability of vehicles and result in a flat rate scale for all parcels delivered anywhere in the U.K.

Contract Hire

In many cases companies feel that for reasons for operating convenience and prestige it is necessary to run their own fleet. A method of doing so without laying out large sums in capital expenditure for purchase, is to hire a fleet of vehicles. Some of the advantages offered are:–

- The company has complete control of operating the vehicles, and in respect of the drivers;
- Considerable flexibility since the vehicles are under the company's control;
- Vehicles are normally painted in the hiring company's livery, and so advertising and prestige are gained;
- The hirer is usually responsible for servicing and maintenance, licenses and other charges;
- The agreement will usually provide for replacement vehicles if any are off the road for any length of time and;
- Costs are known in advance, and can therefore be allowed for in budgets.

Disadvantages of Contract Hire include:–

- Costs may be incurred as the vehicles are limited to carrying goods for the hirer, and return loads may be difficult to obtain. This means that vehicles may sometimes be running empty;

- Charges will continue regardless of the use made of the vehicles;
- Transport facilities, such as garages, offices, loading and routing staff will have to be provided, and will be a cost upon the company, in addition to hire charges and also;
- At the end of the contract period, the vehicles will revert to the company from whom they were hired.

Basis of Charges

In each case there will be a detailed contract between the Hire company and the hiring company, which must be negotiated to suit each particular circumstance. Typical agreements might be:–

- *Heavy Haulage*; A fixed annual charge plus a charge per mile, or a high annual charge but the mileage charge operating after a specified mileage. Period of hire might be for 5 years.
- *Light Vans*: A fixed annual charge up to a specified mileage, and a mileage charge when this is exceeded. Again, the hire period may be for five years.

The agreement must be studied carefully to make sure that it meets the hirer's requirements and the costs intended to be covered are, in fact, covered. Points to check are:–

- That the charges do cover maintenance and license charges;
- Is replacement provided if a vehicle is off the road?;
- Are any advance charges required?;
- Is insurance cover adequate for your requirements?;
- What are the conditions under which replacement vehicles are supplied? and;
- Are mileage charges reasonable?

Owning a Fleet

Many companies prefer to own and operate their own vehicles, since this gives maximum control and flexibility, and may well be cheaper than other methods.

Advantages include the fact that the company has complete control over vehicles and drivers, which gives maximum flexibility in operation. Similarly, the vehicles can be used to project the company's image by it's livery and for advertising particular products.

A company operating it's own fleet will have to provide a transport management function, and the necessary supporting organisation. Workshop and garage facilities for maintenance, and, facilities for storing and issuing fuel are required along with facilities for drivers and mates.

There are of course disadvantages which include:–

- Provision of capital sums to acquire and replace vehicles;
- Difficulty in assessing exact costs of providing a company fleet since some costs will be hidden in general overheads (wages and salaries department etc);
- Vehicles are licensed for company use only, and cannot be used for anyone else (i.e. hired out);
- Charges are incurred whether vehicles are used or not;
- The problem of unbalanced loads, vehicles may run empty due to difficulty in obtaining return loads and;
- The tendency to use vehicles without regard to cost, "as they belong to the company anyway".

Operating Costs of a Company Fleet

All the charges which are involved in the organisation of a transport undertaking, and the costs which are incurred in either the movement of passengers or goods are covered by the term operating costs, and, for the sake of convenience, these are divided into standing charges and running costs.

Standing Charges

Immediately a business is commenced and vehicles obtained, certain expenses will be incurred whether or not the vehicles are operated on the road; such charges are not related to the number of miles run or the number of hours worked.

These charges are as follows:–

- *Interest on Capital*: if allowed, at 1% or 2% above the minimum lending rate.
- *Depreciation*: On cost price of vehicle, less residual value and cost of tyres.

- *Revenue Licences*: Annual cost.
- Road Service Licence and Certificate of Fitness.
- *Licence*: Annual cost should always be considered.
- *Insurance*: Comprehensive policy including third party, fire, Employer's liability, and goods-in transit insurance.
- General Administrative Charges.
- Garage Expenses.
- Wages.

Each one of these components, which together form the standing charges of an undertaking, will be considered separately in the following paragraphs.

Interest on Capital

It has been contended that operators should include in their standing charges a sum equal to that which they would receive if the capital had been invested in government or other high class securities, instead of being invested in vehicles; that the interest on capital should therefore be an element in standing charges. There seems no logical reason why this should be so for it is not the general practice for trading companies to allow interest on fixed assets in assessing costs of production. This should be absorbed by the item allowed for profit. It may be found, therefore, that some operators will allow for interest on capital, while other operators ignore this item completely and rely on the percentage of profit added to cost.

Depreciation

Depreciation is due to three causes, namely, wear and tear, depreciation in value due to fall in market price and obsolescence due to the constant improvement in design. Wear and tear is the common cause of depreciation in value, and, for this reason, there are those who contend that the charge under this heading should be included in running charges, but, even if a vehicle remained stationary all the time it would depreciate in market value, and in the end become obsolete, therefore inclusion of depreciation in standing charges is the general practice.

The cost of tyres must be deducted from the purchase price of the vehicle. As several sets of tyres will be fitted to the vehicle during the course of it's useful life, it is thought proper that these should form an element of the running costs.

Finally, in estimating the amount to be written off for depreciation, the operator must assess the value that is expected to be obtained from the vehicle upon sale at the end of its useful life. Many operators sell, and buy new vehicles, rather than arrange for extensive refits which would make the vehicle mechanically sound for several more years. This value on sale, or scrap value, must be allowed in providing for depreciation.

The charge for depreciation is therefore based on:

Cost of vehicle − cost of tyres − residual value − Dep. charge

The resultant sum is the amount to be provided for depreciation, before distribution of profits, during the expected life of the vehicle. There are several methods of arranging for this.

The necessity for the allowance has previously been explained. If this were not charged, it would be equivalent to returning a proportion of the capital each year to the shareholders.

Insurance

Adequate insurance against all risks is necessary in any business, while third party risk insurance on vehicles is made compulsory by law. Further insurance must be taken out according to the nature of the business and the work undertaken. For the purpose of costing, insurance is included as a standing charge, for it is incurred whether the vehicles are on the road or in the garage. They may be reduced on the vehicle if it is taken out of commission for a considerable time.

Licences

This item covers both the revenue licence and also the licences which are necessary by virtue of the provisions of the Road Traffic Acts. The charges paid for these licences are fixed, but the cost of the revenue licence varies with the unladen weight of a goods vehicle or the seating capacity of a passenger service vehicle. This item must therefore be allocated in accordance with the amount paid for each vehicle. With licences issued under the Road Traffic Acts, these are at a fixed rate per annum, and consequently, the cost is divided proportionately among all vehicles of the fleet.

General Administrative Charges

General administrative charges include the salaries of office staff and managers, directors' fees, rents, rates, taxes, lighting and heating of offices; postage, telephones, stationery, time-keepers and watchmen, garage and depot staff and other essential expenses which are incurred for the benefit of the business as a whole, and which cannot be allocated to any particular vehicle. These items can only be included among the standing charges, and, as such, are assessed on a time basis. Such charges could be allocated to a vehicle in accordance with mileage run, but it would be very difficult to allocate the item precisely.

Garage Expenses

The wages of garage and depot staff may be included under this heading instead of the previous one, together with all other expenses relating to the upkeep of the garage; rents, trades, taxes, lighting, heating and so on. It may be noted that the repair shop is usually treated separately in order that the cost of this may be allocated over the repairs to the vehicles. Day to day maintenance may be detailed to carry out duties in the garage, and the proportion of wages for time so spent should be allocated to garage expenses.

Wages

This item covers the wages of drivers and of statutory attendants or mates in the case of goods vehicles. With road haulers, drivers usually have charge of one vehicle, and their wages can therefore be charged to that vehicle, but where the driver's time is spent on two or more vehicles, then the time must be ascertained and the wage split up accordingly. It must also be borne in mind that drivers are entitled to an annual holiday, and this must be allowed for in making up costs either by charging it up against the driver's own vehicle, or spreading the item over the whole fleet. Wages must be included with the running costs.

The above items form the total cost of standing charges. With road haulers it is usual to find the standing cost for each vehicle, and it is essential to divide some of the items in accordance with the varying tonnage of the vehicle.

Running Costs

Under this heading are included the following charges:–

- Petrol or other fuel lubricants: Quantity used, worked out to a fraction of a penny per mile.
- Tyres: Actual issues.
- Maintenance and Repairs: Cost, or a fixed weekly sum.
- Sundries: Cost.

Fuel

The quantity issued to each vehicle must be acertained and charged to that vehicle, and the mileage for each vehicle must be obtained for each gallon or unit of fuel consumed, and also for lubricating oil.

Tyres

The wear on tyres in accordance with the mileage, and the charge under this item must be assessed accordingly; the manufacturer's assessment of life must be taken until the operator has sufficient experience upon which to base his or her own calculations. Some operators include this item under maintenance.

Maintenance and Repairs

The cost under this heading varies from week to week, and in accordance with the life of the vehicle. Experience has to be the guiding factor in this connection, for a weekly sum must be charged to each vehicle, based on usage, to cover the item, and, by this means, something in the nature of a 'sinking fund' is built up. The total of the weekly charge is credited to this account, and the actual cost of repairs debited thereto.

Sundries

There are many small expenses which cannot conveniently be included under any of the above headings, and must be charged out to each vehicle, or allocated proportionately among all vehicles.

Rail Freight

Railways have certain advantages when arranging for the movement of goods. Among these are:–

- A reliable and speedy service between main cities;
- Collection and delivery to customers can be arranged if this is required and;
- Special contracts for the movement of large regular consignments are possible.

   On the other hand there may be problems in using rail, including:–

- Good and secure packaging is required;
- Delivery times may be lengthy if customers are not on the main line and;
- There is danger of pilferage.

   There are a number of services offered by British Rail.

Ordinary Goods Service

Single consignments which may be delivered or collected from the station. Alternatively, the railways collect goods for despatch, and deliver to the consignee.

Passenger Express Parcels Service

Goods are carried on normal passenger services. This is intended for parcel traffic, and parcels may be handed in at any station. It is also possible to arrange for parcels to be collected and delivered by the railway.

Freight Sundries

British Rail operate this door to door service. They collect from the consignor and deliver to the consignee by road. There is a weight limit of 3 tons on consignments.

Priority, Express Passenger Service (Red Star)

This 'Red Star' service gives priority from station to station. Parcels can be despatched on stated trains by request. Special charges apply to this service.

Use of Containers by Rail

Containers offer many advantages in the depatch of goods. There are many types of containers of various sizes available and this means that a container is available to suit most types of goods.

Containers can be loaded by the consignor, transported by road to the railway, and afterwards taken by road to the consignee. These service are operated by Freightliners Limited, who have a number of "Freightliners Depots", throughout the U.K. Containers are delivered to a depot by road, transported by Freightliner train (operated by British Rail), to a depot near the consignee, off-loaded to road vehicles and delivered to the consignee. Freightliners are on a regular schedule timetable.

Special Arrangements for Large Regular Consignments

British Rail offer special facilities to anyone who has large quantities of goods to move on a regular basis. Examples of this type of consignment are minerals such as iron ore, coal, oil, cement and even motor cars, which are moved to distributors in this way. Anyone who has travelled by rail will have seen trains made up of oil tankers or car transporters; these are company trains operated by British Rail to suit the needs of particular companies. To take advantage of this service it is better if the companies have their own rail sidings, connected to the British Rail system.

Rail Charges

At one time the railway operated an inflexible, rather complicated rate charging system. This has now been abandoned, as British Rail have entered into commercial arrangements on the basis of negotiated rates with customers.

Many customers are very large organisations placing substantial amounts of business, and making individual contracts with British Rail. Examples are:–

- Mail order or other companies with a large amount of parcel traffic; these may arrange a special price per parcel irrespective of distance or parcel weight.
- Large organisations operating "company trains"; examples would

be motor car manufacturers, cement manufacturers and similar bodies with 'bulk' contracts, such organisations can negotiate special contract prices.

Freightliners Limited, also negotiate individual rates with customers for hire or lease of containers, as well as for the transport by Freightliner from 'door to door'. National Carriers operate a system of national distribution in association with British Rail, similar to that operated formerly by the Rail Goods Service.

Sea Freight

Sea services can provide an effective way of getting volumes of product to a central distributions point or a heavy, bulky product to the other side of the world. Other advantages include:–

* A lower cost per tonne of carriage
* A world wide surplus of capacity

Disadvantages include:–

* The need for complicated and expensive loading equipment at ports
* The potential need for specialised vehicle(s) to move the freight from the port to the end user
* Slowness

In terms of the Single European Market and removal of trade barriers, there is concern that V.A.T. could be extended to ships, ships equipment and fuel. Whilst such VAT could well be reclaimable, it has to be paid in the first instance this increasing operators direct costs. In turn this could increase the cost to the customer. A possible "knock-on" effect could be that operators will register with non EC countries and/ or buy their supplies outside the EC.

A possible effect on sea freight is clearly the Channel Tunnel. Whilst such effects are at this stage subjective they could be:–

* Over capacity at UK ports
* Rationalisation of the shipping market
* Southern Uk ports seeking deep sea freight business to replace short-sea ferries lost to the Channel Tunnel
* Depressed shipping and/or port charges

Despite the effects of the Channel Tunnel, EC regulations and general slowness, sea freight can form part of an effective logistics network provided logistics managers can be persuaded to trade off speed against the other benefits.

Air freight

Modern travel means air transport and people now travel by air as a matter of course for holidays, and, for business. Air freight is now as important as passenger travel, and is as convenient when sending goods from one place to another over great distances.

There are disadvantages of air freight when compared to other methods of transport, these include:–

- Higher cost of transport;
- Restriction in size and weight of materials to be sent by air;
- Prohibition of certain items and;
- Possible delays and diversions due to weather.

We must consider against these the advantages of despatching by air:–

- Speed of delivery;
- Reduction in standard of packing is possible;
- Lower insurance rates may be obtained;
- Greater security of goods and;
- Marketing flexibility is obtained.

When considering the advantages and disadvantages of air freight it becomes clear that in the following circumstances, air freight is fully justified:–

- Where goods are urgently required. (e.g. medical supplies or a part required for plant that is broken down);
- The nature of the goods make it imperative that they are delivered quickly (e.g. Daily newspapers, fresh flowers and similar items) and;
- Where the value is high compared with weight or size (e.g. precious stones or modern transistorised electronic equipment).

Regulation of Air Freight

This is carried out by an international body on which are represented various member countries, who have international air lines. It is known as the International Air Transport Association (I.A.T.A.). This organisation fixes rates, and makes regulations observed by all air lines, among the more important are:–

- The Cabotage Principle:–
  This states that all air freight within a country's boundaries must be carried by that country's air lines. This prevents foreign competition on domestic routes. In the case of the U.K. it also applies to traffic to and from the colonies and dependent territories; note that special non-international rates may apply in the case of UK cabotage.
- Determination of Cargo Rates:–
  Air cargo is always calculated per kilogramme gross weight, or, if bulky material, per volume equivalent. Air freight rates are decided by I.A.T.A. on the above basis, and run between airports.
- Minimum charges:–
  These apply to small consignments irrespective of actual weight or volume. They take precedence over charges that would be made if the general cargo rate were to be applied.
- General Cargo Rate:–
  This applies to all goods not in a specific rate grouping. These consist of minimum charges (m) usual rate (n) and quantity rate (q) at various brake points.
- Specific Commodity Rate:–
  This applies to specifically designated commodities carried between two specified points, for consignments at fixed minimum rate. It is lower than the general freight rate.
- Class Rates:–
  These apply to specifically designated classes of goods for carriage between points in a specified area or areas. There is a percentage reduction on surcharge based upon the under 100 Kg General Freight Rate for consignments to which minimum charges apply.
- Special Bulk Unitisation Charges:–
  Where goods are shipped in I.A.T.A. registered and standardised containers, special rates are available. Most routes use pallets and containers, and freight companies will be pleased to discuss the method of transport with customers.

- Documentation:–
  The most important document is the consignment note or air-way bill. This note is a standardised I.A.T.A. document and is in two forms. One for use on domestic routes, and one for use on international routes.

  It is prepared by the consignor in a number of copies, one of which he or she retains. A copy goes to the air line, and also accompanies the goods. It is evidence of a contract and acts as a receipt for the goods.

  Unlike the Bill of Lading used when goods are sent by sea, it is not a negotiable instrument (that is to say ownership cannot be changed by endorsing the Bill), nor is it required in order to obtain the goods.

- Declaration of Value:–
  The value of the consignment must always be stated, although the statement "no value declared" is allowed.

  Valuation charges are made on a weight or volume basis, below this value no charge is made.

- Valuable Items:–
  Where valuable items are to be sent by air, quantity rates do not apply. They are charged at the under 45 Kg rate plus 100% although this may vary with the item value the item type and indeed, the air carrier.

- Hazardous Goods:–
  Certain items are classed as hazardous, and will not be accepted for air freight. Among these are explosives, compressed gasses and inflammable liquids. Full details are given in the I.A.T.A. "Restricted Articles Regulation Manual".

- Other Matters Dealt With by the I.A.T.A.:–
  There are many of these including uniform labelling of consignments, making advance arrangements when necessary, tracing consignments, arranging transfers and so forth.[7]

Other Documentation Required

In order to prepare the IATA air-way bill and generally to make the necessary arrangements for despatch by air, the following are needed:–

- Export license (if applicable);
- Commercial Invoices (In several copies);

- Packing Lists;
- Certificate of Origin and;
- Instruction for despatch goods form, or a similar method of giving despatch instructions.

If receiving goods by air, the following documents will usually be required:–

- Import licence (if applicable);
- Commercial Invoices;
- Packing lists;
- Certificate of Origin and;
- Customs Declaration Forms.

Legislation Relating to Storehouses and Stockyards

The major legislation dealing with people at work is the Health and Safety at Work Act. This Act is most important and many matters dealt with an earlier Acts, such as the Factories Act, and the Office, Ships and Railway Premises Act, are now covered in this new Act. In fact, these earlier Acts, together with some others, have become statutory provisions of the Act.

Those involved with the Health and Safety at Work Act set up "The Health and Safety Commission", which administers the Act. This Commission may direct investigations and hold inquiries, it may also issue 'Codes of Practice' which are not law, but contravention of which would be admissible as evidence in any case brought under the Act. The Commission will recommend to the Secretary of State, that various regulations are made as needed under the Act.

There is also the Health and Safety Executive (HSE) set up under the Work Act. This is an executive body which ensures that the provisions of the Act are implemented. The Factory Inspectorate and others responsible for the enforcement of the Act, are now responsible to the Executive. Both the Commission and the Executive can request information to be supplied as necessary. The inspectors have considerable authority including that of entering premises and taking samples. They can, if they consider personal injury likely, serve a prohibition notice on any activity. They may seize any harmful substance if likely to be a danger. If any Inspector thinks an offence may be committed an improvement notice may be served.

It is a provision of the Act that employers must conduct their business so that the public are not exposed to risks. In addition, the employer must bring a written statement of general policy to the attention of his employees. Provision is made under the Act for safety representatives from among employees who will be concerned with Health and Safety.

The detailed provisions of the Factories Act 1961 still apply, as do those of the Offices, Shops and Railway Premises Act 1963. Therefore, any manager in charge of people at work, should be familiar with them, as they are now statutory provisions of the 1974 Act. Among these are:–

- *A Duty to Fence* – This means that all prime movers, transmission and other dangerous machinery must be fenced. Therefore, if in charge of a stores that has equipment that could be dangerous, it is necessary to ensure that it is safely fenced. This would apply to a guillotine, or hand saw used for shearing or cutting material prior to issue. The rule should be: if there is a foreseeable danger, act to prevent it.

- *Premises Must be Safe* – The Act states that all floors, stairs, passages and gangways shall be of sound construction and properly maintained, and shall, so far as is reasonably practicable, be kept free from any obstruction and any substances likely to cause persons to slip. The implications of this for Storehouses will be obvious, and the Manager must see that the buildings are sound and that floors can carry the loads for which they are intended (fins full of for instance, steel bolts, will be very heavy). "Good Housekeeping" should be the watchwords of the Storekeeper and Manager. Nothing should be left lying about so that people can trip over it, nor should items by left protruding from bins, so that people can catch themselves on them. Drip trays to prevent spillage should be properly maintained, so that people do not slip on spilled liquids.

  Also important in a stores is the obligation to provide safe access to work places and fencing, if a person might fall more than 6'6". Locations to watch are unloading docks, lift shafts and anywhere else in a stores where there is a chance of a person falling.

- *Premises Must be Kept Clean* – All premises must be washed and painted at regular intervals to comply with the Act. In practice of course, Managers will not wish to have dirty premises in their charge, and proper planned maintenance will take care of this aspect. Dirt must be removed daily from floors; whitewash must be renewed every fourteen months.

- *Overcrowding* – A factory must not be overcrowded and adequate space per worker must be provided (i.e. not less than 400 cubic feet of air space per person).
- *Temperature* – A reasonable temperature must be maintained and must not be less than 60°F after the first hour; thermometers should be provided in the workroom.
- *Ventilation* – Effective and suitable provision must be made for maintaining a circulation of fresh air. All fumes must be rendered harmless.
- *Lighting* – Proper lighting must be provided. Good lighting is essential in a store, where order pricing is carried out, and paper work has to be checked. Daylight through roof lights or fluorescent tubes are probably the best forms of lighting available.
- *Drainage* – All floors must be properly drained.
- *Other Provisions* – Sanitary conveniences of a suitable type must be provided and kept in a clean condition. If members of both sexes are employed, separate accommodation must be provided.

There are a number of general welfare provisions under the Act, and among these, the following are of importance to the Stores Manager:–

- Drinking water must be provided at suitable points where it is accessible to workers;
- Washing facilities must be provided for all employed persons. This includes means of cleaning and drying (soap and towels);
- Adequate and suitable accommodation must be provided for clothing not worn at work; in practice this means suitable clothes lockers are needed;
- Seating facilities must be provided where a substantial part of the work may be done sitting down. This would apply, for example, in a stores where packing small parts and certain types of inspection are carried out and;
- A first aid box or cupboard must be provided. First aid must be in the charge of a responsible person, and where over 50 people are employed there must be a person trained to administer first aid available.

Similar matters to those in The Factories Act are also covered in the Office, Shops and Railway Premises Act 1963, but, of course, apply to those particular types of premises.

So far the Health and Safety at Work Act, has been studied in as far as it applies to general management and the operation of stores and premises. However, many of its provisions apply specially to the storing of goods and materials and here again, the 1974 Act has taken over earlier legislation, much of which is now a statutory requirement of the Act.

Among materials which are subject to special requirements of the law are:–

Petroleum Liquids

These are subject to the Petroleum (Consolidation) Act 1928, and a number of regulations that have been added since, including the Petroleum (Inflammable Liquid) Order 1971 and the Inflammable Liquids and Liquified Petroleum Gases Order 1973.

The main provisions of this legislation cover such matters as:–

- The prohibition of smoking and naked lights in the vicinity of petroleum stores;
- The need for electrical equipment such as the pumps to be of a flameproof type;
- Proper warning notices which must be displayed (e.g. 'Petrol Store', 'No Smoking');
- The construction of underground storage tanks;
- The suitable marking of any cans or drums used for petroleum product storage and;
- The need for fire extinguishers of a suitable type (the chemical variety, buckets of sand etc).

If involved in the storage of material of this nature, it will be necessary to ensure knowledge of the law by checking the above mentioned legislation, and also to seek the help of the local Fire Brigade, who are always willing to give advice.

Explosives

Other materials subject to special legislation are any explosive used in connection with work.

The main Acts are the Explosives Acts 1875 and 1923, both of which now form part of the statutory provisions of the Health and Safety at

Work Act 1974. If one is going to store explosives, the exact requirements will depend upon the quantity of explosives one wishes to store. However, the following will always apply:–

- A police certificate is needed to purchase explosives;
- The local authority must licence annually the stores used for explosives;
- Stores for explosives must be substantial and they must not be damp. Iron, steel or grit must not be used because of the danger of sparks. A lightning conductor is also required;
- The Stores have to be built away from other buildings;
- Proper warning notices are required, warning persons of the dangerous nature of the material stored;
- Special forms of lighting are needed to prevent danger from electrical faults;
- People working in Explosive Stores require protective clothing and;
- Smoking is, of course, prohibited.

Any manager of an explosives store must be thoroughly aquainted with these rules.

The stacking of materials generally can provide safety hazards, and so, the Department of Employment has produced a booklet in their Health and Safety at Work series: No. 4 – Safety in the Stacking of Materials. This is an excellent guide to the stacking of a wide variety of materials, and also deals with pallets, shelving and racks, and is well worth obtaining from HMSO.

Bulk Material

These items, such as coal, sand, shale and similar materials are often stored in heaps on open ground. This method of storing materials gave considerable concern following the Aberfan tragedy, when a pit tip collapsed killing most of the school children in the village. The result was the Mines and Quarry (Tips) Act 1969, which regulates the manner of stacking large quantities of materials in this manner. It requires proper advice to be taken before construction and regular inspection when in use.

Many materials are susceptible to spontaneous combustion, such as coal, and precautions must be taken to protect against this. Among these will be limitations on height, and the checking of the internal temperature of the materials.

Before leaving the subject of Health and Safety at Work, there are two innovations in the 1974 Act, that should be noted:–

- The Act covers all places where "persons are at work", and there is no need to worry about whether it is a factory or not and;
- Managers and directors are liable if there is an offence, as well as the company. In fact, anyone in a responsible position may be charged, if he or she is employed by a 'body corporate'.

Control of Dangerous Substances

It is compulsory for employers and self-employed persons to comply with regulations in force since 1st January 1990 with the acronym COSHH. These are the Control of Substances Hazardous to Health regulations.

There is a wide range of substances available today which are capable of damaging health – and not, by any means in industry alone. Some are used, for instance, in the painting and decorating trade, in farms and educational establishments. No work which is liable to expose anyone to hazardous substances may lawfully be carried out unless an assessment has been made and necessary precautions have been taken. This involves:–

- Evaluating the risks and;
- Deciding what has to be done about them.

A sensible step-by-step approach is needed.

A Dangerous Substance

Under the COSHH regulations, this term has a special meaning. It includes those substances which are labelled as dangerous (ie, very toxic, toxic, harmful, irritant or corrosive), agricultural pesticides and other chemicals used on farms, and a range of other substances for which occupational exposure limits have been set. Harmful micro-organisms, substantial quantities of dust and, indeed, any material, mixture or compound which can harm people's health are also included. Because other regulations govern them, asbestos, lead or ionising radiations are excluded.

The printing industry, for example, has quite a number of dangerous substances and illustrates the kind of substances to be considered: inks, varnishes, reducing solvents, blanket washes, ink strippers, adhesives, plate and photographic developers, activators, fixers, deletion fluids and cleaning solvents are all included.

Whatever the type of undertaking, assessment must be made. This is done by a step-by-step approach:–

- Identify the hazardous substances (eg, by labels or ask suppliers);
- Consider how the substance is used;
- Find out the means by which it can harm people (eg, on skin contact);
- Check storage and handling arrangements;
- Consider what might happen in accident or emergency (eg, spillage);
- Compare the standards with those generally accepted (see below);
- Decide what has to be done to control the hazards discovered;
- Consider whether the organisation can "do it alone" or needs expert help;
- Make a written record of the assessment and;
- Review your assessment from time to time.

The problem of comparing the findings with what is generally accepted does not mean checking on what competitors are doing since they could be quite wrong. The standard which is acceptable is that agreed to by the Health & Safety Executive (HSE) and the medical profession. There is an enormous amount of information on the matter and your trade association, chamber of commerce or professional institution should be able to advise. The HSE is ready to give advice on request. It may be decided to employ a consultant and in that case, it must be made sure that the consultant is of high standing.

Having carried out the assessment, the necessary steps should be taken to control the hazards:–

- Control exposure to exclude or, if impossible, to minimise the risk;
- Check that the means adopted are effected;
- Ensure that they are properly maintained;
- Arrange for monitoring of substances to maintain proper limits;
- Keep records of monitoring and;
- Train and instruct employees about the risks and precautions.

Further details and advice are available from HSE and other bodies as already indicated. In addition, the HSE has published a series of leaflets and a booklet to help; the main one is "COSHH Assessments. A Step-by-Step Guide to Assessment and the Skills needed for It".

Legislation Relating to Fleet Management

There is probably more law in this area than any other function of management. However, only those matters which will concern a Stores Manager in their job will be discussed here. A Transport Manager would need a deeper and wider knowledge of all aspects of transport law.

Since the UK is now part of the E.C. and many companies are involved in overseas trade, some international aspects of goods movement will also be dealt with in this section.

One of the main Acts of Parliament affecting the operation of a road transport fleet is 'The Transport Act', which deals with the following matters.

Operator's Licence

The Transport Act, 1968 introduced an entirely new system of goods vehicle licensing which took effect from 1 March 1970. All goods vehicles over 30 cwt unladen weight (this is recorded in the vehicle registration book) or 3½ tons plated gross weight are required to be covered by an Operator's Licence unless specifically exempted. Exemptions include those vehicles which are technically 'goods' vehicles, e.g. vehicles with fixed equipment, agricultural machinery, mobile cranes, ambulances and so on.

The Operator's Licence is issued on no other grounds than that of safety of operation. The Licensing Authority decides whether an Operator's Licence shall be granted, taking into account the adequacy of an operator's maintenance, the arrangements for maintaining these vehicles in a fit and serviceable condition, whether satisfactory arrangements are made to ensure that the law relating to drivers' hours and records will be complied with in respect of vehicles which will be authorised under licence and that vehicles will not be caused to be overloaded. Whether the applicant's financial resources are adequate and whether he or she is a fit and proper person to hold such a licence, i.e. whether he or she has a reasonably clean record of previous conduct in the carriage of goods.

All new applications for, and applications for the renewal of, existing

Operator's Licences will be published by the Licensing Authority, for the Traffic Area in which the applicant is based, in a booklet – 'Applications and Decisions'. The booklet is circulated among interested parties and the application will be open to objections by any of the following persons or bodies:–

- A Chief of Police;
- Local Authority;
- Freight Transport Association
  (trader's own transport association);
- Road Haulage Association
  (a professional carrier's association);
- General and Municipal Worker's Union;
- National Union of Railwaymen
  (ex British Rail employees taken over by
  The National Freight Corporation);
- The Scottish Commercial Motormen's Union;
- Transport and General Workers' Union
  (goods drivers' union);
- The Union of Shop, Distributive and Allied Workers and;
- The United Road Transport Union.

In practice, few of the bodies mentioned have so far taken part in objecting to any applicant's licence. There have been a number of objections initiated by the Licensing Authorities' staff where maintenance facilities and vehicle road worthiness have been faulted.

As an exercise you could examine the grounds each objector might put forward such as:–

- Chief of Police: repeated offences relating to dangerous loads.
- Local Authority   repeated offences of overloading, brought to light by weights and measures inspectors.
- Union: repeated offences of excess hours of work.

A copy of any objection is always sent to the applicant. This licensing procedure applies also to the renewal of a licence or, when the number of vehicles is required to be increased, unless the Licensing Authority considers the variation to be trivial.

An objection can only be made on the grounds set out above. For instance safety, and not purely commercial grounds. The burden of proof however lies on the objector. The Licensing Authority will consider an objection only if he or she is satisfied that it has been properly made and is relevant. In most cases the licensing authority will hold a Public Inquiry at which both sides will be able to state their case. If the application is refused or partly refused there is a right of appeal to the Transport Tribunal. An objector has a similar right of appeal.

Scope of Operation

Under the now defunct 'A', 'B' and 'C' system of licensing the holder of an 'A' licence (public carrier) could carry solely for hire or reward; the holder of a 'B' licence (limited carrier) carried for hire and reward subject to certain restrictions, and carried their own goods; and the 'C' licensed holder (private carrier) could only carry their own goods and not carry goods for hire or reward. This meant that the professional carrier was protected by the licensing system against inroads made by the private carrier into their livelihood.

The situation now is that all operators, properly authorised, may carry for hire or reward without restrictions. In general, there are two classes of operator: the professional hauler and the own account operator.

The User

Under the Transport Act, the user of a goods vehicle on a public road for the carriage of goods whether for haulage work or for own account must hold an Operator's License. It is important to understand the definition of the word 'user'. It makes no difference whether an operator owns the vehicle, is paying for it under a hire purchase agreement, or is hiring it from someone else without a driver; what matters is whether the operator is the user.

The operator is the user when:–

- They are the owner/drivers;
- They employ someone to drive the vehicle and pay his or her wages or;
- They hire, or borrow, the vehicle from someone else, but drive it themselves or pay someone to drive it for them.

As a user the operator has responsibility to maintain the vehicle in a roadworthy condition.

Operatoring Centre

An Operator's Licence is required for each traffic area in which an operator has a base for vehicles. This means that an operator having vehicles based at a depot in Newcastle, Bristol and London will be required to have three 'O' licences. An 'O' licence will normally be valid for up to five years. In some cases, where the Licensing Authority has reason to feel that a certain operator is not as diligent as they might be, a shorter currency period is imposed.

Goods Vehicles

A goods vehicle is a mechanically propelled vehicle which is constructed or adapted to carry a load or burden. When the unladen weight of goods vehicle is less than 3 tons it is called a motor car. The motive power unit of an articulated vehicle is also a motor car when the weight does not exceed $2\frac{1}{2}$ tons unladen. Vehicles are generally classified by size. A small goods vehicle is one where the laden weight is not more than 30 cwt or it's plated weight does not exceed $3\frac{1}{2}$ tons. (A plate setting out the maximum permitted weight limits for each axle and the gross weight is issued by the Department of the Environment at the first annual vehicle test. The plate is then fixed to the vehicle, either in the cab or, in the case of a trailer, to the chassis).

A medium goods vehicle is one where the plated weight exceeds $3\frac{1}{2}$ tons but is not in excess of 16 tons. Two-axle vehicles do not exceed this limit and to drive this vehicle on a public road the law required the driver to hold not only a group 'A' ordinary licence but a Heavy Goods Vehicle driving licence, Class 3. A large goods vehicle is one with a plated weight in excess of 16 tons gross and having three or more axles then the driver is required to have a Class 2 Heavy Goods Vehicle drivers' licence. At present, the maximum permitted gross plated weight of goods vehicles carrying general goods, as distinct from excessively heavy and abnormal loads, is 32 tons, with a limit of 10 tons per axle. The European Community may insist at some later date that the weight be raised to 11 tons. An articulated vehicle being less than $2\frac{1}{2}$ tons may be driven by a person over 17 provided that he or she holds an ordinary driving licence and a Heavy Goods Vehicle driving licence Class 4. Most articulated vehicles require the driver to hold a Class 1 licence and being a large goods vehicle this enables the driver to drive other types of goods vehicles. Coming back into fashion, (now that the law requiring the driver to carry a mate has been repealed), is the draw-bar trailer. If the pulling vehicle has to axles, a Class 3 Heavy Goods Vehicle driving licence is required.

Unladen Weight

This is the weight of the vehicle less the spare wheel, tools and other equipment which may be carried; allowance is made for fuel and water carried.

The Payload

Under the Construction and Use Regulations and the Plating and Testing Regulations, all vehicles are limited to a maximum gross weight. Subtract the unladen weight from the gross permitted weight and this gives the payload. There are problems for the carrier because some aggregates such as sand and hard-core are measured in cubic yards; various types of timber normally carried as packets and standards are difficult to estimate weightwise. In doubtful cases it is best to instruct a loaded vehicle to report first to a public weighbridge. Otherwise if the vehicle is stopped at a roadside check by an examiner and is found to be overloaded, a prosecution could follow and the operator's licence and the driver's Heavy Goods Vehicle licence could be at risk.

The Sale of Goods Act has an important bearing upon the transport of goods. It declares the liability of the sender to:–

- Hand to the carrier first goods to be transported;
- Declare any dangerous goods;
- Declare the nature and weight of the goods;
- Properly address the goods and;
- Accept the liability for payment of the carriage charges.

This act also states that property passes, when goods that are sold are handed to the carrier. This means that when a buyer orders goods, they become the buyer's as soon as the supplier hands them to a carrier for despatch. In consequence, since the owner is the buyer (also the consignee), as soon as the goods are handed to the carrier, the contract is between the buyer (or consignee) and the carrier. The supplier (also the consignor) who arranges the contract, acts as agent for the buyer. If goods are sent from one stores or warehouse, to another stores or warehouse of the same company, then this is a straightforward contract.

If the seller of the goods has been unpaid, then under sections 44–46 of the Act, he or she has a right to stoppage in transit, which simply means that he or she tells the carrier not to deliver the goods and return them. However, three conditions must exist before this can be done:–

- The goods must be in transit;
- The buyer must be insolvent and;
- The seller must be unpaid either wholly or in part

Lien

The carrier also has certain rights in the case of being paid. Under common law the carriers may hold goods if they have not been paid. This is known as passive lien as they can only hold the goods and not dispose of them. It is also a particular lien, since they can only hold the goods on which the charges have not been paid. However, many carriers write into their conditions of carriage a general line. This means that they can hold all the goods of a customer who has not paid, not just the goods on which payment is outstanding. Quite often an active lien is also stipulated, which means that goods can be sold by the carrier to meet any costs.

Common and Private Carriers

Anyone who carries goods for other people is either a common or private carrier. A common carrier has a legal duty to carry goods for anyone who requires them to carry their goods. They are liable for loss or damage to goods during carriage except in the cases of damage caused by:–

- An Act of God;
- The Queen's enemies;
- the consignor or owner of the goods;
- An inherent vice of the goods (the goods are subject to natural wastage or decomposition) or;
- The consignor has been guilty of fraud.

A common carrier has a common-law right of lien. They are subject to the Carriers Act 1830.

Most Road Transport operators are 'Private Carriers'. They have their own conditions of carriage. For instance, those of British Road Services, which are typical of those in use. A private carrier may refuse, or accept, goods for carriage. They are then a 'bailee' of the goods carried.

International Carriage of Goods by Road

It is now commonplace for vehicles to load in, say, Birmingham and drive straight to Milan or other European cities. This increase in through shipment by road made it necessary to look at the law, as up to 1967, a lorry was subject to the laws of each country through which it passed. The Carriage of Goods by Road Act, 1965, means that, throughout it's journey, a vehicle will be subject only to the provisions contained therein. It ratifies discussions taken at the International Convention held in Geneva. A consignment note which meets the requirements of the Act, must be made out and used by the consignor and carrier.

Rail

From their beginnings, the railways were important "common carriers" and thus, subject to the conditions mentioned earlier. This status was altered in 1962 and British Rail is now a private carrier. As such, British Rail accept, or refuse, goods for carriage. They have "General Conditions of Carriage by Goods", (BR18793/ 1) which are British Rail conditions of carriage and are obtainable from them. Anyone using rail transport for goods would be advised to obtain a copy.

It is possible to send goods by rail to the Continent and again, as in the case of road transport, this can cause problems. There are recommended procedures for such traffic, some of which are covered by the Railway Act 1972. A British Rail Consignment Note is available, suitable for this purpose.

1975 TIR Customs Convention on the International Transport of Goods.

This Convention between the U.K. and the European Community countries permitted the movement of goods across national frontiers provided that the vehicle or container in which they are transported is sealed by customs at the consignors and unopened during transit.

One of the aims of the E.C. Common Transport Policy is to reduce or eliminate border delays within the Single Market. In order to assist in the elimination of delays the Single Administrative Document (S.A.D.) was introduced. The S.A.D. is effective within the E.C. and has eliminated the need to apply full T.I.R. procedures.[8]

Notes and References

7. *Transport and Distribution in the Single Market*, TNT Express, Mercury Books, 1992
8. Welford, R. and Prescott, K, *European Business: an Issue-Based Approach*, Pitman, 1992

Chapter 6

Physical Distribution

So far, the operation of Stores and Stockyards, transport operation and the various samples of legislation with which the Stores Manager must comply have been discussed. It is time now to consider the methods of achieving effective planning and control of the distribution of goods, to customers, stores and warehouses by a road fleet.

Distribution

The development of distribution facilities and techniques is increasingly evident in the attention given to this area of company activities, taking into account the need to co-ordinate:–

- Transport: vehicles and routes
- Warehousing: central and local
- Production: batch size and lead time
- Customer service: appropriate level
- Finance: capital investment

In practice, the optimum distribution system may result from "trade-off" agreements within the organisation, combining individual cost advantages and disadvantages to obtain an overall cost benefit to the company and a satisfactory customer service level.

The growing interest in the contribution which an efficient distribution system can make to company objectives has been recognised by the formation of the Centre for Physical Distribution Management sponsored by the British Institute of Management.

It is interesting to note that organisationally, the concept of a totally co-ordinated Distribution System at senior management or director level, is complementary to the Materials Management development of a "linked" system of procurement of supplies, storage and inventory control, production control to obtain the benefits of a total supplies system and access to the early stages of design and development in choice of materials.

Distribution Planning

A number of factors must be considered in planning a distribution system, the first and most important being the needs of the customer. However, it would clearly be impossible to send a vehicle every time a customer required an item and it is necessary therefore, to balance the customer's needs against the cost of providing that service. There are a number of distribution channels by which a product or service reaches a customer, as, illustrated in Figure 15.

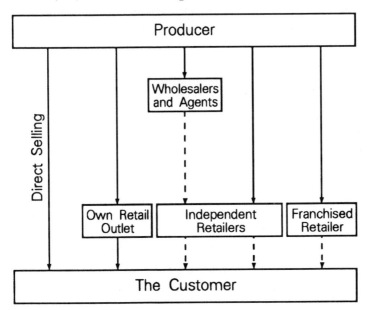

Figure 15.
Channels of Distribution

Customers' needs will be highly varied and it is important to decide the type of transport organisation and distribution system best suited for a particular customer. In many trades a weekly delivery is required, and this is not difficult to plan but it is as well to remember that people expect a delivery on a particular day, and this should be taken notice of and adhered to if possible. In many cases weekly deliveries must be on specified days. There are also trades where daily deliveries are required. Suppliers of drugs and medical item are such a case, as are fresh food deliveries.

In some cases goods are sent out when a full load is made up, but this is unusual since most businesses are based upon a regular delivery service. This is true of deliveries made from Central Stores to sub-stores and depots. Special loads of the type we see taking machinery to a plant with police escort are, of course, "one-offs" and need very careful planning.

Loads

The type of load and the quantity or volume are important factors that must be taken account of when planning the distribution system. The nature of the goods must also be considered. Perishable goods must be delivered right away and will require particular methods of handling. Petroleum spirit and other inflammable or toxic substances will be subject to special regulations. Corrosive loads will also require special precautions to be taken. If any of these goods with special handling problems are to be carried, arrangements must be made when distribution is being planned.

The organisation required

The above factors, together with the volume of traffic involved, will give the basis for deciding the type of organisation best suited for the purpose.

A decision must be made on centralising or having a decentralised method of operating. Where the work is mainly of a local character, it is probably sensible to operate on a de-centralised basis. This means vehicles operating from a depot in each area where there are customers or stores, each depot having its own manager and organisation. This method has the advantage of direct control by local management and it is flexible. However, where a company has a number of vehicle depots, it may be costly, since a number of vehicles must be carried at each depot, some of which may be under-utilised. Where a company is operating on a national basis, it is more likely that a national centralised system will be adopted. This will make maximum utilisation of transport easier, since central planning is possible. It also makes it uneconomical to use management aids, such as computers, for vehicle scheduling and loading. Support services such as private workshops are also possible with centralisation.

We must also consider the method of operating and the type of service, for this will also influence the organisation of the transport service. The company that provides a delivery service to each customer will need more detailed planning than a company that does not provide this service. Many large organisations find it economical to have depots or collection centres at each regional location (e.g. London, Birmingham, Bristol, Manchester and so on). This enables them to use large vehicles which, when fully loaded, are more economical to operate than small vehicles which, when fully loaded, are more economical to operate than small vehicles involved in the same traffic. This method is often known as "trunking", and is popular where the volume of traffic justifies it, as a large vehicle can take a load from one depot to another, and return with a load back to its depot. It is, of course, also necessary to provide a local service, either through own transport or, by using local hauliers on a sub-contract basis. If this system is operated by a company, a local management organisation will be needed. If the job is sub-contracted this is avoided, but the organisation will have lost direct control of delivery to its customers.

Where the traffic is only serving factories or depots within a company or group, the local factories or depots may collect from a central depot in the region at regular times.

There are often localities that have to be served which present special problems. The North of Scotland and the Shetlands are examples of such areas, as well as areas of the UK which, while not remote, may have only a solitary manufacturing unit or customer. It would clearly be uneconomical to send a vehicle on this type of journey, and to incorporate in the plan provisions for the use of commercial carriers for this traffic is essential.

Warehouses and Depots

The provision of warehouses and depots will obviously affect the planning of a distribution sytem. This first point to consider is the necessity of warehouses. Two factors have, in recent years, altered the basis of providing warehouses. The first is the provision of the modern motorway system, which makes it possible to supply a very wide area from a central warehouse. Consider the area that can be serviced from a central warehouse in West Bromwich, which is adjacent to the M5, M6 and M1. The second factor is the recent development of large vehicles which make it economic to move large loads, via the motorway network.

Nevertheless there may well be a case for warehouses to be provided, based upon:–

- The types of goods being transported; perishable goods may require local storage where goods are regional (only sold in some areas);
- The cost of the vehicle operation; it may be that vehicle mileage is sufficiently reduced by providing a local warehouse to make it an economical proposition. Better vehicle utilisation may also be possible and also;
- The customers needs; if customers can be better served by having a local warehouse, or they request such a service, then there are reasonable grounds for providing such a facility.

Among factors that should be considered are the:–

- Cost of order processing;
- Stockholding costs;
- Lead time for the customer and;
- Time taken to process orders.

The Management of the Function

The management of the function will depend upon the needs of the organisation, and there is no general pattern. The needs of the company, the traffic, the customer and the market must all be studied. It is, however, common to have a Distribution Manager but, in some companies, this function may come under the auspices of the Marketing Director.

Logistics and Delivery Planning

In its original meaning, logistics referred to the means of moving and quartering troops and of supplying their needs. Today it is also used as a general term for planning the movement of all kinds of materials. It is the means of deciding the best way of doing this that is considered in this section.

The objective of planning a delivery service is to organise the types of vehicles and the routes to be used in order to achieve the highest mileage at the highest loading. If this can be done the transport cost per load, or per item, will be the lowest possible. This is important since, as noted earlier, transport adds to the cost but not to the value of goods.

Now, having an objective clearly in mind it is possible to plan to reach it. Planning decisions however must be based on realistic facts established by research and investigation. This investigation must include:–

- The operating costs of transport vehicles;
- The distribution and location of customers and collection points. There is a need to list the towns, districts and areas which have customers or collection points and mark their location on a map or by some other convenient means;
- Loads to be carried, size and weight, and also, the nature of the goods to be carried;
- Individual customers methods of ordering and their requirements. If collections are to be made, these too must be studied;
- The number of vehicles available, their type and size and;
- Maintenance and planned servicing requirements.

As a result of investigations into the above mentioned factors, the actual planning of deliveries can be made, and routes decided, on the basis of where customers are, the goods required, customer's particular requirements, and the vehicles available. In practice, this means establishing a routine which will require:–

A Goods Loading Bank

Generally, it is found that operators of parcels services maintain loading banks; but a small loading bank will often be of advantage to the general carrier, for there are occasions when goods have to be off-loaded from a vehicle, upon which repairs must be effected, and the use of a loading bank will then make transference easier. It is not unusual for one vehicle to be backed against another for transfer of goods to be carried out, and, although this may be effective for certain loads, it has disadvantages. Again, where goods have been collected and sent to a distant point and it is found that delivery cannot be performed immediately, as, for example, during a holiday, it may be an advantage for an operator to off-load and store the goods temporarily, thus releasing the carrying vehicle for further service. A simple storage media is shown in Figure 16.

The first point to be considered before constructing a loading bank is the flow of traffic, and this must be considered in relation to the services given by the operator. It is possible that several vehicles will be engaged each day between main towns, so that the time goods remain on hand before being placed on the on-carrying vehicle is very small. On the other hand, the services of the operator may extend over a large rural area, where a vehicle operates over a certain route of alternative days, twice weekly, or even on a five times a week service. In such cases

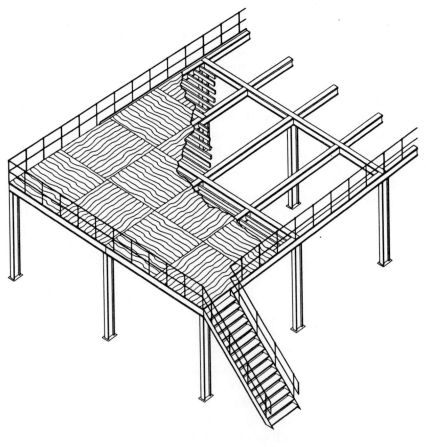

Figure 16.
A typical Storage Platform

parcels must remain on hand and be stored temporarily, and the size of the bank must provide for this temporary storage. One operator may deal with many more packages than another, and yet the need for a large loading bank not be so great.

Other operators, again, accept goods in bulk from rail and arrange for delivery to out-lying districts on receipt of instructions from suppliers; the size of the loading bank must therefore be extended to cope with the temporary storage necessary, or an upper story added to the building for this purpose.

The question of the flow of traffic, or the speed with which it can be cleared must receive first consideration in determining the size of a loading bank.

Siting, Construction and Lay-Out of Depots

The quantity of traffic to be handled, and the speed with which it is to be cleared, must, therefore affect the size of the depot.

In deciding upon the site for a depot, several factors must be borne in mind. The depot must be situated near the principal sources of traffic in order to eliminate empty running as much as possible, for this is entirely unremunerative; it must be so placed that easy entrance and exit is available for all types of vehicle likely to be used – a side road for instance would be better for this purpose than a main road; the ground space should allow for further development, and for a marshalling yard in addition to the space to be occupied by buildings. It must also be decided whether vehicles are to be under cover during the night, or left in the open, as this affects the amount of covered space required.

Upon deciding these points, one may then consider the lay-out of the premises which must conform, to an extent, to the shape of the plot. Within the depot must be placed the loading bank, or banks, for the transfer of goods and, in a separate part of the building, the repair shops, stores, rest room, and so on. The size of the repair shops will be considered in relation to the work to be carried out, for it may be day-to-day maintenance only, or the repair shops may cater for all repairs including chassis, engine, transmission, and body.

Once the lay-out have been determined, the operator can then make plans for construction and, apart from this having a pleasing appearance, the main points to be considered in connection with it are lighting, heating and ventilation, and the provision of the essential services. Buildings must conform to local bye-laws, and so, all plans will need to be passed by the local authority.

There are very few operators of goods transport vehicles that have depot facilities which compare with the operators of road passenger transport.

A loading bank may be single-sided or double-sided, or a number of bays may be constructed in order to make the maximum use of the space available. The advantage of a double-sided bay is that reception of goods can be more easily controlled where a large number of vehicles are engaged; the work of sorting is performed without interruption and goods are stacked in the delivery section. The height of a loading bank must be similar to the platform height of the vehicles, in order to avoid the use of labour unnecessarily in off-loading. Bays containing large unit loads using powered mobile storage are quite common; an illustration is shown in Figure 17.

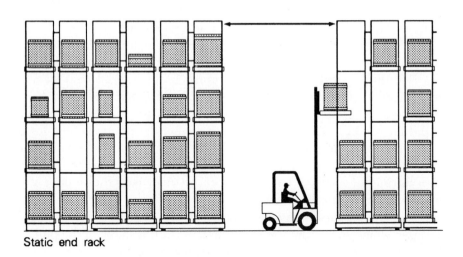

Static end rack

Figure 17.
End-view of Powered Mobile Pallet Racks

Receiving and Dispatching Goods at Depots and Warehouses

Normally it is to be expected that collecting vehicles will return to the depot in the evening after making collection rounds, and delivering vehicles leave on their rounds in the morning, so that a large amount of the sorting work and re-loading is done in the late afternoon, and the balance carried out the following morning. There will be some movement of manufacturers goods awaiting suppliers' instructions for delivery, sorting will be carried out during the day. The question of the amount of labour to be engaged on sorting and checking must be conditioned by the flow of traffic, some early and some late turns being essential.

In order to facilitate sorting, the delivery section of the bank must bear indication boards, plainly visible, showing the various sections of the bank allocated to various delivery points, and, as the work of off-loading proceeds, the goods are immediately transferred to the section of the bank appropriate to the destination.

Within each section of the bay allocated to traffic for delivery, there may or may not be a further sorting required. If goods are to be placed on a trunking vehicle no further sorting is necessary, but, where delivery is to be performed, goods must be placed on the vehicle in such a manner that the driver does not have to search the vehicle for a particular parcel. Goods must be so loaded that the first deliveries are at the rear of the vehicle; the last goods to be delivered must be the first to be loaded. This involves sorting out the goods in the order in which delivery is to be carried out either by first examining and sorting out the consignment notes, if these are available, or by reading the labels on the goods in the stack and making out a delivery sheet or loading list.

Lock-Up

Some of the goods dealt with will be of high value and so need special care; other goods may be on hand for which delivery cannot be made due to insufficient address, or the refusal of the consignee to accept delivery. All such goods must be removed from the loading banks and transferred to a lock-up until such time as the manner of disposal has been decided upon.

Supervision

Much of the successful working of a depot depends upon the manager in charge. He or she will receive their instructions from the depot manager and ensure that they are carried out and will supervise the checkers and sorters under their control to ensure that the work which has been allocated to them is properly done. The safety of goods whilst lying on hand in the depot are also their responsibility, and the manager must take all steps available to reduce damage to goods by handling, and loss through pilferage. The key of the lock-up must be in the manager's possession, and no unauthorised person must have access to it. The order in which waiting vehicles must be off-loaded, and the manner of loading vehicles is also under their control. The manager must be experienced in the handling of the various classes of goods dealt with, and the use of the various appliances which are available for the movement of goods, and must also be satisfied that traffic is securely stowed on vehicles before they leave the depot.

Checking of Goods

The objective of goods checking are first, to see that they agree with the details on the collection or delivery sheets, or, on the consignment notes which may be either prepared by the sender or in the carrier's office. Second, to ensure that only goods covered by consignment notes or load waybills are placed on forwarding vehicles, and third, that the goods are in apparent sound condition, properly packed and labelled.

When vehicles enter the depot after making collections, the drivers should report to the manager, who will allocate a discharging standard and instruct a checker and sorters to deal with each vehicle. The driver of each vehicle will hand all their consignment notes to the checker, who, as the unloading of the vehicle proceeds, will mark off, on the note, that the package or packages have been inspected and are in order for forwarding. Should the checker find any package apparently inadequately addressed, or not properly packed, or suspect that a package contains damaged goods, they should place it on one side. He or she should then obtain instructions from the foreman in charge, or from the office, as to the action to be taken. In many cases it will be necessary to communicate with the sender to clear up any point of doubt. Should no consignment note have been obtained from the sender, a note must be taken of the goods and this note must be handed to the office so that the necessary documents can be prepared. The fleet number of the in-carrying vehicle may be placed on the consignment note as a record for future use, if required. When the off-loading of a vehicle has been completed, all consignment notes should be handed into the office for inspection and to enable the loads for the out-going vehicles to be made up.

The work of checking out-going vehicles is similar. The consignment notes making up the load will be received from the office, and the checker will see that these are placed in delivery order. He or she will then supervise the actual stowing of the goods on the vehicle and again put the fleet number of the out-carrying vehicle on the consignment note. In many undertakings, a waybill is prepared, especially for use on trunk journeys, to which the consignment notes are attached. When loading is complete, the checker should initial the waybill or loading sheet.

Incoming vehicles from other depots must be checked when off-loading as carefully as other vehicles. The waybill should be handed to the checker for marking off and any discrepancy between the waybill and the goods received should be noted on the waybill.

Organisations should always be looking for means of increasing efficiency and one method of ensuring that the depot is still operating efficiently is to review operations. Here it will mean taking each vehicle, the routes used, and recording such factors as:–

- Total mileage per trip;
- Mileage to each delivery point and between delivery points;
- The number of deliveries or collections;
- Time leaving and returning to depot;
- Time at each collection or delivery point and;
- Details of loads, such as weights, handling problems and other relevant information.

As a result of the analysis of this information, improved operations can be developed. Points to look for include such indicators as routes which always take longer than expected; holdups when loading or unloading at the depot or at customers premises; in fact anything which is not normal.

Budgetary Control in Distribution

The Master Budget of a business is the method by which the performance desired is achieved. It is considered a method of management control as it is a method of determining standards in each area of performance, measuring actual performance and comparing results.

A company budget is normally based upon the Sales Forecast, which, after any adjustments for stocks and capacity, becomes the production programme. The cost of meeting this programme is calculated and becomes the production budget. The production budget is in turn broken down into it component parts, such as materials budget, plant budget and labour budgets.

In a similar way, the sales forecast is translated into the sales budget. In order to achieve this level of performance it is necessary for each department to operate at a certain level. This will only be possible at a certain cost, which will become that department's budget.

The Distribution Budget will be one of the departmental budgets, which, combined with all others, will become the overall budget. The objectives of this overall budget are to:–

- Control the performance at each level of the business and to ensure that company objectives are attained;
- To co-ordinate the various activities in pursuit of the common objective and;
- To allow "management by exception" and therefore allow management to concentrate upon areas of deviation from standards.

The Budget Period

For convenience, the budgetary period is usually one year, broken down into twelve, monthly "mini-budgets".

As the period of control is monthly, if the actual expenditure exceeds, or is less than budgeted, action can be taken quickly, certainly within a short time of the monthly figure being produced.

The Distribution Budget

The factors contributing to this budget will be:–

- Warehouse rents and rates;
- Warehouse wages and labour charges;
- Warehouse salaries;
- Warehouse heating and lighting;
- Warehouse maintenance;
- Drivers wages and other related costs;
- Vehicle costs;
- Garage and workshop costs;
- Fuel costs (petrol and diesel oil), and lubricants and;
- Any incidental charges.

Care must be taken to ensure that the budgeted figures are realistic, being based on known facts and anticipated increases in costs during the budget period.

Cost Centres

The Distribution Budget will be broken down into cost centres. This is to enable standards to be fixed for each depot, garage or stores, whichever breakdown of operations is most convenient to control the department effectively. In this manner, the cost of operating a depot or stores can be known each month, and compared with the budget. Action can be taken where there is a difference between the two figures. This is the real meaning of "management by exception"; the management needs only to look at those instances where the actual figure is different from the budget. The majority of cases, where the figures are the same, need not be looked at any further.

In a similar way stocks can be controlled by valuation. A cost centre can be a particular stores or warehouse, and if required, can be further broken down into material classifications. This means that it is possible to see the value of stock in a warehouse and also the value of, for instance, steel, or types in that location.

Thus if labour charges or fuel costs are high at a certain garage, they can be investigated and corrected.

Making sure that products reach customers cannot be regarded by marketing managers as simply the concern of someone else. This distribution activity is as much part of the company's marketing mix as are product, pricing and promotion decisions. In fact in some markets, the impact of the distribution element on sales can exceed that of the other mix elements. Seen in this light, the means whereby the product reaches the customer assumes a vital importance in marketing strategy. The implications of this view of distribution's marketing role are therefore far-reaching, and can involve a considerable reappraisal of attitudes as well as of the means of distribution used. Moreover, the average European manufacturing company spends 15% of its sales revenue on distribution-related activities, it is not difficult to contemplate the benefits of such a reappraisal.

Although place is a convenient shorthand description used to define of the quartet of "P's" which go to make up the marketing mix, it represents the means whereby the needs of the market and the offering of the company are physically matched. As such, it provides the addition of time- and place-utility to the product. Without this added value the product is worthless. Without effective planning and control there may be no products to physically distribute.

Chapter 7

Strategic Purchasing Management

Corporate Planning

When considering a business enterprise it is necessary to ask the following questions:–

- What are its objectives?
- How does it operate?
- What resources are required?
- How are the resources managed?
- What influences bear upon the success or failure of the enterprise?

In so doing, the first steps of Corporate Planning are being considered. All are important questions and it is the responsibility of General Management to consider these matters in terms of long-range planning.

Objectives must be agreed and the provision and management of resources, financial, technical and human, set in motion.

The Corporate Plan

In considering the responsibilities of General Management, planning objectives and controlling resources, the business strategy of the company or governing body, in other words, the CORPORATE PLAN, is under consideration. This involves:–

- Objectives – survival, profitability and social responsibilities;
- Products and Markets;
- Finance;
- Material Resources;
- Human Resources;
- Technical Facilities and;

- Management and Administration.

Within the corporate plan, therefore, lies the important area of purchasing resources.

What is Corporate Planning?

Corporate planning may be described as a careful systematic taking of strategic decision making process. It is concerned with developing a long term view of future developments and in designing a plan so that the organisation can achieve its chosen objectives. During the last decade many of the bigger companies in the United Kingdom had recognised the need to apply a formal approach to this requirement. It means that companies need to prepare "scenarios" or forecasts of future developments in the environment in which they wish to operate, in order to examine whether decisions taken in the present will result in a successful outcome in the future. Changes are taking place at a more rapid rate, but often the effects of decisions taken now may still be influential more than ten years later. Companies, therefore, have been developing more sophisticated techniques to analyse the risks involved in such decisions.

For example, the problem of deciding whether an oil company should invest in a new refinery, which might cost well over £100 million and which might have a life of fifteen years or more. Such a company needs to know whether a market can be assured for the extra volume of its refined products and it needs to know whether they can be produced profitably. In addition, however, it is necessary to study the availability of crude oil and other supplies needed in the operation.

Corporate planning, therefore, is a process concerned with determining the long term objectives of the organisation, with deciding what market opportunities exist and with determining a product to satisfy them. Any plan, however, needs to be firmly based upon a study of supply markets and a plan to ensure that the required resources can be made available at the right price to support such a product policy. In short, an essential element in the corporate plan is a plan for purchasing. In the past, many companies have omitted this element, but problems of supply shortages and rising prices have made top management aware of the need to take into account long term developments in supply markets.

The Need For Corporate Planning

The environments in which companies have to operate today have become increasingly dynamic and they have had to learn to live with and adapt to the changes that are taking place. Some examples of changes that have to be coped with are changes in products, in manufacturing processes, in communication techniques, in data processing techniques, as well as changes in both supply and sales markets. Companies have recognised the need to investigate these changes and to draw up plans in order to adapt to them and to survive. More sophisticated techniques have been developed to analyse the uncertainties and to assess the risks involved in the decisions that have to be made. A further impetus to the need to plan arises from the fact that companies have to invest large sums of money in new plant and equipment and they have to look carefully to see whether such schemes will offer sufficient benefits to justify the expenditure. In order to do so it may be necessary to look far ahead in the future.

The Corporate Plan establishes the basic objectives for the company as a whole and gives guidance to the actions of the various specialist departments, such as marketing, production and purchasing. It is also designed to co-ordinate the work of these departments to ensure that they all work together in order that the overall objectives of the company can be successfully achieved.

The Nature of Corporate Planning

One very important aspect of planning which has not yet been mentioned is the time factor. The consideration of this factor can lead to different perspectives and different types of plan. Most people are familiar with the type of plan called a budget, which is likely to cover, at most, a time-span of twelve months. This is essentially a short term planning device. Plans such as this cover, therefore, only a short period of time and these short terms plans are often referred to as "operational" or "tactical" plans. However, many companies have recognised the need to look much further ahead (investment in new plant and equipment today may have significant implications for a long period of time into the future – often ten years or more). In recent years, especially, therefore, there has been growing support for the need to develop long term plans for companies, covering at least five years into the future. These plans may be referred to as "Strategic" or "Long Range Plans".

It is likewise important to develop strategic plans for the specialist functions. From the purchasing point of view, it needs to be stated here that many companies have been slow to develop such a strategic perspective of the purchasing specialism. It has to be admitted, too, that many purchasing personnel have been slow to see the need for and to develop the vision required to construct a strategic plan for purchasing.

Many companies adopt only two planning horizons – "operational" and "strategic" – some companies view the problems as being concerned with three planning horizons, namely:–

- Up to one year – operational, day to day.
- One to two years – short-term, tactical.
- Three to ten years or more – long term, strategic.

Having identified the time characteristics of corporate planning, it is essential to consider the basic approach to the preparation of corporate plans. It should be noted that the emphasis in this Chapter will be on the longer term, strategic type of plan.

Typical studies need to be carried out:

External Factors affecting both Sales Markets and Supply Markets	*Internal Factors*
- General Economic Conditions	- Product Development
- New Product Developments	- Production Facilities
- Key Suppliers and Competitors Activities and Plans	- Process Developments
	- Transport Facilities
	- Industrial Relations
	- Personnel Development
- Mergers and Changes to Market Structure	- Financial Resources
- Government Legislation on International Factors e.g. Exchange Rates, tariffs.	
- Industrial Relations	

The objectives of these studies are to:–

- Develop a clear picture of existing markets and future opportunities and threats which are beginning to emerge, and;

- Carefully analyse the resources that the company at present possesses. Once this work has been completed, it is possible to proceed with the development of the plan itself. Some companies employ specialist Corporate Planners, but others rely on departments to develop the plan.[9]

The Contents of a Corporate Plan

The contents of a Corporate Plan will vary according to the nature of each company, taking into account whether for instance the company is in manufacturing or distribution. The complexity of the company may also vary depending upon whether the company operates on more than one site and whether it is involved in more than one product area. Corporate plans may need to be drawn up for separate divisions or subsidiary companies.

The overall objective of the plan will be to set overall profit objectives and to show how these are to be achieved. In outline, this involves identifying the market opportunities that are to be pursued and showing how the resources of the company are to be utilised and developed to satisfy the target markets. In arriving at the details of the plan the following aspects will need to be considered:–

Marketing

- Products to be offered – types, range, degree of flexibility;
- Project volumes;
- Distribution policies and methods and;
- Promotional strategies.

Production

- Product developments;
- Process developments;
- Manufacturing facilities and location;
- Manufacturing strategy
  e.g. "Make-for-Stock"
  or "Make-to-Customer Order"
  or "Mixed Strategies" and;
- Quality and Reliability.

Purchasing and Supply

- Make or buy strategies;
- Research and development of new materials and suppliers;
- Price Cost Analysis Studies;
- Inventory requirements and;
- Sourcing strategies.

Finance

- Development of a financial plan;
- Investment Plans and;
- Financial Requirements.

Organisation

- Structure;
- Personnel development;
- Company Development with regard to mergers and Takeovers;
- Growth Strategies – horizontal and vertical integration or diversification into related or unrelated fields.

It is important that the plan shows a coherent competitive strategy on which the detailed plans for each function can be based. It is perhaps also important to allow a certain amount of flexibility because of the uncertainties of predicting the precise nature of future operating conditions. Risks need to be carefully assessed and contingency plans drawn up, where these might be needed.

Planning has long been regarded as an essential function of management and this applies at both the highest level in the company organisation and within specialist departments of the company. Planning can be understood quite simply as deciding *what* to do, *how* to do it, *when* to do it and *who* is to carry it out. It involves, therefore, the setting of objectives or goals which are to be achieved and the plans or methods to be used in their attainment. If companies fail to pay sufficient attention to this function they cannot hope to have a clear sense of purpose and to be able to exercise any control over their destinies. This applies both in public, and private, sectors.

Purchasing Planning and Purchasing Strategies

This chapter has concentrated on the general aspects of corporate planning and it has stressed the need to integrate functional or departmental plans with the overall corporate plan. Purchasing aspects must be taken into account if the corporate plan is to be realistic and effective. A strategic perspective of this specialist function should, therefore, be developed. Unless the appropriate material resources are made available at the right time and the right price, no corporate plan will succeed.

It has to be admitted, however, that companies and writers have been slow to appreciate the strategic role that purchasing plays. Indeed many purchasing personnel themselves have not fully appreciated this aspect. Thus, many have regarded purchasing as being only concerned with short term, operational problems. However, the need for a strategic perspective has now been more widely recognised and it will be the purpose of this chapter to support this change of view.

Several factors in recent years have given strength to the development of the strategic perspective of purchasing. Amongst these are the following:–

- Rising prices and the need to control inflation;
- The need to control investment in inventory more effectively;
- Recognition of the importance of purchasing costs to profitability, especially in "purchasing intensive" companies where material costs, as a percentage of total costs, are very high;
- Shortages of materials and;
- Growing scarcity of some key materials.

Although purchasing will form part of the short-term plan as represented by the annual budget, it is still important to develop the long term view. The long term strategic plan for purchasing provides a framework within which operational decisions can be made. Recognition of longer term implications of a decision should prevent the long term supply position of the company from being put in jeopardy. In this particular chapter it will be useful to identify the basic stages involved in the development of a strategic plan for purchasing.

Stages in the Development of a Corporate Plan for Purchasing

- Collect information, and monitor factors in supply markets and the external environment of the organisation. It will be necessary to investigate, for example, what new materials are being developed, what changes in supply and demand can be expected, and, what price trends are to be expected;

- Collect information and data concerning demand for materials and equipment within the company;
- Develop a long term plan which establishes objectives and strategies to be adopted and which also covers short term tactics and goals;
- Design an organisation and devise procedures and policies to implement the plan;
- Construct a manpower plan so that the required human resources are available to put the plans into operation and;
- Monitor the performance of the department and of the staff to check that results are in accordance with the plans. It may become necessary to modify actions in order to get back on course to achieving the objectives of the plan.

It was stated earlier in this chapter that "planning" is a key element in the task of the manager. In the above framework the other key functions of management can also be identified, namely, organising, staffing, and controlling. This chapter will also be concerned with these other functions, but it is the planning function which gives a sense of direction and purpose to the activities of people in the department.

Corporate and Environmental Factors

If we consider, for example, purchasing strategies, we are faced, in the long term, with the problems of:–

- Inflation;
- Physical shortages and;
- Energy crises.

The general need, therefore, is for flexibility by alternative plans, and so, continuous control and reassessment is essential as a major factor of *Flexible Strategic Planning*, with alternative objectives positively introduced to meet changing circumstances rather than passive acceptance of the changes.

A strategy long-term plan with no provision for change may lead to costly and disastrous emergency action. In-built flexibility by shorter-term progressive reassessment of the long-term plan gives meaning to the term:–

Strategic Planning

The need for a considered approach to flexibility, as an important factor in long-term planning, is evident when we consider the two-fold influences which may affect the performance of any business:–

- Internal and;
- External

Internal Flexibility

Basically, this involves pressure on finance to meet unanticipated contingencies and can be referred to as the *liquidity* strength of the company, measured by the relationship, or ratio, of equity to debts and asset position, current to fixed assets.

External Flexibility

This involves:–

- Markets and;
- Research – Sales and Supply.

Market Strategic Flexibility

This can be explained in terms of:–

- Sales spread amongst customers – the avoidance of over-dependence on a single customer or a few large areas;
- Diversification of products;
- Diversification of markets – domestic and overseas and;
- Technological research into opporunity areas.

Objectives and Responsibilities

It is as well to define the areas covered by what appear to be similar aims – those of objectives and those of responsibilities. Whilst they are important corporate considerations, in modern management thought they pose different approaches, but, contain interacting factors. As we have already seen, these constitute aims and purposes inherent in the company processes of management, and, consist of planning economic developments and available resources on a long-term basis.

Responsibilities

These are in the nature of social or moral considerations. For example:–

- Conservation of the environment;
- Avoidance of pollution;
- Employment security;
- Social welfare and;
- Philanthropic contribution to the general community.

Although classed as non-economic objectives, these responsiblities can affect the strategic planning of a company.

Good environmental conditions, internal and external employment security and social welfare can contribute to productivity.

Philanthropy, whilst appearing to use resources otherwise available for development, often appears in the later stages of company growth, as a reflection of stability and the primary satisfaction of economic objectives.

Social Accountability

Business, essentially focused on profitability and economic viability, is giving increasing attention to its further role of social accountability. An enterprise has responsibilities directly to the customer, which demand a social awareness of the need to consider the quality of life through the product, including safety, but also responsibilities towards the many small suppliers who depend on larger organisations for their continuing existence.

Socio-Economic Factors

The question of pollution has exercised the minds of past generations and is today a matter of prime importance with governmental checks and controls. Most companies are conscious of their responsibilities in this area and have, in many cases, taken the opportunity to derive economic advantage from waste polluting materials by converting them to saleable by-products, thus avoiding environmental problems, ensuring economic returns and strengthening their position both economically and in the community.

Social Welfare

There is today an accepted awareness in modern industry of the responsibility of business enterprise to the welfare of employees – the result of enlightened management, governmental control and the Trades Unions:–

- Security of Employment, for example the Employment Protection Act 1975;
- Health and Safety, for example the Health and Safety at Work Act 1974 and;
- Social Security, namely the Social Security Pensions Act 1975.

These are the main legislative acts which have fostered industrial relations. Legislation is contained in the Acts covering the Employment Protection (Consolidation) Act 1978 and the Employment Acts 1980 and 1982, including an important section on the individual employment rights of employees.

Business and the Community

Referred to earlier was the contribution of business enterprises to the community at large, mainly in terms of philanthropy by established and successful concerns in the form of charitable and artistic trusts. There is, however, the further contribution made by the business managers themselves, in giving time and energy to support company participation. Whilst in most cases the extra-mural activities spring from the company awareness of responsibility to the public environment, there is often a "trade-off" effect of enhanced company image and increased trade.

The Effectiveness of Social Considerations

Whilst it appears at first sight that in long-term planning there are restrictive influences involved in financial outlay in matters of social accountability and philanthropy, the question of "trade-offs" in terms of public image and trade potential must be given full consideration.

Job satisfaction, participation, profit-sharing, the question of machines and manpower, technical advancement and employment security are social matters of grave importance for employment and competitive strength.

"Swot" and "Gap" Analyses

Swot

SWOT means, quite simply, Strengths, Weaknesses, Opportunities and Threats. It is an analysis of any supply chain which will show quite clearly if any SWOT elements exist within it. A typical approach to SWOT is shown in Figure 18.

Internal		External	
Strengths	Weaknesses	Opportunities	Threats

Figure 18.
SWOT Analysis

Strategic planning involves the collection of relevant data, the identification of alternatives, the selection of the most attractive of these and the enactment of those selected. "SWOT" is necessary to recognise problems and opportunities. A simple technique which is also useful in this connection is called gap analysis.[10]

Gap Analysis

Gap analysis shows graphically what the company or organisation concerned is trying to achieve and what outcomes would be likely if its current strategy continued to operate. It shows the gap between what is desired and what is likely to happen.

Gap analysis is best undertaken at corporate level. Purchasing has a significant impact on business results and needs to be involved at the planning stage. Often, the Purchasing function can make significant contributions towards closing the gap. Such contributions may be an examination of supply sources, prudent made or buy decisions, value engineering and acquisition cost reduction. A typical example of gap analysis is shown in Figure 19.

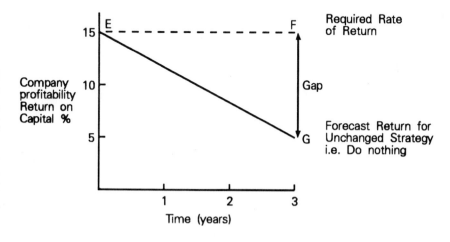

Figure 19.
Gap Analysis

Functions Involved in Corporate Planning

It must not be assumed that a corporate plan emerges as the product solely of a high-level "think tank". If the main areas of the company audit are taken into consideration:–

- Production;
- Finance;
- Technology and;
- Administration

and the external activities of marketing and purchasing involved in growth, it can be seen that these are considering functional areas of company management. Corporate Planning therefore rests on functional support, in the main factual.

Corporate Policies emerge as decisions to operate in those areas which are considered best for successful achievement of objectives. For example, the following alternatives may present themselves:–

- Market penetration by development of the existing market, that is, effort concentrated upon obtaining a larger share of the existing market at the expense of competitors;
- Limiting product utility to a particular section of the market, either industrial or domestic and;
- Diversification into new products and new markets.

Notes and References

9. Porter, M., *How Competitive Forces Shape Strategy*, Harvard Business Review, March/April 1979
10. ibid

Chapter 8

Purchasing Policy

Functional Contribution to Corporate Strategy

Consider the corporate audit in the light of functional activities and their particular contribution to corporate management.

Marketing

This is intimately concerned with growth and profitability. Demand regulates turnover, which must be supported by adequate and suitable administration of:–

- Manufacturing;
- Logistics;
- Technology;
- Purchasing;
- Manpower and;
- Finance.

Manufacture

The corporate audit will look into adequacy of production facilities and the need to expand both operationally and in the use of advanced technology and equipment to produce in economically visable quantities in time to satisfy the market.

Logistics

Linked both with marketing and manufacturing operations in the movement and storage of goods at all stages to meet projected sales programmes.

Technology

Research and development of products functionally and visually to satisfy the need for economic production and to promote sales. Product reviews to support the company image for reliability and innovation.

Finance

Costs administration and cash management are important in promoting attractive product prices, combating inflation and conserving cash resources.

Purchasing

Efficient Purchasing Management is vitally necessary in ensuring free flow of materials at economic prices and in suitable quantities to meet production schedules and sales programmes.

Manpower

Assessment of manpower levels to meet operational and administrative growth – recruitment and training. Management development and the need for functional managers trained to think in corporate terms.

Monitoring Performance

Master Plan and Functional Plan

The two-way provision of support data for the functional level and long-term plan of the corporate strategy becomes evident in the Master and Functional Budgets.

Appraisal of resources, their potentialities and limitations, in deciding upon objectives leads to:–

- Corporate Plans;
- Estimates of Financial Implications and a;
- Master Budget.

All in the long-term, with emphasis on profitability and Return on Investment (ROI). From the Master Budget stems the capital

allocation of departmental budgets appropriate to support programmes functionally achievable to bring success to the Corporate
Strategy and fulfil the company objectives. At both levels, corporate
and functional, the monitoring of performance is of prime importance.
Whilst many of the departmental budgets are short-term, involving the
"tactics" of annual programmes and day-to-day decisions, the longer-
term aspect of Management by Objectives ensures that the corporate
plan is fully supported.

For example:–

- Personnel contributes to the Manpower Survey and is budgeted
  accordingly;
- Finance projects and monitors progressive Return on Investment;
- Research and development combat the possibility of shortages of
  supplies and demand change by seeking material substitutes and
  improved designs;
- Purchasing seek new supply sources, new materials, promote
  standardisation and rationalisation, with emphasis on cost reductions and economic materials management and;
- Manufacturing is concerned with techniques and equipment to
  ensure production support and meet the problem of economy with
  flexibility.

Purchasing Needs and Corporate Strategies

The demand for goods and services to be satisfied by the Purchasing
Department is derived from the demand in the company's market.
Corporate plans must take into account marketing strategies on the
output side. Production plans to support such strategies will also be
drawn up; from these it is possible to determine input requirements. It
is necessary therefore, to develop an understanding of the implications
for Purchasing arising from production and marketing strategies.

Marketing Strategies and the Demand for Inputs

During the last two decades the importance of marketing to a company
has been recognised, both as a general business philosophy and as a
specialist function. It embodies a recognition that the success of an
organisation is dependent on satisfying a market demand for particular
goods and services. It follows, then, that a company should identify

market opportunities and then develop a corporate plan based upon an appraisal of those future market needs. "Produce what you can sell", rather than "sell what you can produce". Within the marketing function, therefore, the activities of market research, advertising and promotion have been added to the selling task. Market research plays an important part in gathering intelligence about the nature of demand and the potential of particular product designs. On the basis of this information a number of different strategies can be considered, designed particularly to meet a corporate objective of growth, which many companies regard as the best way to achieve profitability in the long run.

Marketing Strategies to Achieve Growth

If growth is set as an objective, marketing plans can be drawn up to achieve this, based upon for possible alternative strategies:–

- Market Penetration –
  This aim here is to increase the use of the Company's existing products or services in the present markets. This increased demand may arise by increasing customers' rate of usage, attracting customers from competitors and attracting non-users.
- Market Development –
  This strategy is concerned with marketing present products in new markets. These new markets may be opened up by expanding on either a regional, national or international basis. Alternatively, an existing product range can be sold to a new segment of the market.
- Product Development –
  This third strategy involves the development of new or modified products designed to satisfy existing markets in which the firm operates. It may involve a broadening of the product range as well.
- Diversification
  This final approach covers the addition of both new products, and new markets, to the firm's operations.

Implications for Purchasing

We can now analyse the effects of these alternative strategies on the demand for materials from which these products are manufactured.

Market penetration and Market Development strategies lead to an increase in sales of an existing product range. Therefore, there will be an increase in the volume of materials of existing specifications to meet this expansion.

Product Development and Diversification strategies involve the development of new and modified products and, therefore, will change the specifications of the material inputs. New and modified inputs will be required and research and development work will be needed to prepare new designs. Diversification, especially, may require the application of different technologies, and, purchasing may become involved in new supply markets. The supply of old ingredients will need to be phased out and new material inputs brought on stream.

So far the direct effect of marketing strategies on material requirements have been considered. It is necessary now to look at the effect of marketing strategies upon production and further consequences arising from production plans for purchasing.

Production Strategies and Implications for Purchasing

Plans affecting the output of finished products have direct implications for the production facilities needed to produce them. An increase in output will need an increase in capacity to produce the required volumes. Thus, additional equipment, buildings and even new factories may be required. Old equipment may also need to be replaced during the period covered by the corporate plan. Plans for capital investment, therefore, will create a demand for the purchasing department to purchase the necessary plant and machinery. The search for, and installation of, efficient modern equipment can make a valuable contribution to the effective implementation of the corporate plan. Changes in the level, and methods, of production will also affect the demand for consumable supplies needed in the conversion processes.

Expansion plans may require the construction of a new factory, and this leads to the problem of where this should be located.

It is essential in analysing this problem to take into account, not only marketing factors and labour factors, but also an assessment of supply conditions. The location of suppliers and the cost of transporting supplies can have a significant influence on the economies of the location decision. The high costs of transporting a large volume of low value goods or a high consumption of energy can attract factories close to the supply sources, for example. The relative costs of transporting supplies and transporting the finished product, thus, need to be studied in order to find out whether the factory should be located near the market for the finished goods or near the sources of supply. The British Steel Corporation, for example, is anxious to locate basic steel-making plants on coastal sites because of the need to import iron ore.

When opening up new markets in other countries the possibility of building new factories in those countries may arise. It is essential, particularly when possible sites are in relatively undeveloped countries, to investigate the supply situation. Do such countries have potential suppliers who have the necessary skills to produce the right quality goods, at the right price, at the right time? If not, is it feasible and economic to import supplies? There is evidence to suggest that companies have ignored these factors when taking investment decisions and have been faced with unexpected supply difficulties as a result.

Corporate plans to implement marketing strategies can affect the demand for future supplies of bought-out requirements. Now the problem of devising purchasing strategies that are designed to ensure that those requirements can be satisfied should be considered. If insurmountable supply constraints are foreseen then the corporate plan, if it is going to succeed, must reflect this. However, if future supply difficulties are anticipated in advance, then solutions to overcome them can be found in most cases.

Purchasing Strategies

In order to provide the required resources to support the corporate plan, it is necessary to assess the existing supply situation and then devise strategies to ensure that these resources can be obtained. This approach is more rational than merely reacting to emergencies on an 'ad hoc' basis when they arise. The first stage is to appraise the existing supply environment and to identify trends, threats and opportunities within it regarding the availability, design and prices of future supplies. Strategies need to be developed to exploit these opportunities and to find ways of overcoming threats regarding possible shortages and adverse price movements. There is a need to consider such aspects as the development of new materials, the opening up of new sources of supply and negotiating strategies in supply markets. 'Make or Buy' will be considered in depth as another important strategic decision in what might be called 'resource management'.

The Development of New Materials and Equipment

There are two reasons why buyers should be concerned with identifying and helping suppliers to develop new materials and equipment. First, innovations are an important source of cost savings and of improvements in performance. Secondly, the substitution of new materials and equipment for products bought on previous occasions can overcome anticipated shortages and adverse price movements.

The development of new designs can take a long period of time in which materials have to be investigated and tested. Purchasing personnel need to work closely with their own research and development engineers as well as the technical experts of supplying companies. Plans need to be drawn up to control the development and to introduce the changes on the basis of forecast lead times. The initiative in the development of new materials can arise either from the suppliers firm or within the buyer's firm.

The Development of Supply Capacity

Changes in supply conditions and changes in expected demand for materials may create a gap between existing capacity and the volume required. Buyers, therefore, need to take steps to increase supplies in line with the corporate plan. This may be done either by arranging for existing suppliers to expand their facilities or by developing new supplies. Discussions should be held with suppliers regarding long term requirements, so that suppliers can also plan ahead to meet their customer's needs and install new plant and equipment if necessary. A programme of 'supplier development' can also be drawn up to create new sources of supply which have the correct production and quality control facilities to supply goods of the desired quality. Suppliers should, therefore, be closely involved in the corporate planning process so that both supplier and buyer can benefit from symbiotic growth.

Price Strategies and the Structure of Supply Markets

An audit of existing supply market structures may show that the buying company may be in an unfavourable position. Monopoly and oligopoly situations could restrict competition and thus weaken the power of the buyer as regards choice of suppliers and the negotiation of prices. Purchasing departments, especially in the larger organisations, therefore, need to develop strategies to control the flow of supplies at favourable prices. 'Counter-vailing' power can be developed in the following ways:–

- Develop price-cost analysis techniques to improve negotiating ability with existing suppliers;
- Allocate business to more than one supplier as a means of preserving competition;
- Encourage new suppliers to enter the market or develop foreign sources of supply to increase competition;
- Contact the Director General of Fair Trading to investigate monopolies and restrictive agreements if the public interest is considered to be in jeopardy;
- Consider the possibilities of the buyer's own company making the product;
- Investigate the possibility of takeover or merger with a supplier in order to increase control of essential supplies and;
- Develop substitute materials from other suppliers to overcome shortages and resulting price rises.

It can be seen therefore, that buyers should not merely adapt to changes as they occur in the supply environment, but should take positive steps to ensure that developments are favourable to their needs and protect their interests. The pursuit of short term price advantages may have unfavourable consequences in the long term if the price-cutting tactics of suppliers are designed to drive competitors from the market and to build up a dominant position.

Flexible Strategies

The dynamic character of the world today means that it can be difficult to forecast future conditions and, thus, flexible strategies may be needed to cope with uncertainty. Consider flexibility in the context of having several suppliers available and the possibility of maintaining flexibility in the choice of materials.

Single Versus Multiple Sourcing

Multiple sourcing can be seen as a response to the uncertainties of relying on the deliveries of one supplier, which can be delayed by such contingencies as strikes, transport problems and fires. A further advantage of multiple sourcing arises from maintaining contact with research and development undertaken by several suppliers. In addition, there may be tactical benefits from being able to alter the division of business between them to encourage a high performance as regards delivery and quality. Purchasing strategy, therefore, involves a policy decision regarding situations in which multiple sourcing should be adopted. Essentially this should include items which are critical in the production process and which incur high costs if the production lines are stopped. The higher unit costs which might arise as a result of splitting the business can be seen as an insurance against the higher total costs of stopped production. There is also a need to guard against buyer inertia.

Multiple Choice of Materials

It is never possible to forecast future trends with complete accuracy and, in the face of a high degree of uncertainty, a plan which allows a flexible response is preferable. A good example arises in the choice of fuels. Technological change and competition between producers, as well as other disturbances such as strikes and OPEC controlled price rises, has made it difficult to forecast future price movements. A flexible approach, therefore, is to invest in equipment which can use more than one type of fuel. Such a strategy relegates the choice of fuel to a tactical problem of choosing the lowest cost fuel when an order has to be placed. A second example concerns the development of new materials and components. Predicting the time needed to carry out research and development projects is hazardous and plans may thus be needed to carry on using previously tried materials as an alternative. When developing the RB 211 jet, for example, Rolls Royce has to consider using fan blades made out of conventional metal material as well as the development of the new material, carbon fibre. Insurmountable obstacles meant that the new material could not be used in the end.

Plans for Stores and Stock Control

It is also important to consider the implications for stores and stock control when developing the corporate plan. Changing demand rates for materials and other goods, and consequent changes in supply rates, put different pressures on the stores function. Changing lead times are also relevant. It is necessary to draw up plans, therefore, to provide the physical facilities for the anticipated scale of operations. Problems such as what to stock, how much to stock and where to stock need to be analysed, as well as defining the levels of service that are required. Materials handling techniques have evolved rapidly, and thus, methods need to be investigated and improved. Finally, we must not ignore the major aspect of costs, which can be as high as 25% of average inventory value. Forecasts of working capital needed to finance planned inventory levels must also be prepared. Thus, the objective of planning in this area is to provide a 'least cost service' to meet the planned levels of production.

'Make or Buy'

For many companies, particularly in the engineering industries, 'make or buy' problems are important strategic issues. This type of problem can arise as a short term question when spare manufacturing capacity is available in times of slack demand. Technical considerations may be similar, but the financial aspects differ according to whether it is a long term strategic issue or whether it is a short term tactical difficulty. The former situation is of prime importance.

All too frequently in the past, companies have not taken a serious look at what should be made in the company and what should be bought from outside suppliers. Manufacturing policy has been determined by previous traditions and has not taken into account the present and future possibilities. The 'make or buy' decision is not one that the purchasing function can take in isolation. It is important that both purchasing and production information is considered together, and thus a committee approach which allows all interested parties to express their view will be advantageous. Some important decisions may need to be resolved at Board level. Nevertheless, the purchasing function should play a significant part in finding the right answer.

First, the strategic problem needs to be clearly stated. It may be concerned with the question of how existing production facilities should be used in the future, or, it may also be concerned with whether an investment should be made in additional plant or equipment. The tractical short term problem, however, is concerned with how to use spare capacity, or, indeed, what to subcontract if existing capacity is fully utilised in times of an unexpected jump in demand for the finished product.

The Company must first, make a full appraisal of its technical capabilities with respect to proposals of what should be manufactured. This should cover existing strengths and weakness's as regards knowledge and skills, availability of labour, materials, and finance as well as suitability of plant and equipment. If there are any deficiencies in the present picture, which mean that the company cannot produce the products in the required volumes, then a further appraisal must be made of the feasibility of acquiring the extra resources.

At the same time the purchasing department should make a similar assessment of the supply market. Have there been difficulties regarding quality, delivery and price which can be solved by internal manufacture? Are there any particular advantages that external suppliers have regarding research and development expertise, long production runs and specialist equipment? The volume required by the company may be insufficient to benefit from the specialisation which suppliers can indulge in when supplying to a much wider market.

Finally, assuming that there are no major technical barriers to making the product, a comparison of the total cost of manufacture needs to be compared against the cost of acquiring the product from external suppliers. It may also be possible to compare the alternative costs and savings from a number of 'make' proposals. When the issue is a strategic question, full costs of internal manufacture (i.e. capital or fixed costs as well as variable costs) should be taken into account. In the tactical situation, however, a case can be made for leaving out fixed costs for use of machinery and equipment. This approach is based on the assumption that equipment will remain idle in the short run, if the particular product in question is not made internally, but that overhead charges will, nevertheless, be incurred by the company. The financial analysis will, therefore, reveal whether it is more economic to purchase from an outside supplier or whether it should be made internally.

The purchasing function can make a valuable contribution to the decision-making process with regard to 'make or buy' problems. It should also be prepared to initiate proposals to reverse previous policies if changes in supply markets indicate that the company can gain from doing so. The Corporate Plan should be based upon a careful analysis of what it should produce and what it should purchase from outside.

International Trade – the Implications for Purchasing Management

International factors may have a significant effect on a company either directly, in relation to the products that are bought or sold overseas or indirectly, by influencing government actions and the activities of suppliers and customers. Purchasing Management is more involved with influences affecting supplies, though changes in demand for the finished products cannot be entirely ignored.

Factors Directly Affecting Purchasing

- Availability of Foreign Products
  The changing pattern of world markets affects the availability of goods that can be purchased abroad. It is necessary to study changes in supply and demand and to identify new products and new markets as they develop. As a result of improvements in transport techniques, of changes in the relative competitiveness of overseas producers and of technological advances made elsewhere, the potential for sourcing overseas has increased. However, it is also important to be aware of factors which may reduce availability, for example, political changes in a country, adverse weather, exhaustion of resources, and also official or unofficial quota restrictions. Finally, it must be emphasised that buyers should be looking for possible overseas sources for not only raw materials and foodstuffs, but also manufactured goods.

- Prices of Foreign Products
  Factors influencing the supply of goods mentioned above will also affect the prices of such goods. Thus, reductions in supplies will lead to price rises, as will a growth in demand. The opposite trends will lead to the reverse effect. There may be time lags before adjustments in supplies can be made to adapt to changes in demand. Thus, price fluctuations can be large, particularly for foodstuffs and raw materials on the commodity markets.

- Government Policies
  Government measures can also have a direct effect on prices of imports through tariff policies and international trading agreements. The activities of the Bank of England, in addition, may be important with regard to exchange rates. Thus, entry into the EC affects the tariffs charged on imports into the UK. It is essential for

buyers to take into account tariff and exchange rate consideration when analysing overseas opportunities and to assess the implications of changes in these factors. Devaluation, for example, may lead to a significant increase in costs if a company purchases a substantial quantity of imports from overseas.

Indirect Factors

- Suppliers

A purchasing department may use suppliers located within the United Kingdom, but the latter's operations may be affected substantially by international factors if they are dependent on overseas supplies. The effects of international events cannot be insulated from their customers, therefore, and thus prices and deliveries of goods produced in the United Kingdom will also be affected. It follows, therefore, that buyers need to take international matters into account when analysing home markets in which goods have a substantial imported content.

- Government Economic policy

International factors and, particularly, balance of payments difficulties may influence Government economic strategy in managing demand in the domestic economy. The implementation of government strategy via fiscal, monetary prices, and income measures can affect home markets. If the strategy is aimed at expanding the economy at a faster rate, the growth in demand may lead to supply shortages, lengthening lead times and higher prices. A deflationary policy on the other hand may make supplies more easily available and prices may fall.

Difficulties of Importing Goods

The expansion of international trade has increased the opportunities of sourcing overseas, but it is also important to bear in mind difficulties which may arise when using a foreign supplier which do not affect domestic suppliers. Some examples of these problems are:–

- Communication problems arise because of differences in language, distance, and time factors and these may be costly;
- Increased transport problems because of increased distance and because the United Kingdom is surrounded by water;
- Full transport costs, tariffs and exchange rate factors must be

considered when comparing prices with suppliers in the United Kingdom;
- Difficulties of obtaining spares and replacements quickly;
- Difficulties in visiting suppliers and;
- Complications of administrative procedures needed for imported goods to pass smoothly through customs.

Specialist knowledge and expertise is useful in handling imports and if a company is not large enough to develop this, it may be advisable to buy foreign products through distributors and agents in the United Kingdom. Larger companies have "shipping departments" which take responsibility for organising transport (unless this is arranged by the supplier) and for handling importing procedures.

The international environment is an extremely important influence and cannot be ignored in the development of a purchasing strategy. An implicit assumption of this Chapter has been the need to obtain supplies for an organisation located within the United Kingdom. For some multi-national companies, however, it may be necessary to develop a purchasing strategy to provide supplies for locations in many different parts of the world. International factors have significant effects on the national economy, in which the intervention of the UK Government has become a significant feature.

This chapter has covered particular purchasing strategies that can be considered in the corporate planning process. It is vital that purchasing activities should be concerned with long term plans as well as immediate operating problems. The next chapter is concerned with purchasing policies to implement these strategies.

Policy Issues

In addition to the various strategies described in the previous chapter, there are several policy issues which can influence the operations of the purchasing department.

Policies regarding 'reciprocal trade', 'intra-company trading' and 'purchasing ethics' should be established as part of the plan for purchasing management. These, allied to selecting a policy, the structure of the purchasing function, centralise or decentralise activity and interface with materials management are all relevant to effective purchasing management.

'Reciprocal Trade'

Reciprocity involves a two way flow of trade between companies so that each is both a seller and a buyer. A potential reciprocal trading situation is one which can cause conflict within the company between the purchasing department and the selling department. Let us consider a hypothetical example. Company A will only buy from Company B as long as B will agree to buy goods from A. The sales department in Company B will, therefore, apply pressure on their purchasing department to buy from A. How should buyers react to such an attempt to restrict their freedom choice as regards source selection? As long as the product offered by Company A is satisfactory, competitive (from a price point of view) and if company A is reckoned to be a reliable supplier, there is no difficulty and they can be given the contract. Buyers should, however, insist on carrying out a full market appraisal to identify the strengths and weaknesses of all the possible suppliers. Any disadvantages of using Company A can then be clearly presented and weighed against the possible gains to be made by making the sales to Company B. The ruling criteria should be "what is right for the company", and not "what is right for purchasing or marketing" in isolation. Thus, a policy decision should be made concerning the approach to be adopted in analysing reciprocal trading situations. If supplier A is chosen, even though they are not seen to be the best supplier in the market, then the reason for such a decision needs to be recorded and their performance needs to be monitored. A final point is that a decision should also be taken with regard to the provision of information from the purchasing department or the marketing department concerning the values of purchases from particular suppliers.

Intra-Company Trading

The growth of multi-product companies has increased the opportunities for internal trading between different parts of the same company. A policy decision is needed to state how such possibilities should be handled. There has been a tendency in the past for arbitrary policies to be established giving preference to internal sources and, thus, restricting the choice of the buyer. However, a preferable approach is one by which each case is examined on it's merits to find where the balance of advantage lies. The cost of using an internal source should be compared with the costs of using an independent supplier. A 'profit centre' approach, which regards each manufacturing division, or subsidiary, as a separate accounting unit, means that each must be self-supporting and should not receive subsidies from other parts. In effect, if a subsidiary buys from another part of the company at a higher price than from an external supplier, then the difference in the prices can be regarded as a subsidy. If the supplying division is not competitive, therefore, it should not be given the business (at least in the long term). Where there is no external supplier to act as a check on price, negotiations should be conducted to identify the true costs of manufacturing the product, and to set realistic 'transfer' prices. Further difficulties regarding quality and delivery can arise in intra-company trading situations and the manufacturing division may give preference to independent suppliers. The correct policy should be to buy from the best source inside or outside the company.

Additional complications can arise in multinational companies due to the fact that supplies may cross international boundaries. Setting 'transfer' prices will involve the consideration of exchange rates, tariff duties and tax differentials in the various countries. An overriding objective in this case may be to minimise the total tax liability of the company. Decisions may need to be taken at headquarters in such companies, since only there may all the necessary information be available.

General Comment

This chapter has provided information about the various purchasing policies that can be adopted to support a firm's corporate plan. It is important that a long term view of activities should be prepared and that this should provide a framework within which day to day problems can be tackled. It is especially important for large companies to develop conscious long term strategies in order that their monopolistic powers should be used wisely. Concentrated buying power may be able to dictate to smaller suppliers in the short term, but it is essential to estimate the long term effects. The pursuit of low prices may bankrupt suppliers and such tactics may, therefore, alter the market structure and reduce competition. Other detrimental effects, albeit less severe, such as poor service and a high rejection rate may also arise as unwanted side-effects of the pricing policy. Purchasing, therefore, must decide whether their long term objective on continuity of supply is more important than achievement of price objectives in the short term. The dominant buyer should seeks to maintain 'effective' or workable competition which produces fair prices in relation to cost, prompt service and a reasonable rate of innovation.

Selecting Overall Policy

The ability of the organisation to develop, and apply effective purchasing policy depends partly on the perceptions of managers at all levels. The manager charged with the development of a policy should recognise that these perceptions are affected by the existing company structure, the quality of its internal communication system, the past experience of the company and its managers, and, the resources available.

As has been suggested earlier, the development of a policy involves company-wide considerations. These considerations differ by industry and by company. What should be common, however, is the need to develop advantages over the competition and use them effectively.

The ability of the organisation to develop and apply effective purchasing policy will be conditioned by several factors, and, there are roles for a purchasing manager which relate to the development of policy. Among these are:–

- Generating alternative solutions to procurement problems;
- Protecting the cost structure of the organisation;
- Minimising purchasing costs;
- Assuring long-range sources of supply and;
- Maintaining good relationships with suppliers.

Each of these has a strategic as well as an operational facet. This emphasises the important point that development of a policy necessitates a co-ordinated operational response. It is of little use defining and developing a policy unless the day-to-day actions of the organisation are geared to the strategic approach. This is a deceptively simple concept, for it is not uncommon to find companies which purport to have policies where the behaviour of managers is contradictory to the stated approach.

Structure of Purchasing Organisation

An essential part of policy development and selection is to devise an organisation to carry out the activities embodied in the policy.

Classical management writers have emphasised the importance of organisation as a key function of management. Whilst their views have been modified in many respects, this function is still important and, therefore, the purchasing manager should pay close attention to the development of the organisational structure for the purchasing function. Organisation is concerned with the division of work and the delegation of authority and responsibility in such a way that the objectives of the organisation can be achieved. It also involves defining the duties of personnel and the relationships between them.

The task of developing an organisation structure has become a complex one and there is no longer a simple prescriptive model that can be applied in all situations. The business environment is now populated by a wide variety of different types of organisation. It is recommended, therefore, that an organisation structure should be tailored to the particular circumstances of the particular organisation. What is suitable for one would not necessarily be copied by another. In discussing organisational problems for purchasing management, it is essential to take into account some of the important differences. Of course, the development of an organisation for the purchasing function is only part of the general problem of developing an organisation structure for the organisation as a whole. Thus, purchasing considerations will reflect the needs of this broad framework as well as internal factors.

Structure of the Purchasing Function in Simple Organisations

In this example it is necessary to concentrate upon the organisation of a centralised purchasing function within a relatively simple, single product, single site firm; assess the advantages of specialisation and then map out the possible range of activities that could be included. Having portrayed a typical structure diagrammatically, the place of the purchasing manager within the overall management structure of the organisation will be examined.

Benefits of a Centralised Purchasing Function

In very small firms the scope for specialisation is limited and purchasing activities would not be sufficient to occupy a person full time. Once a firm employs around a hundred personnel or above, however, it should be possible to introduce purchasing as a specialised area. As the volume of work expands, so the number of purchasing personnel will grow and the opportunities for specialisation within the function increase. Parallel with this growth, therefore, the problem of organisation assumes greater importance.

The introduction of a specialist department to handle purchasing activities means that it's members see purchasing as their major responsibility and can develop expertise in conducting their work. Previously, purchasing jobs would have been done by other people for whom it would have been a major activity and for which they had no particular skills. Thus, full time specialists can develop their abilities and use progressive purchasing techniques to obtain better value for money. The department can co-ordinate the previously fragmented purchasing pattern and can introduce a common system of procedures. Knowledge of supply markets can be built up, an efficient record system introduced and negotiated skills can be applied. What may have started as a simple clerical function can become a sophisticated independent department.

The basic argument for the development of the centralised function rests upon the point that efficiency in controlling the flow of inputs to the firm is increased by the application of specialist expertise. The opportunities to make such improvements in efficiency can be found in different types of organisations in all sectors of the economy. Most large organisations already appreciate the advantage to be gained by effectively controlling purchasing activities, but, many medium sized and small organisations have yet to reap the full rewards because insufficient recognition has been given to this function. The purchasing function can make a major contribution towards the achievement of corporate objectives in both the public, and private, sectors.

Activities in the Purchasing Function

A wide variety of arrangements can be found concerning the activities which should be included under the control of the purchasing manager. The most effective pattern is one in which the purchasing manager is given authority for all those activities which lead to the supply of goods and services to user departments. Such a range might include:–

- Categories of Goods Purchases

With reference to basic categories of goods purchased by an organisation it can be shown that the area of authority concerning this range varies in different organisations. In manufacturing companies, the purchase of industrial materials is regarded as the major area of expenditure to be controlled but many purchasing managers, however, have no control over the purchase of plant and equipment at all. In spite of this difference in delegation of authority, the arguments in favour of the application of specialist purchasing skills are relevant to all purchases. It follows that the purchasing department should be given responsibility for purchasing all bought out goods that are required. This does not mean that other departments should be excluded from the decision-making process, but that the purchasing department should contribute it's commercial expertise to this process in order to complement the technical skills of the other departments. A purchasing research team should also be attached to the buying area to provide information to the buyers which may include cost analysis.

- Progressing or Expediting

An essential phase in the purchasing process, for the more important needs at least, is the progressing activity, to ensure that goods arrive at the desired time. The organisational problem here revolves around whether buyers should also progress the orders they have placed or whether a specialist or specialist team should be formed to carry out these duties. The division of work between buying and progressing sections allows each to develop its own particular skills for the different activities. The buyer can concentrate attention on market analysis and contract negotiation, and the expeditor can build up contacts and persuasive skills to obtain deliveries from suppliers. On the other hand, some argue that having to do the progressing work disciplines the buyer in selecting reliable suppliers. On balance the first approach is preferable (as long as the workload is sufficient), and as long as the buyers are informed about poor delivery performance.

- Purchasing in Distributive Organisations

Whilst the principles of purchasing management apply equally to the wholesale and retail sections of industry, procedures differ within manufacturing. Since there are normally no production processes involved (the raw material stockholder may offer a cutting or shearing service), sales and purchasing personnel are involved in product selection and programming as a total merchandising operation. Many large organisations are headed as far as supplies are concerned by a Merchandise Executive or Director responsible for both Sales and Purchasing, organised to coordinate the expertise and information available to both. In a dynamic, consumer demand situation – retail, multi-stores or supermarket – purchasing requirement forecasting and expenditure, based on product sales, subject to changing preferences, promotions and seasonal peaks and troughs, requires continuous updating of data and flexible purchasing arrangements. Product knowledge, ability to interpret sales data, both short and long term, allied to continuous supply market research, are essential to successful buying for direct re-sale to the consumer.

- Stores and Stock Control, Including Goods Receiving

It can be argued that there are advantages to be gained by grouping stores and stock control activities under the control of the purchasing manager. The achievement of the objective of lowest cost of supply implies that both purchasing and stock control considerations are relevant in deciding how many, and when to purchase, goods required to reprovision the stores. It is easier to develop an integrated system of procedures and exchanges of information in a unified purchasing organisation than in two separate departments. Goods receiving activities complete the purchasing cycle and transfer the purchases to user departments or, more frequently, to the stores. These, too should be integrated into the purchasing organisation.

A Typical Structure of a Purchasing Department

It can be seen from the foregoing information that the structure of the purchasing department can be varied to give an assortment of different configurations. The following diagram shows a typical structure for a supplies organisation in a medium to large sized company.

Division of Work Amongst Buying Groups

The division of work between buying groups and buyers should be made on a logical basis. In single product, single site organisations the

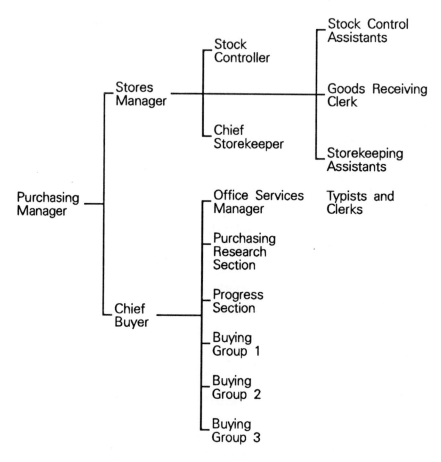

Figure 20.
Division of work amongst Buying Groups

major principle adopted is to divide purchasing work according to commodities. Each section, and each buyer, would be given responsibilities for particular groups of products. Thus, Buying Group 1 might be authorised to purchase all the Industrial Materials, Group 2 might be responsible for Industrial Equipment and Group 3 might be given responsibility for Industrial Supplies and Services. Individual buyers would then be given narrower ranges within each section. However, a second principle might also be followed in so far as more senior buyers would be responsible for high value orders. Specialisation on a commodity or product basis allows buyers to build up expertise in a limited number of markets and to gain the opportunity to get to know the nature of these products and the characteristics of the suppliers.

In more complex multi-product, multi-site companies, however, two further principles, which can be adopted in the division of work, may arise. Buyers may be appointed to handle purchases for a particular product line or manufacturing division. In addition, workloads can be divided up according to geographical locations.

Arrangements in the Automotive Industry

The nature of the large volume production systems and the methods of control adopted throughout the organisation have led to the emergence of a different type of structure on the purchasing side of the automotive industry. The method of control is based upon a set of interrelated computer programmes linking market forecasts, production programmes and materials schedules (for example, lists of products required to meet the production programme that also take into account stocks on hand). A scheduling group is responsible for obtaining the necessary quantities, at the required time, from suppliers by sending out delivery schedules (usually on a monthly basis). A purchasing group has responsibility for initially arranging 'blanket order' contracts with suppliers when the items are first introduced, as part of a new or modified model programme. These contracts over the specification and price arrangements with the suppliers and provide the framework for subsequent scheduling operations. Some companies have a third group concerned with supporting research and development projects for new designs and prototypes. Finally, other purchasing groups will control the acquisition of equipment and supplies following more conventional practices. Within this scheme there are variations as to whether the scheduling group is part of the supplies department or whether it is part of Material Control (embodying production control and inventory control) and falling under the jurisdiction of the Production Manager.

The Position of Purchasing Management in the Organisation

Where there is an integrated supplies organisation or, indeed, where there is a significant purchasing team, a case can be made for the Purchasing Manager or Director of Purchasing to have a high position within the management structure. This allows the Manager and his or her department to give full weight to commercial aspects of purchasing decisions. If the Purchasing Manager is subordinate to the Production Manager there is a danger that too much importance will be attached to the technical matters. As an independent department, the supplies department can make it's full contribution towards the achievement of corporate objectives. It can be argued, therefore, that the Purchasing Manager should be a member of the senior management team, with a direct reporting responsibility to the General Manager. The Purchasing Manager may also be a member of the Board of Directors. Thus, the management organisation might be as follows:–

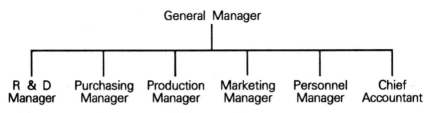

Figure 21.
Position of Purchasing Manager in the organisation

The position of the Purchasing Manager within the organisation hierarchy is an important determinant of the impact that the department can have. A high position and high status enables an effective, progressive approach to purchasing work to be implemented. Support from the general manager helps to increase recognition for the function and encourage good horizontal relationships with other departments. In the end however, it is successful performance that earns the respect of others in the organisation.[11]

Structure of the Purchasing Function in Complex Organisation

The emergence of large multi-product, multi-site organisations, and, marketing strategies that can alter products as they seek growth means that organisations have moved away from the relatively simple situation of operating one production site to manufacture one product line. For this reason, some organisations have diversified into other product areas on one or more sites, and others have duplicated production facilities by opening establishments in different geographical locations. Policy decisions which have brought about these transformations have also influenced the development and adoption of different organisational structures to cope with the added complexity. The emergence of huge, multinational conglomerates, in which international differences magnify the problems of geographical dispersion has also been seen. One of the major organisational innovations of the twentieth century has been the introduction of the multi-divisional structure.

In the simple organisation, the basic breakdown of tasks was achieved by splitting work up according to the main functional activities. In the multi-divisional organisation, function tasks are grouped around different product lines, thus, several quasi-independent organisations are created and each has a reporting relationship to a central headquarters organisation. Each product organisation might be a separate, limited company, with, as headquarters, a holding company. In others, each division and the head office may all be part of the same legal entity. At both divisional and head office levels, further divisions of work can be made on a functional basis. Thus, a system such as the one shown in Figure 22 is formed.

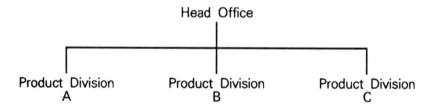

Figure 22.
A typical Divisional Structure.

Each division may have a management structure as above and the same functions may be present at the head office level to act in a co-ordinating capacity. However, the extent of the head office activities of the divisions tends to vary. Some multi-level organisations are relatively centralised and the head office personnel play a detailed part in the activities of the divisions. Other decentralised arrangements, however, give more autonomous powers to the divisions. These are established as separate profit centres, with minimal interference from headquarters, and the relationship between the division and the headquarters being mainly a financial one. The division is responsible for achieving satisfactory profit figures and must apply for approval of corporate plans and investment finance. It can be argued that the more unrelated in terms of technology, materials requirements and markets the division is, the more decentralised should be the method of control. There is little scope for central co-ordination as each division operates in an entirely different sphere.

The opportunities for central co-ordination are greater in situations when organisations are manufacturing the same product or offering the same service at multiple locations. Production technology, marketing problems and purchasing problems are similar and there is potential for more centralised control of operations. In this multi-level situation, therefore, more power and more activity will be located at head-quarters. Indeed, some of the functions can be located solely at the head office.

Alternative Structures for the Purchasing Function in Complex Companies

There are three possible solutions to the problem of organising the purchasing function in complex organisations. Each will be examined in turn to establish the advantages and disadvantages inherent in each solution. The three solutions are as follows:–

- Complete Centralisation – one central purchasing department controls the purchasing of all supplies for various scattered units or factories.
- Complete Decentralisation – each separate unit or factory has its own purchasing department and is responsible for obtaining its own requirements.
- Multi-level Structure – each unit has its own purchasing department, but a central purchasing department has some powers to co-ordinate the activities of the local departments.

Advantages of Centralisation

The advantages to be gained from the establishment of one central purchasing department are as follows:–

- Economies of bulk buying of items commonly used at each unit. The central department can negotiate cheaper prices on the basis of total consumption throughout the company.
- Avoidance of 'competitive' buying by individual departments of materials in short supply.

- Opportunities for development of greater knowledge about products because buyers can specialise in a narrower range of commodities which can be handled more expertly, for example buyers place orders for the whole company for a small range of products, whereas local buyers have to handle a more general range of local requirements.
- Savings in operating costs. Fewer, but larger orders are placed and hence a reduction in administrative costs can be made.
- Development of common procedures, forms, standards and specifications.
- Simpler relationship with suppliers as a result of single, direct contact.
- Investigations of new products and materials can benefit all units in the company.
- Centralisation of stock control can reduce overall stock levels through greater flexibility and establishment of strategic reserves, such as flow of stocks between factories to meet shortages.
- Development of improved support services made possible, for example, purchasing research and statistical information services.
- Enhanced importance of the Supplies Department and higher position of the Supplies Manager in management hierarchy.
- More scope for purchasing strategy and contribution to corporate plans.
- More scope for manpower planning in the function and development of training programmes.

Advantages of Decentralisation

The advantages of decentralisation can be seen as a remedy for the weaknesses of centralisation. The main advantages are as follows:–

- Closer co-ordination with local organisation, and, buyers can build up close contacts with other departments.
- The buyer is in direct contact with the problems where they arise and can handle emergencies more easily than a distant office.
- Local buyers are better informed about local markets, which may offer possibilities to a local customer which could not be offered on a national basis.
- Clear responsibility of buyers to local management.
- Local plants may need a different range of products and, thus, a local buyer may have a more specialised knowledge of these.

A Multi-Level Structure for Purchasing Management

The multi-level approach attempts to obtain the advantages of both the previous models. The division of duties between the two levels which is designed to achieve this are:–

Central Office

The following tasks may be allocated to the central office:–

- Determination of purchasing policy and development of purchasing strategies;
- Standardisation of procedures, specifications, codes and forms;
- Negotiation of contracts for commonly used items against which local departments can place delivery orders for supplies as required;
- Purchase of major plant and equipment;
- Importation of supplies from overseas;
- Responsibility for legal matters;
- Inter-plant stock transfers and stocking policy;
- Responsibility for training and;
- Research and information service.

Local Offices

- Responsibility of placing orders for 'non-contract' items and;
- Place delivery orders for contract items.

In this group purchasing system, the manager at the local level would be responsible to his or her local line management. The Manager at the central office would act in a staff capacity usually. That is to say, the latter would not have executive authority, as such, over the local manager, but would act in an advisory capacity.

A number of difficulties can arise in this multi-level approach. First, there is a danger that local initiative will be stifled by having group contracts imposed by a remote head office. The relationship between the two levels may be difficult to control. The local department may resent interference and there may be a conflict of interest between local interests and the views of the head office. The staff/line division of responsibilities does not successful resolve the problem of the local purchasing manager who has dual responsibilities to his other local management team and to the group purchasing manager, when the latter has a more senior position, but no executive authority.

In spite of these problems, however, where a large range of items are commonly used, the benefits of having a central office outweigh the difficulties. When the range of commonly used items is small, other methods of achieving a common approach have been devised. These methods do not involve the formation of a permanent central department as such.

Other Methods of Achieving Co-ordination

Several other approaches have been developed to take advantage of the purchasing power of large companies without developing a central purchasing office. These include the use of a 'lead buyer' strategy and the use of committees of local purchasing managers.

● Lead Buyers' Contracting

The essential feature of this strategy is that the major user division or factory negotiates a contract, which is made available to the other parts of the company to use if they wish to do so.

● Committee of Purchasing Managers

Regular meetings of Purchasing Managers can be held to discuss common problems and to co-ordinate activities. Tasks of negotiating bulk-contracts can be allocated to individual departments.

● Informal Communication

Informal communication between local departments can also lead to the formation of common policies.

These three approaches can be seen as being of a less formal kind than setting up a permanent central office. They also lack the scope of the central office for providing all the additional services indicated previously. In some cases local purchasing departments may be large enough to afford some of the specialisms that may have been given to head offices.

The Selection of an Appropriate Structure for Particular Circumstances

There is no single method of organising the purchasing function which is appropriate for all complex organisations. In developing a suitable structure, it is important to analyse the circumstances of the particular organisation for which it is intended. Perhaps the key question that needs to be asked is how common are the purchasing problems that have to be faced at each site? The greater the similarity of purchases, the greater is the potential for centralising control. Conversely, the greater the variety, the greater the opportunity to decentralise activities. Four different situations are worth examining:–

- Single Product/Multi-site operations;
- Multi-Product/Multi-site operations in which products are related;
- Multi-Product/Multi-site operations in which products are un-related;
- Very large multi-product/multi-site operations in which there is scope for multi-level structures in each division.

Single Product/Multi-Site Operations

Where each factory is concerned with manufacturing the same products, the purchasing requirements are the same. Demand arises for the same products which are purchased from the same markets. There is scope for a fully centralised purchasing function, therefore, to gain the maximum benefit of the purchasing power of the company and to provide common solutions to common problems. In the tertiary sector, a central purchasing department would be able to control the purchasing for individual branches of a retail or distribution network and organise central storage points from which supplies of many items could be delivered. Buying consortia for several local authorities base their arguments on such a premis.

Multi-Product/Multi-Site Operations in which Products are Related

In organisations which have several product divisions, but whose products are related, in the sense that similar technology and similar materials are used, a multi-level purchasing system could be used. Sufficient common items and associated purchasing problems exist for a central department to make a valuable contribution, whilst local supply departments maintain close contact with local factories.

Multi-Product/Multi-Site Operations in which Products are Unrelated

Conglomerate or diversified organisations may consist of manufacturing divisions which are entirely different in terms of technology and materials used. In such a situation, few common problems arise and there is little to be gained, therefore, from having a central department. Each divisional purchasing manager, however, should be given a high position of responsibility within the divisional management structure and should play a significant part in the planning process for the division.

Very Large Multi-Product/Multi-Site Operations

In very large organisations, individual divisions may themselves have a multi-level organisational structure. In such a situation, there may be local purchasing departments under the control of a divisional Purchasing Manager. On top of this there may be a corporate purchasing department to co-ordinate the activities of the divisions, depending on how similar their needs are.

Multi-National Supplies Structures

The multi-national character of big organisations creates additional complications. Wide variations in terms of political, economic, social and industrial conditions may exist in the countries in which operations are located. It may be necessary, therefore, to allow a local purchasing department wider latitude in determining it's own supply policy and controlling it's own supplies. Nevertheless, if there are opportunities to be gained from closer co-ordination, such objectives should not be ignored and the local department should be encouraged to follow group policy. The central office could be used to organise the supply of goods being imported into other countries for local factories.

Public Sector

Both in central government and local authority purchasing, the emphasis is on *public accountability*. This is not to underestimate the vital necessity for efficiency in purchasing, as in the private sector, and the move towards centralisation is evident in both central and local organisation.

Central Government

The Procurement Executive provides a central technical and procurement service for the armed services, within the framework of co-ordinated assessments of service needs and the financial constraints of budgeted allocations.

To assist in the study of requirements, two advisory committees have been formed:–

- The Operational Requirements Committee (ORC) and;
- The Defence Equipment Policy Committee (DEPC).

The actual purchasing of equipment is made by contract, preferably on a "fixed price" basis and, as is apparent by the very nature of the equipment, the range of contractors able to fulfil requirements is limited.[12]

Local Government

The method of operating the purchase of supplies is made the subject of local authority *standing orders* on procedures for competitive tendering and acceptance rules. The Purchasing Officer, whilst appearing to operate under more constraints than a colleague in the private sector, is able to combine the formality of laid-down procedure with purchasing skill. Whilst in the 1990's there are several E.C. Directives regulating public purchasing, initially the stimulus to efficient procurement within local authority organisations was fostered by the *Local Authority (Goods and Services) Act 1970*. The main points of emphasis were:–

- A recommendation of the need for functional purchasing as a specialist operation and;
- The advantages which could be obtained from co-ordinated purchasing by combined authorities – centralised purchasing.

Materials Management

The materials management concept is based on the potential advantages to be obtained from controlling the flow of materials and goods from the supplier, through stores and production, to despatch. The overall control would thus embrace:–

- Purchasing;

- Stores;
- Inventory Control;
- Production Planning and Control and;
- Physical Distribution.

The functional managers would operate under the co-ordinating expertise of a Materials Manager or Director. There has been a strengthening "lobby" for some time to give inventory control responsibility to Purchasing, and Materials Management appears as a wider aspect of this development. Arguably, both functions could be part of Logistics Management.

Alternative structures can emerge based on functional managers responsible for:–

- Purchasing: With responsibility for supplies research and acquisition;
- Inventory: stores, warehousing, movement of materials and inventory management;
- Production: control of programmes, work schedules and material quantities, and;
- Physical Distribution: limited either to inwards and despatch transport facilities or the wider concept of external warehousing and customer service.

The benefits of this wider concept of *materials management* are reflected in:–

- Higher level of departmental co-operation;
- Efficient communications;
- Improved inventory control by centralised non-duplicated records, with the possibility of data-processing support;
- Personnel development with wider experience and;
- Strengthened support for purchasing.

There are no simple prescriptions to help designers prepare a plan for the organisation of the purchasing function in a complex organisation. It is necessary to examine the conditions in which each is operating. An additional determinant will be the view of senior managers at the corporate level who are the key decision-makers regarding the structure of the organisation as a whole. A further feature which may require diplomatic treatment is the relationship between the parent company and newly taken over subsidiaries. Personnel in the latter are often reluctant to alter systems and procedures and adopt new policies. Even within old established organisations, plans to restructure an organisation can also cause much conflict unless the task is carefully carried out.

This chapter has been concerned with the problem of policy and organisation with respect to the purchasing function. There are generally no simple solutions which can be applied generally to all organisations. It is, nevertheless, extremely important to design an effective structure if purchasing activities are to make a significant contribution to the success of the company. Structural arrangements have a significant effect on the performance of individuals in the function, because it is these arrangements which circumscribe the duties to be carried out by them – it is, ultimately, individuals who select and implement policy.

Notes and References

11. Baily, P., *Purchasing and Supply Management*, 5th edition, Prentice Hall, 1991

12. Quayle, M., *Prime Contractorship*, Purchasing and Supply Management, April 1991

Chapter 9

Managing the Logistics Function

Directing the Function

The Logistics Manager is concerned not only with managing the flow of materials and resources but he or she is also concerned with managing the human resources through which control of materials is achieved. In this chapter the problems associated with staffing the positions or roles that have been defined within the structure will be investigated. The various aspects of recruitment and training and the preparation of job descriptions and operating manuals will also be considered.

In addition to the elements of the staffing problem attention shall also be focused upon a closely related managerial requirement. This concerns techniques of directing and motivating the staff to achieve departmental and corporate objectives and to provide opportunities for members of the logistics function to satisfy their own individual goals at the same time. This topic is a controversial one and in the social environment of today, traditional views have come under severe attack. These opposing views shall be studied in the context of logistics management.

Staffing the Logistics Department

Audit

In an established organisation structure, a periodic audit of company resources must include a survey of personnel, in terms of adequacy of numbers and skills to meet the needs of changing programmes, particularly in a period of growth.

Responsibility rests, therefore, with the departmental manager to determine the effect of corporate plans on the department and in conjunction with the Personnel Department to arrange participation in the Training and Development Programme and for recruitment where necessary.

The Logistics Department audit will need to relate workload to current staff, and assess future needs. This can be achieved via a programme of training and experience obtained through job rotation (particularly an advantage to the specialist in developing product knowledge), visits to suppliers to obtain first-hand experience of industrial processes and formal education courses for professional training.[13]

Job evaluation for recruitment and grading require a description of the job, and a job specification describing the personal skills and attributes required for the duties and responsibilities to be undertaken (matching person to job and therefore important in recruitment and training).

Job Description

One of the classical principles of organisation is to carefully define the duties and responsibilities of each position in the organisation structure. Job descriptions specify what the holder of the position should do and they are a major determinant of the behaviour of the holder. They provide a broad statement of the purposes, scope, duties and responsibilities of particular jobs and allocate job titles. The need for such descriptions increases with the size of the organisation, but even in smaller organisations it is important that the occupants of job positions know what is expected of them. They act also as a guide for recruiting staff and for the assessment of training needs.

For organisations who have not yet developed job descriptions, the following steps should be taken. The first task is to prepare an analysis of existing jobs by a series of interviews both with job holders and other staff. Job analysis is concerned with establishing why a job exists, its objectives and how they are to be achieved. It is also necessary to establish its relationship with other jobs in the department, what supervision is given and received and what qualities are needed by the job holder. On the basis of the information which is collected, job descriptions can be compiled.

The following list includes the headings which could be included in a plan for the preparation of job descriptions.

- Job title;
- Title of immediate supervisor;
- Brief summary of the job;
- Detailed description of duties;
- Specific reports or information to be provided;
- Decisions and recommendations made by the holder;
- Responsibility for work of others;
- Responsibility for accuracy of work and the effects of any errors that may occur and;
- Education and experience required.

In many organisations, job descriptions form the basis of job grading schemes, which in turn are related to salary and wage structures. The ultimate objective is to prepare a rational salary shceme which gives similar pay to jobs of a similar grade throughout the company. In order to do this, it is necessary to compare the content of jobs in different departments. Various methods have been developed to evaluate jobs, such as ranking, points rating and factor comparison, with respect to such features as duties, supervision given and received, the nature of decisions taken, and the qualifications needed by the occupant. Such exercises are likely to be carried out by Personnel Departments, with the possible assistance of Organisation and Methods (O & M) specialists.

Staff Appraisal

The staff appraisal meeting between managers and supervisors and between supervisors and individual staff members, gives an opportunity for:–

- Setting objectives and targets jointly in key areas of the individual's duties and responsibilities;
- The supervisor or staff member to participate in choice and setting of targets, promoting job interest and confidence in planning and in handling of problems;
- The manager to be supplied with facts on individual performances in support of personal judgements and;
- The setting of key objectives. The discussion and counselling involved at this stage, and at the end of the period under review, involves leadership and motivation, benefiting management and staff in a common purpose.

Examples of objectives agreed might be:–

- A specified percentage of on-time deliveries to customers;
- A specified percentage saving against standard costs within a given period;
- A reduction in administrative costs per £100 of expenditure on transport and;
- A warehouse stock reduction through improved supplier relationship and supplier development.

Operating Manuals

Many organisations have found it useful to prepare logistics manuals as a guide to company personnel. These act as a guide, firstly, for the logistics department itself, secondly, for employees in other departments and, thirdly, for suppliers. Manuals describe the procedures to be adopted to achieve particular purposes and the rules for making particular decisions. They will also usually contain information about job responsibilities and reporting relationships, inform people about the service provided by the department and act as a guide to departmental policies regarding such issues as business ethics. The objective of such a manual is to provide a clear statement of how things are to achieved and it also is a useful help to newcomers. The operating manual can help to resolve disputes that may arise. The drawback with this approach, however, is that it might lead to a stifling of initiative and a reluctance to tackle new problems which do not seem to be covered by the manual. Thus, it is possible to argue that an operating manual is a more useful device in relatively static conditions, but less appropriate in a rapidly changing environment in which old methods and procedures may quickly become ineffective.

Qualities of Logistics Personnel

Discussion of organisational aspects of logistics work has indicated the wide variety of jobs that exist within the function. The desired qualities of job occupants need to be tailored to the needs of particular positions. In other words, it is not possible to prepare a simple blueprint of the ideal person for logistics work. Skill and personality profiles should vary according to the nature and complexity of the job. In spite of these reservations, however, some general comments about the characteristics apparent in a member of the logistics function can be made.

It has often been said that the logistician is a "jack of all trades, master of none". In the sense that an effective logistician needs a sound general business knowledge this is true. He or she needs a thorough understanding of the commercial and economic background to logistics work, he or she must develop a detailed picture of the particular markets in which they are operating and be able to make a careful analysis of the abilities of suppliers within them and he or she must also develop sufficient product knowledge to gain an appreciation of the alternative possibilities, and the commercial implications.

Technical Expertise

The extent to which detailed technical knowledge is required is a controversial issue and policies differ from organisation to organisation. On the one hand, it has been argued that the main contribution of the logistician is that of providing and analysing commercial information and playing a leading role in distribution. Supporters of this view suggest that logisticians should not attempt to become "pseudo-technologists" and take on the roles of designers and engineers. On the other hand, there is the belief that logisticians can only make a full analysis of the commercial aspects of a logistics problem if they have got a detailed knowledge of the technical features. Other departments may gain a greater respect for the logistician and may co-operate more closely with a person who demonstrates an understanding of the technical problems. Thus, some organisations do see a technical training as an essential quality for some posts in the logistics department. It is not possible to make a judgement that would be valid for all situations. The degree of technical knowledge required can be expected to vary.

The expert logistician will have a sound understanding of advanced techniques and should be able to apply a creative approach to logistics problems. In applying such techniques, competence in accounting and financial areas is also important. Increasingly it is becoming more and more important to develop skills in mathematics and statistics for the purpose of undertaking analytical work. Finally, in this list of required skills and knowledge, the addition of managerial skills, as logisticians move into more senior positions involving supervisory and planning work should be referred to. We can now consider personality traits that are appropriate to logistics work.

Personal Qualities

It is apparent that one of the most important characteristics which is necessary in a professional logistician is integrity. Communication skills play an important part in relationships. These involve the ability to perceive and understand points of view and points of information presented by other people, as well as being able to express points in a concise and easily comprehensive manner. Logisticians must be able to work closely with other people, both inside and outside the organisation and at times patience and diplomacy may be necessary when working under pressure. Logisticians have to be able to cope under pressure, particularly in situations which may threaten to stop an assembly line from operating because of logistics shortages.

Recruiting Personnel for Logistics Function

In developing a personnel policy in the logistics function it is important to plan for internal recruitment as well as external recruitment. Individual members of staff should be encouraged to develop their abilities by providing them with training facilities and an appropriate work programme with a view to future advancement to positions that will become available as a result of expansion and the retirement or promotion of existing incumbents. Records of existing members of staff should be kept and reviewed for training and recruitment purposes. Records showing educational qualifications, specialised technical skills, appointments within the organisation and career experience with other firms, training received and a summary of appraisals and personal particulars should be maintained. Internal promotion can improve morale and act as a spur to better performance.

Careful planning should precede interviewing work, to decide what questions should be asked and how assessments are to be made. Many organisations like to use intelligence tests and aptitude tests as additional devices. It is important to get the applicants to talk and to provide an opportunity for them to ask questions. Two possible schemes for interviewing can be outlined:–

The Seven Point Plan

The National Institute of Industrial Psychology (now defunct) suggested a scheme for selection interviews, covering the following features, which are still valid:–

- Physical characteristics;
- Attainment with regard to education, training and previous experience;
- General intelligence;
- Special aptitudes;
- Interests;
- Disposition – personal characteristics with regard to manner, and ability to get on with people and;
- Circumstances – domestic situation.

The Five Fold Grading Scheme

An alternative scheme places more emphasis on the dynamics of personality and motivation. It also involves the use of a five point scale for each of the five headings.

- First Impression and Physical Characteristics. This covers appearance, speech, manner and personal method of dealing with others.
- Qualifications and Expectations. This includes details of education, training and previous experience, but also expectations for the future.
- Brains and Abilities. Much will have been learnt from qualifications, but the results of tests can also be included.
- Motivation. Concerned with finding out the type of work the applicant likes and the "interest pattern" of the candidate.
- Adjustment. This covers distinct qualities such as integrity, reliability, acceptability to others and behaviour under stress or difficulties.

If, after considering the internal potential, it is decided to recruit externally, the logistics manager will, in most cases, call in the Personnel Manager to assist. External recruitment is expensive. Adverts should be placed in the papers or journals which are likely to be read by the type of person that is required. Particularly in times of high employment, this is a competitive process and the advertisement must be carefully prepared to attract the right person by giving a clear account of the nature of the post and future prospects, as well as giving a specification of the required quality. If applicants are asked to fill in a standard application form, the task of comparison is easier. A short list of candidates for interview can be compiled from this initial screening.

Recruitment is a costly process and it is important, therefore, to fully utilise the abilities of staff once they have been recruited, otherwise, they will leave. Further development of their skills is another objective and so therefore, training and education of staff as a further aspect of personnel policy in the logistics function, will be examined.

Training and Education

Successful training and development policies will enable the organisation to attract and retain able people. In today's rapidly changing world, with developments in knowledge and techniques, it is also important that staff at all levels in the organisation are provided with facilities that enable them to keep up to date. In the last analysis, better trained staff will give a better performance. No longer can organisations rest content that employees have received sufficient education and training before entry into the organisation. Many organisations have developed a training department to help in this area and to assist departmental managers in devising the right policy.

During the last two decades or more, there has been a rapid expansion of facilities to provide education and training. The government, through the 1964 Industrial Training Act, gave active encouragement towards this and, through the state education system, has provided various courses at colleges of technology, polytechnics and universities. Under the act, Industrial Training Boards collect levies from organisations, which are then used to pay the costs of training and which can be claimed back by organisations as grants towards approved forms of training courses that they offered, including correspondence courses. The major problem today is to diagnose training needs and to select the appropriate course from the wide variety that are available. Various training agencies have superseded or complemented training boards; the concept however, remains the same.

A number of steps are important in developing and supervising training. The first task involves identifying the training needs of individuals. An assessment of individual strengths and weaknesses in relation to existing and possible future jobs is a starting point. The emergence of new knowledge, new techniques and new legislation must also be monitored. Having analysed the needs, a programme of how these training needs can be met must be drawn up. The training programme, once in operation, must be evaluated in terms of the benefit accruing to the individual and the organisation.

In discussing the various types of education and training that can be given, it will be useful to distinguish between internal and external training, although some schemes combine aspects of both.

Internal Training

As regards internal training, commercial, undergraduate or graduate apprentices should be first considered. Such programmes are run mainly for employees upon entry into the organisation and are concurrent with attendance on external courses. The training in the organisation may commence with an induction course to introduce the newcomer to the structure and activities of the company as a whole. This will be followed by special work assignments under the supervision of senior staff to provide experience in the different types of work involved in the function. Commercial apprentices may be on sandwich degree courses. In addition, they may be involved in specialised courses such as that offered by the appropriate professional body.

Other internal training courses can be devised for other members of the logistics function. The emphasis of these courses, usually intensive and of short duration, would be placed on specific aspects relevant to the particular needs of the organisation. These courses, frequently of a participative kind involving case studies and role playing exercises, can be used to develop knowledge and skills, but, also to influence attitudes and encourage co-operation. Courses can be organised and run by the organisations personnel or by consultants and can be tailored to the particular needs of the organisation.

External Courses

External courses can take several forms. First, there are part-time or full time courses provided by the state education service. These cover HNC, HND, and Degree courses in Business Studies as well as the specific courses by professional bodies. These provide a general education in commercial aspects of business and a more specific education in logistics management and the techniques used in this field. Several European Universities now offer Masters Degrees covering Logistics and Logistics Management. In addition, courses in technical subjects may also be considered. Correspondence courses provide another route by which the student can gain these qualifications.

The importance of providing the right training in order to operate an effective logistics department is crucial. Attention must also be given to the qualifications of employees upon entry, but these abilities must be supplemented and built upon by further programmes tailored to their needs and to the needs of the company. The human resources of the organisation, and of the logistics department, should be regarded as valuable assets which need to be carefully cultivated. The maximum benefit can only be gained from providing the right environment in which the knowledge and skills of personnel can be properly applied. Often the benefits of training courses are lost because those attending are not permitted to practice what they have learnt.

Managing the Logistics Department

When considering the managerial function of directing, guiding or supervising the work of subordinates, one of the most controversial topics in business comes into consideration. The relationship between managers and their subordinates is at the heart of what has been called industrial relations. Whilst attention in the media, tends to concentrate on industrial relations on the shop floor, relations within "white collar" work are just as significant. During the Second World War, ideas concerning how managers should direct their staff have undergone many changes. In addition, social changes have taken place so that attitudes affecting the expectations of employees towards their jobs have been transformed. In particular, different views concerning the nature of authority in organisations have emerged and the importance of employee interests has received increased attention.

The following should be studied when considering the development of ideas with regard to the supervision and motivation of the work force:–

- The classical and neo-classical management tradition;
- The human relations tradition and;
- More recent ideas concerned with participation.

The Classical and Neo-Classical Management Tradition

The school of writers and ideas that can be labelled in this manner has been, and still is, extremely influential. Indeed, the framework of ideas upon which this chapter has been based has been drawn from this tradition. Many of the ideas concerning the function of management, with regard to planning, organising, staffing and controlling, remain as key thoughts in the organisation of an employer in general or a logistics department in particular. However, the major weakness in these traditional ideas lies in the area of manager to worker relations and the somewhat naive ideas of earlier writers concerning motivation and leadership.

The cornerstone of this tradition, with regard to industrial relations, lies in the view of authority and the prerogatives that this appeared to confer upon managers. Authority within the structure of organisations in the private sector was seen to be derived from the shareholders and this delegation of authority gave the Board of Directors, and the executive managers, authority to issue instructions and direct activities designed to enhance the interests of the shareholders. In turn, they were held responsible for achieving or failing to achieve the objectives of the shareholder. In return for the material rewards of the wage or salary agreement, employees were expected to accept without question instructions that were given to them. The pursuit of efficiency and the pursuit of profit was conducted with little attention to other interests of employees. In the public sector, managerial authority was seen to be derived from either parliament or the local council and, ultimately, from the electors. Strict adherence to this hierarchical view of authority has led to what might be called an "authoritarian" or "dictatorial" style of management. However, this view of an arbitrary style of management has come under fierce criticism for a number of reasons.

First, the view of authority itself has been challenged, particularly by the Trade Unions. The essence of this opposition is that insufficient attention is given to the rights of employees and these need to be protected, particularly through collective bargaining processes. Other ways of extending the powers of the employees, such as representation on boards of companies, works councils and an extension of collective bargaining have been put forward. Government legislation has already been passed to protect the rights of employees and it is possible that other measures to increase democracy will emerge in the near future, particularly in view of existing legislation.

Secondly, the authoritarian style of management has been attacked on the grounds of expediency. It is argued that it is based on a misconception of human nature and that it does not contribute to maximum effectiveness. Indeed, this view classifies authoritarian or dictatorial rule as being inefficient and warns that undesirable results will emerge, such as strikes, poor performance and a high turnover of staff.

The Human Relations Tradition

The foundations of the human relations tradition are generally accepted to rest upon the Hawthorne Studies, which were conducted in the United States during the 1930s. The essential finding of these studies conducted by Elton Mayo, is that individual performance can be affected by the attitudes formed by informal work groups in which the employees are located. It was discovered that the morale and attitudes of such groups could be either favourably or unfavourably disposed towards the achievement of corporate objectives and the acceptance of managerial instruction. Furthermore, it was suggested that workers are concerned with obtaining not only monetary rewards, but also satisfaction of social needs from belonging to the group. The implication for management of this point of view is that attention must be given to techniques of supervision. Instead of relying on coercive methods, using only financial incentives and punishments, supervisors are recommended, by this school of thought, to develop ways of influencing group attitudes and gaining the support of employees for organisational objectives. The emphasis is placed, therefore, on the social skills of supervisors, designed to remove any antagonism in informal groups towards the formal requirements of the organisation. Importance was attached to communicating a sense of purpose and developing teamwork.

However, difficulties attached to this view have become apparent; it tends to underestimate the importance of material rewards and it ignores some of the factors which can influence group attitudes. In particular, it ignores the influence of external forces, such as Trade Unions. Nevertheless, the development of this tradition was a useful counter-balance to the instrumental view of employees adopted previously.

Participative Approaches

New ideas have emerged during the last ten years or so which have their origin in both the findings of the human relations school and in the more general opposition to authoritarian rule in society as a whole. These ideas are also based upon a different conception of the basis of characteristics of human nature. The thrust of these views is to allow individual employees greater scope to exercise their basic talents and sense of responsibility. Instead of giving a rigid prescription of what job holders should do, it is advocated that more discretion should be allowed so that they can use their initiative in solving problems. This extension of responsibility has been called "job enrichment" and to it others have added "job enlargement". The notion, underlying this second term, is that jobs should not be divided up into too narrow a task, which might lead to boredom and monotony. Furthermore, the roles allocated to employees should include participation in the setting of objectives and the making of decisions which affect them. The essential features for management in this school of thought is that managers should adopt a consultative style and encourage a joint problem solving approach.

Psychologists agree that this participative approach allows individuals the opportunity to develop the full potential of their abilities and satisfies their wishes to exercise more control over their work. It is argued that this desire for autonomy is increasing in advanced industrial societies. On the basis of this analysis, managers, in designing organisations, should establish a less rigid structure in order to create an environment in which abilities can be developed. Too much reliance on prescriptive and coercive techniques will not utilise the full potential of employees. Rewards should be closely related to the achievement of objectives, but employees should be given freedom to select the means of achieving them. They should also be allowed to participate in the setting of the objectives in the first place.

The right of the manager to manage through the following of these later ideas is justified less in terms of managerial prerogative and more and more in terms of expertise. Acceptance of managerial authority by subordinates may also, therefore, be based on the competence of the managers. Concern for people as well as concern for results is important in motivating people according to this third school of thought.

The drawback of these later ideas concerns the problem of whether all people want, or feel happy with the participative approach. Some people prefer to be given detailed instructions of what to do and experience stress if they are left to decide for themselves. Also, in situations which are straightforward and unchanging, there is evidence to suggest that firm decisions taken by the managers are more effective.

Implications for Logistics Management

In the dynamic and rapidly changing environment that exists today, there are no simple prescriptions to guide the logistics manager in directing the work of the department. It is necessary to develop a sensitive perception of the needs of both the organisation and of subordinate staff. Attitudes need to be based upon an analysis of the situation which exists, and situations vary from organisation to organisation. In some organisations, in which unions play an important part, a different approach is required from others in which employees are accustomed to a more authoritarian style. However, it is possible to argue that the task of the logistician is one which can be carried out more effectively by people who are permitted to exercise initiative. Very often, within their particular commodity range, they are the ones with the most expertise. There is scope, therefore, for encouraging a participative approach, at least in the higher levels of the logistics department. It is important that the logistics manager maintains an awareness of new developments and, in particular, an awareness of new legislation. Many people have suggested that social technology lags behind advances in other forms of technology. Nevertheless, it is of fundamental importance to develop a personnel policy and a managerial style that effectively utilises the talents of members of staff and that satisfies both organisational and individual objectives. In achieving this, ideal managers need to develop a sensitive awareness of the factors influencing performance. It is important to provide the appropriate training support to increase the value of these human resources.

Management and Implementation of Change

In order to achieve objectives within an organisation, changes are likely to become necessary from time to time. These changes are achieved through the staff. The outcome will depend upon the effectiveness with which this process is managed.

Strategic Change

Internal and/or external factors are likely to signal the need for change.

External factors might include legal changes, socio-economic changes, technological changes and so on.

Internally, it might be a change of objectives or mission, new men with different ideas, and such like.

Managing strategic change is concerned with a change in the "culture of the organisation". One can identify two main stages in the process of change:–

- Unfreezing, or breaking down, previously held beliefs and assumptions and;
- Reformation of new sets of beliefs.

Recipe for Change

The recipe is a set of beliefs and assumptions which form part of the culture of an organisation, and have been called:–

- Paradigms;
- Recipes and;
- Interpretative schemes.

Unfreezing Process

It is possible to identify from the above, a number of ways of unfreezing the existing recipe, such as:–

- Signal – downturn in performance;
- Challenge and exposure of the existing recipe;
- Reconfiguration of newer structures and;
- Intervention of an outsider for instance, someone with little commitment to the existing recipe.

Other Methods

Change can be implemented by:–

- Changing formal control mechanisms;
- Structural changes;
- Symbols of change, such as ICI change, Harvey Jones a

flamboyant character, bright ties and not in the traditional ICI mould and;

- Organisational structures, because they communicate "readily understood" visions of the organisation's mission or role.

Political Nature of Change

Management of change has political implications. If change is to be successful, it will be necessary to "manage and manipulate" the political power structure.

Logistics and Change

Increasingly, proactive organisations are recognising that logistics, far from being just another operational variable, is uniquely placed within the organisation to manage the inter-relationships of all the factors which affect the flow of both information and goods necessary to fill orders. This flow begins when the customer decides to place an order and ends when the order is fulfilled and the monies collected.

Organisations which believe that the single output of any organisation is customer service, understand the strategic significance of logistics in this process. They know that, to succeed in today's environment, they must adopt a disciplined and systematic approach to the market, create carefully considered priorities, allocate resources in the strictest possible manner and make often difficult trade-off decisions.

It is not yet common for the logistics manager to be involved with the initial phases of an organisation's strategic planning. However, the size of the corporate profit slice which logistics affects is sufficiently large to suggest that the logistics manager should be a key figure at the strategy formulation stage.

In describing strategic planning as the process of formulating plans which ensure the long-term profitability of an organisation, actions taken in anticipation of customer needs were referred to. The logistics manager is the only person in the organisation charged solely with managing the interactions and flows of information and materials in the conception to consumption chain. It is this unique position that provides the logistics manager with an appreciation of the organisation's capacity to respond to expectations.

Strategic planning forces management to reconcile two almost contradictory tasks: long-term (visionary) planning with short-term responsiveness to customers. To achieve this seemingly impossible balance it is necessary to focus on the "strategic" side of planning and not consider strategy to be just another word for "long-term".

Strategic planning covers three steps as far as logistics is concerned:–

- Vision or mission statements (what the organisation stands for);
- Aims (directions the organisation wants to go in) and;
- Objectives (specific quantified targets).

The chief executive is in the best position to understand the expectation of "stakeholders" (shareholders and employees) and the organisation's long-term goals. Accordingly, he or she must be the one to articulate the vision statement.

The difference between aims and objectives is the difference between quantitative and qualitative analysis. Aims are the qualitative statements, the expression of desires and goals. Objectives are quantitative and therefore must be measureable. It is not enough to set an objective as "increasing sales" because there is no way to determine if the objectives has been met. Increasing sales may be the aim, but, increasing sales by 3 per cent within six months should be the objective. This gives a finishing point and a specific target. Once the aims and objectives are established, operational plans can follow.

Proper procedures for implementation, control and evaluation are needed to translate plans from mere words on paper to actions on the ground. This is where effectiveness of the logistics manager will determine the success or failure of the whole planning effort.

The creation of a strategic plan does not provide a guarantee of success, rather, it provides a frame of reference against which changes in the environment external to the organisation can be evaluated. In this way the organisation can respond to both anticipated and unexpected changes in the external environment in a planned manner. It is this ability to evolve and adapt that distinguishes the strategically oriented organisation from its endangered counterpart.

The strategic planning process points the way forward for organisations which aim to be progressive and protective in the years ahead. Logistics, and the role of the logistics manager, are being recognised by strategically oriented organisations as key ingredients in successfully meeting the challenge of these increasingly turbulent times. Logistics managers must adopt a strategic approach if they are to be equal to the challenges that await them in the future.

Chapter 10

Electronic Data Interchange (EDI)

A Definition of Electronic Data Interchange (EDI)

In its broadest definition, Electronic Data Interchange (EDI) is the exchange of information between two different computer systems. For the purpose of this chapter, however, the most commonly used definition of EDI will be used.[14]

During the 1980's, the introduction of information technology into companies has enabled significant change to take place within the business – change in working practices, change in organisational structure and change to business strategies bringing improved efficiency, management control and customer service – and with them, a bottom line.

Technologies such as the Personal Computer (PC), Local Area Network's (LAN's) and, latterly, more widely based Corporate Networks have been adopted. Within the organisation this has enabled the application (such as a Material Requirements Planning System) to be brought closer to the end user and has facilitated the sharing of information between applications across common databases. This implementation of technology has brought with it real business benefits to the organisation.

There is, however, a further dimension to the implementation of information technology which has emerged over the last 7 years in particular. This is the electronic exchange of information between the applications of different organisations – Electronic Data Interchange (EDI). The business requirement for EDI is clear.

Whatever the business, organisations need to trade in order to survive. In order to achieve this, documents such as orders, delivery instructions and invoices must be interchanged and processed. Furthermore, because market conditions can change rapidly, these communications must be fast and accurate, with administrative processes minimised to ensure that, at all times, market opportunities are exploited and profits are maximised. In other words, the organisation needs to communicate effectively with all of its trading partners, whatever their function in the supply chain, whatever their sizes and wherever they are.

Electronic Data Interchange (EDI) services allow the exchange of trading data, such as orders and invoices, directly from one computer system to another, regardless of its make, size or location and without the need for manual intervention. As such, the consequential benefits to be obtained from the use of EDI are very significant. In the ordering process alone, the speed of movement of information means the supply chain can work together to ensure that the correct stock is in the right place; that the order is delivered on time; the market opportunity has been captured and to minimise working capital in the process. In short, it gives competitive advantage in competitive markets.

The sinners of the 1990's will be those organisations that not only implement, but exploit, information technology, and particularly, EDI more creatively, more efficiency and more successfully than their competitors. They will be those companies that form much closer working relationships with their trading partners, customers and suppliers alike and, EDI will be a key enabler in this process.

The Fundamentals of EDI

There are many different ways in which two businesses can communicate with one another: face to face meetings; paper transactions; telephone conversations; the telex or the fax; and, more recently, electronic mail. In each of these cases an "operator" is required within each organisation for the communication to be completed – in essence, they are all forms of person-to-person communications.

In addition to personal communications, Information Technology has allowed organisations to offer to trading partners access to their computer systems by a variety of communication methods. Examples include airline reservation systems and insurance quotation systems. Whilst one "operator" becomes a computer system, it is still in essence being interrogated by a person at the other end. Hence we also have person-to-computer communications.

EDI takes this one step further, being a dialogue between two computer applications without the need for any personal intervention.

EDI transactions are designed to be generated by a computer application, not a person. Likewise, an EDI transaction coming into a company is not designed to be printed and read, but rather to be entered directly into a computer application.

EDI has two main components. These are outlined below:–

- Data Standards

  If organisations are to exchange commercial data such as orders and invoices with trading partners, there needs to be some formal, explicit definition of the document. This enables the sender to know what information to send in what order, and the computer receiving the transactions knows exactly what was contained within the transaction and therefore how to process the information.

  As EDI has developed over the years in different parts of the globe there are, understandably, many different data standards available. In the UK there are only three widely acceptable standards, namely, "TRADACOMS" "ODETTE" and "EDIFACT". The standard that an organisation should use depends upon the standard used by the trading community. In an industry sector where there is no accepted standard established, the choice will depend on the business requirements of the sector. For example if business was international in nature, this would favour the use of the new international "EDIFACT" standards.

- Communication

  There are many different ways in which data can be exchanged between computers without the need for manual re-keying. Computer diskettes or magnetic tape, for example, can be used to exchange data, but this still relies on some kind of courier service to relay them between trading partners. This obviously has time delay implications.

  Discounting these options therefore, the choices are: point-to-point connections or leased lines between organisations; packet-switching services, usually offered by the public telephone service providers (commonly known as the PTI's); or Value Added Network Service providers (VANS).

  Whilst all three options are used in the UK, most of the inter-organisation EDI is conducted using the services of VAN's. With respect to communications, the main reason for this is that the EDI services deal with the differences in computer protocols of the various trading partners, and, provide store and forward facilities, so that a data exchange does not have to be scheduled for times when both partners have their computer systems available for the task.

Why USE EDI?

External and Internal Pressures

There are two groups of triggers driving EDI which can work independently or together. One group is external, the other internal.

The major pressure driving organisations into EDI is external, that is, pressure from major customers. Some are building EDI capability into conditions of contract, others are imposing financial penalties for each paper document submitted. The other external drivers competition and the need to match or stay ahead of the competition – particularly in servicing customers leads to the introduction of EDI.

Internal pressures are much more diverse. Organisations seeking to reduce the cost of purchase are attracted to the cost of savings EDI provides. Inventory reduction programmes, support for Just in Time (JIT) programmes, order-cycle and lead time reductions and the need for greater productivity are all supported by EDI.

EDI Benefits

EDI offers substantial benefits for improving the efficiency and effectiveness of the purchasing and logistics functions.

Most organisations focus on the cost saving aspects of EDI. These include:–

- Stationery;
- Postage;
- Mail handling;
- Data entry and correction and;
- Inventory reductions.

The speed of EDI transactions also brings benefits. Reduced purchase and delivery cycle times contribute to reduced lead times with a subsequent reduction in inventory.

EDI Activity in the UK

There are over 5,000 organisations, across some 40 major industry sectors in the UK, currently involved in Electronic Data Interchange through open, third party clearing house services. Many other organisations also use EDI both within their organisations and with their major trading partners or using direct telecommunications connections (such as permanent or leased lines).

Industry Sectors currently active with EDI include:–

Aerospace	Brewing & Leisure	Builders' Merchants
Chemicals	Clothing	Construction
CTNs/Newsagents	Distribution	DIY
Education	Electrical	Electronics
Engineering	Energy/Oil	Export and Transport
Food/Grocery	Garden Products	Healthcare
Home Shopping	Household	Local Government
Manufacturing	Motor Manufacturing	Motor Parts Distribution
Office Products	Pharmaceuticals	Publishing
Retail Chemists	Retail Departments	Variety Stores
Stationery	Sound & Vision	White Goods

The largest of these industry communities are foods and groceries, DIY and Motor Manufacturing, each with EDI communities ranging in size from 300–500 organisations.

Organisations involved across the 40 sectors range from the UK's largest multi-nationals (approximately 75 of the Times Top 100) to firms employing only one or two people. They come from all parts of the industry supply chain – retailers, distributors, wholesalers, importers, manufacturers and transportation firms.

Legal Issues

The information being exchanged in the EDI chain is, in some instances, part of a legal process. Purchase orders, invoices and some freight documents have legal, as well as business, purposes. If nothing else, EDI eliminates the battle of the forms. Documents with terms and conditions referenced now disappear. The legal structure and rules, however, are built to serve a paper based trade system, it has not yet caught up with the technology.

In the UK there are no restrictions on the use of EDI in the legal code, save for the requirement that land and bond purchasing should be effected under seal. No one has yet found a way of applying a seal to an EDI message. The 1981 Finance Act was changed at the request of the EDI lobby to amend clauses which would have outlawed EDI-based invoices. Whilst there are no significant restrictions on EDI, it must be pointed out that, to date, EDI has not been tested in the courts. When EDI software and services are selected, it is necessary to ensure that full audit trials are provided.

To help remove the uncertainty caused by this lack of legal precedence, the UK-based EDI Association (EDIA) has produced a model interchange agreement. The agreement is designed to supplement existing terms and conditions of contract when EDI is used. It includes clauses covering security and integrity of data, use of intermediaries (EDI service providers) and disputes.

Whether the EDIA or another interchange agreement is used, it is important to review existing terms and conditions of trade. Many include reference to paper and postal systems which must be removed. As most EDI transactions relate to term contracts, contract negotiation is not an integral part of the transaction, terms and conditions having been agreed upfront.

Organisations seeking to use EDI in an international arena will need to be particularly careful. The legal status of EDI differs, even within the European Community. The United Nations has produced guidelines – the UNCID rules – to help draft interchange agreements. The European Commission is currently trying to harmonise the Community's legal position on EDI but that work is not yet completed.

Finally, to pull all of the above into context, it must be said that the UK now has a community in excess of 5,000 organisations clearly demonstrating that legal issues have not restricted the growth in the use of EDI.

Degree of Integration

Supply chain operations involve vast quantities of information. Efficiency in supply chains demands efficient means of handling this information. Information Technology has been, and is, used extensively in certain sectors of the supply chain: inventory control, logistics, manufacturing planning, distribution, purchasing, and sales order processing are commonplace. In some organisations, these functionally based systems have been integrated to reflect more accurately internal supply chain operations. With EDI it can be seen that this integration expands across organisations, continuing the trend of directing information technology investments in order to facilitate greater degrees of integration. This relationship is illustrated in Figure 23.

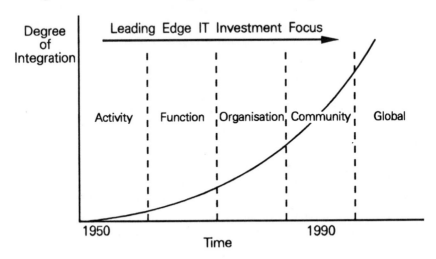

Figure 23.
Changing Focus of IT Investments

   EDI will significantly improve the efficiency of information across the supply chain, bringing great benefits to both purchasing and logistics operations. By creating a link between business processes in different organisations (or disparate parts of the same company) EDI will result in significant changes. Not since the introduction of Just in Time (JIT) has a concept been devised that will have such far reaching implications.

Notes and References

13. Gattorna, J., *The Gower Handbook of Logistics and Distribution*, 4th edition, Gower Publishing, 1990
14. *Electronic Data Interchange*, IPS, 1990.

Chapter 11

Marketing Research

It has been shown that distribution is an integral part of logistics. Distribution channels and their availability is also an essential element of effective marketing research. It is appropriate therefore that such research should be thoroughly understood. The aim of this chapter, therefore, is to provide an overview of this.

With the increasing acceptance of the marketing concept which places clients and customers NEEDS central to the task of marketing, research to determine these needs in detail has expanded enormously over recent years. The number of organisations having their own market research department varies by industry, such departments being most common in consumer organisations.

For those organisations without expertise there are many specialist consulting firms available. These fall into several categories:–

- Full-time market research organisations whose clients are too small to have their own reseach department;
- Specialist firms concentrating in particular areas such as market analysis and forecasting, survey research work, packaging research, brand name testing. These tend to specialise in either consumer or industrial goods and;
- Information selling organisations who gather continuous trade or consumer data to sell to client organisations on a fee-subscription basis.

Definition

Market research can be defined as – "The process of systematic investigation into markets to:–

- Establish present, and potential, demand for consumer and industrial products and;
- Provide a basis for management decisions."

Information from research reduces the element of uncertainty and thus sets limits on the decisions which have to be made.

Research undertaken needs to be sound and scientific, that is, logical in method and objective in outlook; if must be careful not to give a false sense of security. Judgement still has to be exercised.

Some organisations have employed researchers and been reluctant to believe their results since they do not "fit in" with the organisation's ideas. This may be because the client organisation does not know its market, although, it is possible that incorrect bases have been employed in the survey.

Sources

Sources of information can include the organisation's own sales statistics, information published by competitors, and, Trade Associations. Government statistics can provide useful sources of information although some care is necessary in using this source in terms of the need to check definitions carefully. Many general publications such as newspapers, The Economist and trade journals provide further sources.

Interviews of many types provide detailed information on the needs, preferences and perceptions of clients. These may take the form of:–

- Personal interviews carried out by independent consultants, or, interviewers from a specialist agency;
- Group interviews and discussion. This can be very useful in ascertaining attitudes;
- Consumer panels. Members of such panels need to be changed frequently to prevent bias;
- Telephone surveys are popular, particularly in the USA, for consumer surveys. Often a telephone call may be used to discover if a visit would be worthwhile.

Surveys by post can be unsuccessful since they may be dealt with by someone of little importance and without suitable detailed knowledge. Many questionnaires are thrown in the waste paper basket, whilst others get an irrelevant reply.

It is worth while at this point distinguishing industrial market research from consumer market research.

- Consumer research is used in the highly competitive consumer market for foodstuffs, soap powers, cosmetics, toothpastes and the like. Only a small sample of consumers can be questioned and the sample must therefore be statistically representative. Questions asked are normally predetermined and fixed for the survey. Attitudes may be tested as well as buying characteristics.
- Industrial research. The number of businesses in an industry are relatively limited, and purchasers of equipment and materials are generally experienced and knowledgeable in the trade. These circumstances call for quite a different approach to that followed for consumer research. Information is obtained by personal interview and the interviewer must be experienced and able to ask relevant questions and note pertinent data which may be revealed in the course of the meeting.

Research Methodology

This can be summarised by considering the stages in the research process.

Problem definition is a preliminary statement of the research objectives which are, normally, to provide information. Information needs are identified at this point.

This information can be gained from:–

- Primary data sources from "fieldwork" and;
- Secondary data sources from both outside the firm and from within.

The information required may be about products, brands, companies, retail stores, services and charitable organisations as well as about individuals. The information required may relate to:

- Opinions
- Values
- Beliefs
- Motivations
- Attitudes
- Intentions
- Knowledge
- Behaviour
- Lifestyle
- Social grades
- Minority groups

Secondary Source Data is available from:–

- Company records and previous research findings;
- Research organisations and government departments or trade and professional organisations;
- Market research agencies;
- Trade or professional conferences and seminars or;
- Technical literature, periodicals, government statistics and newspapers.

New or primary information will be obtained through:–

- Surveys by personal interview, telephone or post;
- Observation and experiment and;
- Motivational research methods including in-depth interviewing group discussion and group interviews.

Other stages in the process will define the research method, locations and size or type of sample, collect the data, analyse the data and evaluate the results and set down recommendations for action.

Field and laboratory experiements are used to evaluate the affect of changes in the product or service, its price, type of packaging, outlet or methods of sales.

Laboratory experiments provide a controlled method of determining the effect of price, packaging and other stimuli on individual consumers or groups of consumers. Whilst laboratory tests are somewhat artificial, valuable information can be made available to suppliers of goods in terms of measured attitudes to the product, price, packaging, advertising and promotion compared with competing products. Such tests provide an indication of customer reaction and behaviour in the market place.

Selective observations of people using mechanical devices can provide valuable insights to behaviour, although, not necessarily to motivations. Observations in shops, for example, children's reactions to toys or clothes provides information on attitudes, preferences and intentions. Since interviews are not conducted there are obvious problems associated with the interpretation of observations. Mechanical devices such as eye cameras, which measure changes in pupil size, can measure interest and reactions to adverts. A tachioscope, a projection device to present visual stimuli for a brief period, can be used to measure brand-name awareness. The use of tape recordings of discussions between sales staff and customers and the use of movie cameras and video tapes can all provide valuable research data. The use of traffic counters and television and radio audimeters are other examples of mechanical devices being used to observe physical phenomena.

Physical phenomena that are observed by people include the use of store and retail audits, "pantry" audits and information on brand and stock levels. Products and brands on hand provide basic information for the supplier company.

Research using questionnaires is widely used – and often abused. Surveys may be carried out by mail, telephone or personal interview and the method used will be dependent upon the type of information sought, the amount of information needed, the levels of cost accuracy required and the ease of questioning. The decision made will require the sample size to be determined and the method of analysing results to be decided upon.

Questions that should be considered when designing mailshot questionnaires should include:–

- Who is the respondent? Are they industrial buyers, consumers or professional advisers?
- Will the motivation to respond be high?
- What will be the length of the questionnaire and will it be simple to complete?
- What sample size is required?
- If a rented or purchased list is used, how up to date and accurate is it?
- Will a reply device be enclosed and;
- What will be the response rate?

The covering letter is very important and should, among other things, ask for co-operation, and possibly, give instruction and guidance.

Questionnaires

The preparation of a questionnaire requires considerable skill and, in industrial selling, often a good deal of technical knowledge. Too many open-ended questions will invite many responses and make analysis difficult. Questions may be structured – Yes/No, multiple choice, rankings or paired comparisons. When wording questions, it is important to avoid ambiguity in order that the question should mean exactly the same to all respondents. The respondent's ability to answer depends upon his or her education and language and he or she may exhibit an unwillingness to answer blunt questions on personal matters.

In posing questions, it is necessary to use language that does not influence the answer and in sequencing questions, the initial questions need to be designed to provide motivation and encourage co-operation. There is a need for a logical order, from general to specific and the rotation of questions and sub-questions will eliminate bias. Personal questions may be left to the end or inserted in the middle when appropriate.

Motivated Research

Motivated research techniques try to find the underlying motives, desires and emotions of consumers that relate to their behaviour. The techniques penetrate below the level of the conscious mind and uncover motives which consumers are not aware of, or, tend to hide. Two approaches to motivated research are:–

- The psychoanalytical approach. This technique relies on what is drawn from individuals via in-depth interviews and projective tests and;
- The psychosociological approach relies on group behaviour of consumers and the impact of culture and environment.

The techniques used are:

Depth interviewing – This uses interviewing and observational methods. The interviewer chooses topics for discussion and, through non-structured indirect questions, leads the respondent to free expression of motives, attitudes, opinions, experience and habits in relation to adverts, products, brands, services and such.

Good interviewing – In this technique, the interviewer stimulates and moderates group discussion to encourage freedom of expression and interaction between individuals.

Projective techniques – Here the respondent sometimes reveals what he or she may cover up in direct questioning. Verbal projectives may seek answers to questions such as "What do you think people do in a situation . . . ?" When a person is asked about someone else, their answer may reveal their own view. Other methods use word association tests, response to pictures, and sentence completion of the type "people buy on credit when . . .".

Assistance with Export

As an introduction to exporting, the Small Firm's Service offer a free, and very useful booklet "How to start Exporting". A good deal of literature is also available from the main high street banks, which deal with export finance, foreign exchange, letters of credit and associated topics. Local export clubs can also provide valuable information and practical help.

The British Overseas Trade Board (BOTB) is a good source of information and provides free booklets on many overseas markets giving detailed information which is regularly updated.

Foreign Embassies and Consulates are another useful source of market information and can save a firm's time and money in researching the market abroad for its products or services.

The Statistics and Market Intelligence Library at the Department of Trade and Industry is a source of information about the needs of overseas countries and their development plans, and this can be invaluable to the exporter. Also at this London based library is the BOTB's Product Data Store which provides data on many product headings, according to the Standard Industrial Classification.

The BOTB can very much reduce the effort on the part of the firm who's ambition is to export and who wish to find the potential for their product in specific countries. The Market Prospects Service and Export Representatives Service have been profitably used by firms starting to export and needing information on the prospects for their product or service, competing products, identifying potential customers as well as advice on price, quality and distribution methods. Full details of this service can be obtained from the nearest BOTB office. The Export Representative Service will also give assistance in selecting agents.

Market Research at low cost is available through the BOTB's Export Marketing Research Scheme. The scheme contributes to the cost of market research commissioned from consultants, to travel costs for employees of the organisation carrying out research outside the EEC as well as substantial financial help towards research commissioned by trade associations.

Having chosen a potential overseas representative to handle the firm's product or service, the BOTB can supply, at very low cost, an assessment of the agent or distributor through its Overseas Status Report Service. This report, obtainable from the local BOTB office, gives details of the interest and capabilities of the overseas company, its commercial standing, territorial coverage and facilities.

Further help is available from department of The British Standards Institution that supplies help to Exporters, giving information on foreign standards and requirements; a translation service is also available. Some help is given free of charge but the BSI will charge for detailed research.

Other Survey Methods

Omnibus surveys ask questions on behalf of many different client organisations and thus cut costs, since the individual client pays for their particular questions. Several research organisations conduct surveys on a regular basis and client organisations list their questions, and receive the answers, usually in the form of a computer print-out. The surveys are carried out by personal interview or telephone. General omnibus surveys and specialist surveys are available; the former interview is a representative sample of 1000–2000 people on a regular weekly or monthly basis. Because some clients may require less than the whole sample, or require a sample composed of females only (such as housewives) this is usually available at a lower cost.

Specialist surveys are sold to organisations who are interested in a specific market sector such as farmers or motorists. Omnibus surveys allow a firm to test the reaction to a modified product, or, a new method of packaging. The use of a regular omnibus survey will allow an organisation to gauge if it is gaining market share (and who it is gaining it from) or who is reducing its market share.

Most omnibus survey providers charge an initial entry fee followed by a charge per question asked. Help is offered by the survey organisations in designing the form of questions. The initial fee is payable usually on a once only basis. For general omnibus surveys using personal interviews the entry fee is of the order of £100 at 1990 prices. Telephone surveys, as well as some specialist surveys, do not charge an entry fee.

Question charges are priced depending on:–

● The size of sample required;

- The number of questions to be asked;
- The number of people answering them and;
- The type of question to be asked.

General omnibus surveys charge, under 1990 economic conditions, £150–£250 per question for "pre-coded" questions, and, for specialist surveys, £90–£350.

A good response provides a relatively low cost method but the speed of response may be slow; reminders may be necessary to speed up and increase response.

For telephone surveys, similar considerations will apply. The telephone is increasingly used as a relatively quick and cheap method of communicating with the prospect but suffers from the disadvantage of being impersonal and, usually, only permits speaking to one person when the respondent cannot consult other people or company records and so forth. Personal interviews are usually associated with high costs. The respondent may be interviewed in the home, office, in the street or in a theatre queue. The factors affecting motivation to participate in an interview are numerous and include:–

- Pressure of competing activities, embarrassment or ignorance, consequences, invasion of privacy and;
- Liking of interviewer, interest in content, loneliness, prestige of research agency.

Marketing – Does the Single European Market (S.E.M.) Matter?

Marketing strategy does not differ from market to market. The tools and frameworks applied to marketing in France do not differ to those used to market products in Brazil. Why then, is it necessary to discuss marketing in the light of the Single European Market? Principally, there are certain issues associated with it which will impact on specific factors of marketing strategy. Identifying these issues and assessing their effects on strategy provides the basis for the future direction of marketing in Europe.

Marketing strategy provides the framework for planning business activities to develop and sustain competitive advantages. A large number of tools and systems have been developed by marketing managers and theorists to assist in this process. These fall into three main generic categories: defining market opportunities, fitting the capabilities of the firm to the identified opportunities, and the "marketing mix" – the strategies adopted and implemented, including, product, price, promotion and distribution issues.

The Single European Market has had a marked effect on strategies for competitive advantage. Most importantly, it has changed many of the parameters of competition and thus enforced a period of reassessment and adaptation. The opening-up of the market, and the resultant increased competition have widened the perspective of the planning framework with profound implications.

The removal of physical barriers to trade, and new-found freedom of movement around the European market have served to catalyse European expansion, and, in so doing, raise the degree of intra-EC trade and investment. With greater numbers of competitors in each market, and more competition coming from non-indigenous competitors, the pressure that firms create in order to develop effective strategies and it's liberalisation of European-wide competition, the enhancement of competitiveness must feature highly on the list of most firm's policy objectives.

Operating on a pan-European basis involves addressing the issue of cultural difference and, consequently, developing a balance between standardisation and adaptation. This not only involves product development issues, but also the nature and location of production, the price charged for the goods, the form and content of advertising and promotion and the nature of distribution channels. Successful competitive strategy, therefore, does not depend on finding a strategic approach which works in one market and replicating it for others. A market-by-market approach is required to determine the appropriate marketing strategy for each market. This is further compounded by the differences in competitive structures of the Member States of Europe which have arisen out of historical, economic, political, fiscal and cultural regimes.

Harmonisation of markets is expected to be reflected in the convergence of prices and, ultimately to erode the differences between the Member States in terms of the prices charged for the same goods. As prices converge around the lowest common denominator, the scope to centre marketing strategy on price competition will be reduced. For some, an increase in efficiency will be necessary if they are to profitably match the new market price. For others, in order to preserve profit margins, competition will be biased more towards differentiation than price competition.

Although there is some evidence to support the notion that tastes are increasingly harmonising on a global basis, in many product sectors this is not likely to be achieved in the short term. Therefore, the immediate challenge is to ensure sensitivity to local market needs, which, in some instances, may mean adaptation. In the longer term a more standardised approach may prove possible. This raises another important issue. As markets are dynamic, with changes in economic conditions, political influences and consumer behaviours constantly shaping and reshaping demand and supply conditions, marketing strategy needs to be flexible and responsive.

Clearly, then, there are specific factors associated with the Single Market which will continue to have an important impact on the marketing strategy. But how can organisations ensure that their strategies will enable them to survive in the increasingly competitive markets of the EC? By highlighting the factors which appear in each generic group – defining market opportunities, fitting the capabilities of the firm to market opportunities and the marketing mix – it is possible to conceptualise the future marketing challenges for Europe.[15]

Clearly, marketing research and strategy are only two elements of marketing per se. This chapter has provided a brief overview of the research methods currently available and should assist in any overall strategic understanding of one of the integral subfunctions of Logistics.

Notes and References

15. Welford, R. and Prescott, K, *European Business: an Issue-Based Approach*, Pitman, 1992.

Chapter 12

Quality

The aim of this chapter is to provide a brief overview of a lengthy aspect of Logistics – that of quality. After defining quality and the costs of failure, methods of getting it right such as BS5750 and Total Quality Management are covered.

Defining Quality

The reputation attached to an organisation for the quality of its products and services is accepted as a key to its success and the future of its employees. To prosper in today's economic climate, any organisation and it's suppliers must be dedicated to never-ending improvement, and more efficient ways to obtain products or services, that consistantly meet customers' needs, must constantly be sought. The consumer is no longer required to make a choice between price and quality, and competitiveness in quality is not only central to profitability, but crucial to business survival. In todays's tough and challenging business environment, the development and implementation of a comprehensive quality policy is not merely desirable – it is essential.

Quality is often used to signify "excellence" of a product or service – some talk about "Rolls-Royce quality" and "top quality". In some engineering companies, the word may be used to indicate that a piece of metal confirms to certain physical dimension characteristics, often set down in the form of a particularly "tight" specification. If quality is defined in a way which is useful in it's management, then it is necessary to recognise the need to include, in the assessment of quality, the true requirements of the "customer".

Quality is simply meeting the customer requirements, and this has been expressed in many ways by others:–

- "Fitness for purpose or use" – Juran.
- "The totality of features and characteristics of a product or service that bear on its ability to satisfy stated or implied needs" – BS4778, 1978 (ISO 8402, 1986) Quality Vocabulary: Part 1. International Terms.
- "The total composite product and service characteristics of marketing, engineering, manufacture, and maintenance through which the product and service in use will meet the expectation by the customer" – Feigenbaum.

There is another word that should be defined properly, that is "reliability". Why does someone buy a particular car? "Quality and reliability" may be the answer. The two are used synonymously, often in a totally confused way. Clearly, part of the acceptability of a product or service will depend upon its ability to function satisfactorily over a period of time, and this aspect of performance is known as "reliability". It is the ability of the product or service to continue to meet the customer's requirements. Reliability ranks with quality in importance, since it is a key factor in many purchasing decisions where alternatives are being considered. Many of the general management issues that relate to achieving product or service quality are also applicable to reliability.

Quality requires that both the actual needs of the customer and his or her perceived needs are explored. Frequently, a choice of product or service is made upon apparently irrational grounds; identical offerings, presented in different ways, will sell in vastly different quantities, and will have different qualities ascribed to them. The detergent which sells better in a blue box than a red box, and the bank account which has a higher status because of the leather chequebook waller, are well known. Similarly, a quality judgement is often related to the price paid without any regard to the discernible properties being purchased. The reasons for a purchase may be difficult to identify, yet their reality must not be denied.

The quality of products and services is important not only for users, but also, for suppliers. For manufacturers, quality deficiencies result in additional costs – for inspection, testing, scrap, re-work, and the handling of complaints and warranty claims. In the service industries, errors, checking, enquiries and complaints account for losses in efficiency and productivity. Repeat sales and future market share will also be affected, with significant effects on profitability and survival.

Quality must, therefore, be taken into account throughout all the areas of marketing, design, purchasing, production or operations, and logistics. It must be controlled in all these functions, and their activities co-ordinated to achieve a balanced, corporate quality performance. Quality performance will not just happen; effective leadership and teamwork is the only sure recipe for success. Real understanding and commitment by senior management, together with explicit quality policies, lead to an improvement throughout the entire organisation which, in turn, generates a momentum for the improvement of products, services and performance.

Achievement of quality relies upon consideration of both the external environment and the internal resources: the identification of the customer's requirements must be matched by the ability to produce a product, or generate a service, which will be recognised as satisfying the needs. In the event of a conflict between these two determinants, the intended marker segment may have to be changed, or the internal resources may have to be re-examined. The customer's perception of quality changes with time and any organisation's attitude to quality must change with this perception. The skills and attitudes of the producer are also subject to change, and failure to monitor such changes will inevitably lead to dissatisfied customers. Quality, like all other corporate matters, must be reviewed continually in the light of current circumstances.

A traditional approach to many transformation processes is to depend on "production" to make the product and "quality control" to inspect it and divert that output which does not meet the requirements. This is a strategy of detection and is wasteful because it allows time, and materials, to be invested in products which are not always saleable. This post-operation or post-production inspection is expensive, unreliable and uneconomical.

It is much more effective to avoid waste by not producing unsaleable output in the first place – to adopt a strategy of prevention. The prevention strategy sounds sensible and obvious to most people. It is often captured in slogans such as "Quality – right first time". This type if campaigning is, however, not enough on its own. What is required is an understanding of the elements of a systematic control system which is designed for the prevention of products or services which does not conform to requirements. Management must be dedicated to the ongoing improvement of quality, not simply a one-step improvement to an acceptable plateau.

A quality policy then requires top management to:–

- Establish an "organisation" for quality;
- Identify the customer's needs and perception of needs;
- Assess the ability of the organisation to meet these needs;
- Ensure that supplied materials and services reliably meet the required standards of performance and efficiency;
- Concentrate on the prevention, rather than detection, philosophy;
- Educate and train for quality improvement and;
- Review the quality management systems to maintain progress.

The quality policy must be publicised and understood at all levels of the organisation.

Design and Conformance

Quality has so far been defined as the degree of satisfaction of customer needs. So the quality of a motor car, or washing machine, or banking service is the extent to which it meets the requirements of the customer. Before any discussion on quality can take place, therefore, it is necessary to be clear about the purpose of the product, in other words, what the customer's requirements are. The customer may be internal or external to the organisation and his or her satisfaction must be the first and most important ingredient in any plan for success.

The quality of any product or service has two distinct but inter-related aspects:–

- Quality of design and;
- Quality of conformance to design.

Quality of Design

This is a measure of how well the product or service is designed to meet the customer requirements. If the quality of design is low, the product or service will not satisfy the requirements.

The most important feature of the design, with regard to the achievement of the required product quality, is the specification. This describes and defines the product or service and should be a comprehensive statement of all aspects of it which must be present to meet customer requirements.

The stipulation to the correct specification is vital in the purchase of materials and services for use in the transformation process. All too frequently, the terms "as previously supplied" or " as agreed with your representative" are to be found on purchase orders for suppliers. The importance of obtaining quality inputs cannot be over-emphasised and this cannot be achieved without adequate specifications.

A specification may be expressed in terms of the maximum amount of tolerable variation on a measurement, the degree of finish on a surface, the smoothness of movement of a mechanical device, a particular chemical property, the number of times the phone rings before it must be answered, and so on. There is a variety of ways in which specifications may be stated and ingenuity must be constrained in order to control the number of forms of specifications present in any organisation.

Quality of Conformance to Design

This is the extent to which the product or service achieves the quality of design. What the customer actually receives should conform to the design, and direct production or operating costs are tied firmly to the level of conformance achieved. Quality cannot be inspected into a product or service; the customer satisfaction must be designed into the whole system. The conformance check then makes sure that things go according to plan. A high level of final product inspection or checking of work is often indicative of attempts to inspect in quality, an activity which will achieve mostly spiralling costs and increasing viability.

The area of conformance to design is largely concerned with the performance of the process, which transforms a set of inputs, including actions, methods and operations, into desired outputs – products, information, services, and so forth. In each area, or function of an organisation, there will be many processes taking place, and the output from one is often the input to another. Clearly it is essential to have an effective system to manage each process. The recording and analysis of data play a significant role in this aspect of quality.

The Costs of Quality

Manufacturing a product, or generating a service, which meets the customer requirements must be managed in a cost-efficient manner, so that the long-term effect of quality costs on the business is a desirable one. These costs are a true measure of the quality effort. A competitive product based upon a balance between quality and cost factors is the principal goal. This objective is best accomplished with the aid of competent analysis of the quality costs.

The analysis of quality costs is a significant management tool which provides:–

- A method of assessing the overall effectiveness of the management of quality and;
- A means of determining problem areas and action priorities.

The costs of quality are no different from any other costs in that, like the cost of maintenance, design, sales, production and operations management, information and other activities, they can be budgeted, measured and analysed.

Having specified the quality of design, the task is to achieve a service or product which matches it. This comprises activities which will incur costs which can be separated into the categories of failure costs, appraisal costs and prevention costs. Failure costs can be further split into those resulting from internal and external failure.

Internal Failure Costs

These costs occur when products fail to reach designed quality standards and are detected before transfer to the consumer takes place. Internal failure includes:–

- Scrap – defective product which cannot be repaired, used or sold;
- Re-work or rectification – the correction of defective output or errors to meet the required specifications;
- Re-inspection – the re-examination of output which has been rectified;
- Downgrading – product which is usable but does not meet specifications and may be sold as "second quality" at a low price;
- Waste – the activities associated with doing unnecessary work or holding stocks as the result of errors, poor organisation, the wrong materials and so on, and;
- Failure analysis – the activities required to establish the causes of internal product failure.

External Failure Costs

These costs occur when products or services fail to reach design quality standards and are not detected until after transfer to the consumer. External failure includes:–

- Repair and servicing – either of returned products or those in the field;
- Warranty claims – failed products which are replaced under guarantee;
- Complaints – all work associated with the servicing of customer's complaints;
- Returns – the handling and investigation of rejected products and services, including any transport costs;
- Liability – the result of product liability litigation and other claims, which may include change of contract and;
- Loss of goodwill – the impact on reputation and image which impinges directly on future prospects for sales.

It can be seen then, that external and internal failures produce the costs of getting it wrong.

Appraisal Costs

These costs are associated with the evaluation of purchased materials processes, intermediates, products and services, to assure conformance with the specifications. Appraisal includes:–

- Vertication – of incoming material, process set-up, first-offs, running processes, intermediates, final products and services, and includes product or service performance appraisal against agreed specifications;
- Quality audits – to check that the quality system is functioning satisfactorily;
- Inspection equipment – the calibration and maintenance of any equipment used in appraisal activities and;
- Vendor rating – the assessment and approval of suppliers of all products and services.

Appraisal activities result in the costs of checking that it is right.

Prevention Costs

These are associated with the design, implementation and maintenance of the quality system. Prevention costs are planned and are
incurred prior to production. Prevention includes:–

- Product or service requirements – the determination of quality
  requirements and the setting of corresponding specification for
  incoming materials, processes, intermediates, finished products
  and services;
- Quality planning – the creation of quality, reliability, production
  and operation supervision, verification and other speical plans
  (such as trials) required to achieve the quality objective;
- Quality assurance – creation and maintenance of the overall
  quality system;
- Appraisal equipment – the design, development or purchase of
  equipment for use in appraisal;
- Training – the development, preparation and maintenance of
  quality training programmes for operators, supervisors and
  managers and;
- Miscellaneous – clerical, travel, supply, shipping, communications
  and other general management activities associated with quality.

Resources devoted to prevention give rise to costs of getting it right
first time. The relationship between these costs and how they change as
quality improves is illustrated in Fig. 24.

Total direct quality costs, and their division between the categories
of prevention, appraisal, internal failure and external failure, vary
considerably from industry to industry and from plant to plant. The
work of Juran, has suggested that total quality costs in manufactoring
average 10 per cent of sales turnover. Another writer on quality,
Freigenbaum, has introduced the idea that in the average organisation
there exists a "hidden plant", amounting to approximately one-tenth
of productive capacity. This is devoted to producing scrap, re-working,
correcting errors, replacing defective goods and so on. Thus, a direct
link exists between quality and productivity, and there is no better way
to improve productivity then to convert this hidden plant to truly
productive use. A systematic approach to the control of quality
provides an important way to accomplish effective contrrol. One such
approach may be to use British Standard 5750.

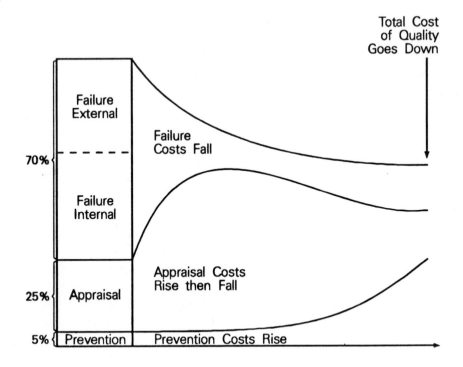

Figure 24.
The Cost of Quality

BS5750

The BS5750 series are the national standards which promulgate, for
use by UK suppliers and purchasers, the ISO 9000 series international
standards for quality systems. They tell suppliers and manufacturers
what is required of a quality-orientated system. They do not set out
extra special requirements which only a very few organisations can – or
need – comply with, but are practical standards for quality systems
which can be used by all of UK industry.

The principles of BS5750 are applicable whether an organisation
employs 10 people of 10,000. They identify the basic disciplines, and,
specify the procedures and criteria to ensure that products or services
meet the customer's requirements.

The benefits of applying BS5750 are real; it may save money –
because procedures may be more soundly based and more efficient; it
may ensure satisfied customers – because the organisation may have

built in quality at every stage; it may also reduce waste and time-consuming re-working of designs and procedures.

Constituent Parts

- Part 0: Section 0.1/IS0 9000 is a guide to the selection and use of the appropriate part of the BS5750/IS0 9000 series.
- Part 0: Section 0.2/IS0 9004 is a guide to overall quality management and the quality system elements within the BS5750/IS0 9000 series.
- Part 1/IS0 9001 relates to quality specifications for design and development, production, installation and servicing when the requirements of goods or services are specified by the customer, in terms of how they must perform, and which are then provided by the supplier.
- Part 1/IS0 9002 sets out requirements where a firm is manufacturing goods or offering a service to a published specification or to the customer's specification.
- Part 3/IS0 9003 specifies the quality system to be used in final inspection and test procedures.

Purpose

BS5750 sets out how it is possible to establish, document and maintain an effective quality system which will demonstrate to customers that organisations are committed to quality and are able to supply their quality needs.

It is an internationally accepted standard and is simply common sense set down on paper in an organisation way. It has been broken down into sections to enable manufacturers to implement it easily and efficiently.

Using BS5750 may bring real economies in its wake; economies in production because sustems are controlled from start to finish, economies in resources and in time spent on planning or modifying designs. The organisation may also have a complete record of every stage of production – invaluable for product or process improvement and in relation to any product liability claim.

Who Uses BS5750?

Suppliers can use BS5750 when setting up their own quality systems; customers may specify that the quality of goods and services they are purchasing shall be controlled by a management system complying with BS5750 and customers, or third parties, may use it as a basis for assessing a supplier's quality management system, and thus, ability to produce satisfactory goods and services. In fact, it is already used in this last way by all major public sector purchasing organisations and accedited third party certification bodies.

The direct benefits to firms who have been assessed in relation to BS5750 and who appear in the Department of Trade and Industry's Register of Quality Assessed United Kingdom companies are considerable; reduced inspection costs, improved quality and better use of scarce resources. Exporting firms who have been assessed may find that assessment helps them to obtain reciprocal recognition of certificates where needed by overseas authorities.

Comments

A slavish adherence to sources being BS5750 approved can screen, from the buyer, organisations that have the integrity and ability to deliver reliability. Bluntly, it can deny access to "quality" companies, reduce choice and eliminate flexibility. A cynic might argue that it allows "ordinary" companies to masquerade as "quality". Perhaps there is a more obvious need to ensure integration of the organisation and total commitment to quality. One method is Total Quality Management.

Total Quality Management (TQM)

Competitiveness is often measured by three things: quality, price and delivery. It is often a misconception that quality costs extra money in terms of inputs. The theory behind a TQM system is that, as quality improves, costs actually fall through lower failure and appraisal costs and less waste. TQM involves much more than assuring product or service quality, it is a system of dealing with quality at every stage of the production process, both internally and externally. TQM is truly a system requiring the commitment of senior mangers, effective leadership and teamwork.

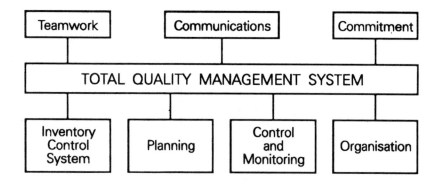

Figure 25.
The Total Quality Management System

The TQM system requires that every single part of the organisation is integrated and must be able to work together. The main elements of the system are:–

- Teamwork: This is central to many parts of the TQM system where workers have to feel that they are part of an organisation. In addition, teams of workers will often be brought together into problem-solving groups, quality circles and quality improvement teams;

- Commitment: To be successful, TQM needs to be truly organisation-wide and, therefore, commitment is required at the top, from the chief executive, as well as from the workforce. Middle management have an important role to play in not only grasping the concepts themselves but also, explaining them to the people for whom they are responsible;

- Communication: Poor communication can result in organisational problems, information being lost and gaps occurring in the system. A good flow of accurate information, instructions and feedback is vital in maintaining the cohension needed by the system;

- Organisation: A cohesive system needs to be an organised one, with clear channels of responsibility and clearly-defined reporting procedures. Quality-related errors can be quickly rectified if an efficient organisation structure is in place;

- Control and monitoring: The TQM system will not remove the need to monitor processes and sample outputs, neither will it simply control itself. Many organisations use after-the-fact control, causing managers to take a reactive, rather than proactive, position. The TQM system needs a more anticipative style of control;

- Planning: Processes need to be planned carefully if they are to be efficient. This usually requires the recording of activities, stages and decisions in a form which is communicable to all. A clearly-defined process reduces the scope for error, and provides the basis of an analysis into possible improvements that might be made;

- Inventory systems: It is in the storage of raw materials, components or the finished product that quality can diminish. The keeping of stocks is also physically expensive and can lead to cash-flow problems. An inventory control system is, therefore, required to keep stocks to a minimum, whilst ensuring that supplies never dry up. One such system is the "Just in Time" system.

A breakdown in any part of the TQM system can lead to organisational gaps where wastage may occur or quality may be overlooked. Errors have a habit of multiplying, and failure to meet the requirements of one part of the organisation creates problems elsewhere. The correction of errors is time consuming and costly. TQM can provide a company with a competitive edge, which will be important given the increases in competition resulting from the Single European Market. This means that managers must plan strategically, both externally and internally, and that internal strategic planning has to involve everyone in the workplace. TQM is an approach aimed at improving the effectiveness and flexibility, of business as a whole through the elimination of wasted effort as well as physical waste (that is, improving the effectiveness of work so that results are achieved in less time and at less cost).

Overall, TQM appears to be a better integrative process. Below is a reminder of the benefits: TQM:–

- Focuses the individual's role on customers and constant improvement;
- Develops teamwork, commitment and innovation as vehicles for employee ownership of improvement process;
- Identifies and eliminates waste of resources and costs and;
- Provides a basis for management development and training

focused on company values and the shift from policing to enable style.

Generally TQM will increase profits and the market share the positive way – by delighting the Customer and doing it RIGHT FIRST TIME!

Chapter 13

Operating Environments

– A Case Study.

Understanding Logistics in operating environments is important to understanding the total concept. To be able to do this we need to examine a new method and compare it to the problems of existing methods. In order to illustrate this, a specific example of logistics support in the aircraft industry will be considered; the principles however, are the same for any capital equipment project in manufacturing, public services, the armed forces and construction industries.

Integrated Logistic Support (ILS)

ILS is a structured and co-ordinated approach to support planning that will produce the most technically efficient and cost effective support solution for the aircraft industry.

ILS is an American concept that was introduced by the US Government in an attempt to combat their spiralling support costs and to give a structured approach to support planning so as to let it influence the design process.

The concept was developed and became Mil.Std.1388. This standard now provides a frame work which can be tailored to suit individual projects and user requirements dependant upon budgets, time scales and project size. We shall not mention "1388" again but bear in mind that all the concepts are based on this Mil.Std.

The reason for adopting ILS is that the customer will make it a contractual requirement of the project with the aim of meeting the same objectives.

Integrated Logistic Support – Main Objectives

So, what is wrong with present systems and why do we need ILS?

Past problems can be grouped together to give three main objectives. These are:–

- Reduce Support Costs
  – past project support costs have now risen to an unacceptable level.
- Ensure Support Influences Design
  – so that the product is designed to be as supportable as possible at the first attempt.
- Ensure the Timely Development and Acquisition of Resources
  – all the required resources are to be in the right place at the right time.

So, let us look at the first of these objectives.

Reducing Support Costs

What exactly is a Support Cost? The "Support Cost" is the cost, incurred by the customer, through owning and operating a product, for example, an aircraft. It includes repairable components, technical publications, Aerospace Ground Equipment (AGE), Petrol Oils and Lubricants (POL), contractor site representatives, and largest of all, the customer's labour costs.

Previous Support Costs

As products have become more complex so the support costs have risen. The effects of these high support costs seriously jeopardise the chances of a company being awarded export contracts.

Potential Export Contract Support Costs

Let us take aircraft manufacture as an example of the effects of high support costs on a quote for an export contract.

If we allow £20 million per aircraft then the support costs, at present rates, come to approximately £11m for each aircraft.

In order to keep costs within the customer's budget the present support rates mean that the customer will be limited to eight aircraft. A fleet of eight aircraft means that no more than six aircraft are available on the line at any one time.

The effectiveness of this in air defence terms, in relation to the total cost, is not a viable defence option compared to other national budget demands. In any national budget squeeze an early cancellation of the aircraft sale is likely and the result is loss of important export revenue for the manufacturer.

Potential Export Aircraft Support Costs

To emphasise how support costs dictate the number of aircraft a customer can purchase it is necessary to consider them in detail. The effect is that high support costs can affect the actual numbers of aircraft that the customer can purchase. Bear in mind that these support percentages are expressed as a proportion of the cost of an aircraft.

At 100% support costs, the customer gets 6 aircraft for £120m and £120m worth of support.

At 50% support costs the customer gets 8 aircraft for £160m and £80m worth of support.

If we reduce the cost of support to 33% of the aircraft costs then we could supply 9 aircraft.

But the bottom line – and this is where we should be aiming – is that if we managed to reduce the cost of support to 20% of the cost of that aircraft then we could supply the customer with 10 aircraft – a more realistic figure with which to form a visable defence policy.

Manufacturers do not lose orders through poor product performance – they lose orders because prospective customers cannot afford to keep the product in service.

Costs – Initial and Recurring

Having established the effect that the support costs can have on a project, and that they must be kept to a minimum, let us look at what support costs consist of.

Support costs fall into one of two categories:–

- Initial costs
  – those borne at the time of the initial purchase such as Test Equipment, Training, Spares and Publications.
- Recurring costs
  – those costs that are continued throughout the Life Cycle of the project. The major cost drivers in recurring costs are usually the

upkeep of documentation, the cost incurred by the need to keep training manpower, but invariably the major cost driver is labour in the form of maintenance and repair.

It is therefore easy to see that the more we can improve the reliability of the product, the less would be the requirement for maintenance and repair, thus the lower the recurring costs.

The main reason for keeping recurring costs to a minimum is that they are subject to inflation and as such can considerably influence the support costs throughout the life cycle.

How Support Can Influence Design

As well as trying our best to plan the support requirements it would help if the product was designed to be as supportable as possible in the first place. Let us look at an example of how costs escalate because of a poor supportability design and failure to rectify it.

In this particular example, a small alteration is needed to make the fitment of an item easier by changing the size of a securing bolt.

If, during the design stage a possible alteration is identified that could make the product more supportable it would take £10 to alter the drawing and no more than that would have been required.

Had the project been in the development phase a Modification (Mod) Kit would have been introduced – and the drawings altered – it would have taken £100. During the Production Phase the stores quantity would have been altered, the Mod. kit purchased – and the drawings altered – the cost would have been nearer £1000.

If the product had been in service and the same bolt size changed to improve the products supportability, by the time you take into account the modification kits, stores catalogues, stores changes, product downtime, retrospective fitting and labour – the cost of the change is nearer £10,000.

The costs quoted are fictitious but the effect is not. If we can influence the design savings of more than a factor of ×1000 can be made in certain areas and we shall end up with a design that has been influenced by support – not support that is influenced by design.

The Final Objective – To Ensure The Timely Development and Aquisition of Support Resources

Acquisition of Support Resources

The date that the product using the example of an aircaft once more will enter service is called the In Service Date – ISD. Three months before this occurs, all the agreed support requirements, facilities and equipment are to be in service and ready for use. This date is called the Logistic Support Date – LSD.

To achieve the requirements for LSD there is a large amount of work to be carried out. Try and imagine the planning that is required to ensure that everything is ready to go:–

- All the necessary training must have been carried out so that both aircrew and engineers are competent.
- The National Publications data base must be compiled and up to date, and publications must be printed and available as required.
- All Support Equipment should have been identified, developed and in place at the correct levels ready for use.

This must be so for all the support requirements for the aircraft or for any other significant product.

It is the job of ILS to ensure that the agreed support package is ready, in all respects, for LSD.

Three Main Objectives

There are therefore three main objectives that we need to concentrate on. To re-cap they are:–

- to reduce support costs
- to ensure that support influences design
- timely development and acquisition of resources

As well as our 3 main objectives there are always mistakes that have been made on previous projects that under no circumstances can be allowed to happen again.

Past Problems

In the past the various support disciplines have often been left to their own devices in producing support plans for their particular area. These are just a few examples of what went wrong in the fictitious aircraft programme.

The initial intention stated that in-service repair would run from day one (ISD). So, all the planning for the provisioning of spares necessary to support this date was carried out only to find that the ISD had slipped 3 years. This may look like a "God send" in that it provided a lot more time, unfortunately, it also allowed numerous modifications to be introduced which meant that the support disciplines were planning for targets that had long since changed.

The Technical Publications Department of the various partner companies were working together to compile a joint set of publications. Unfortunately, these partner companies were not interested in Batch 1 aircraft, as their respective airforces were not going to receive aircraft until Batch 2. Therefore the three partner companies were working to widely differing Logistics Support Dates.

It is a prime objective of Integrated Logistics Support to ensure that the lessons have been learnt and that we don't allow these same mistakes to occur again.

Un-coordinated Logistic Support

There has been very little use of Automatic Data Processing systems in Logistic Support and when they have been used they have been for individual needs rather than as a coordinated attempt to construct a common support data base.

It is possible to picture this unstructured and uncoordinated approach to support planning with some disciplines 'talking' to each other and others not at all.

This along with an unstructured approach to Support Project Management, has contributed much to the problems encountered.

Co-Ordinated Logistic Support

What we need is to bring everyone together and pool all their efforts into one coordinated and planned structure. That structure is:

"INTEGRATED LOGISTIC SUPPORT"

This focal point is the means of achieving the objectives of ILS – it is:

"LOGISTIC SUPPORT ANALYSIS" (LSA)

We shall look at LSA in more detail later but first let us see how the structure of ILS Management will help us achieve our objectives. For consistency the example is an aircraft; the principles remain the same for any major product.

ILS Management Structure

Integrated Logistic Support Management is divided into three groups:

- Aircraft Support Group
- Supplier Control Group
- Programmes and Budgets Group

The ILS Manager can be responsible to two directorates; to the Support Director and also to the Project Director.

Although it may seem unusual for a manager to be responsible to two different directorates, if we are to accomplish the objectives then the ILS manager needs to be on equal standing with the technical managers on the project.

This is normally a condition of the contract placed upon the manufacturer to ensure that ILS and the support directorate has equal standing along side the technical areas.

Aircraft Support Group

The Aircraft Support groups' main task is to ensure that progress towards the "Total Support of the Aircraft" is kept in view at all times and that the support disciplines work towards this concept. To this end we undertake various tasks:–

- Ensure that the costs of support are reduced and that only the most technically efficient and cost effective approaches are adopted.
- Review the maintenance policies as produced by LSA.
- Monitor the Reliability and Maintainability targets and help propose ways that any shortfalls can be recovered from.

- Carry out Life Cycle Costing between comparable procedures and policies.
- Introduce ILS procedures into Aircrew Synthetic Training Aids (ASTA) and Groundcrew Training Aids.
- To ensure that interfaces are established between disciplines using Automatic Data Processing Systems (ADP).
- Act as interface for queries; particularly from the customer but also from any section in the company involved in the support process.

Supplier Control Group

The supplier control group acts as the ILS/LSA interface with the suppliers of aircraft equipments and, in due course, the suppliers of test equipment for these Equipments.

Their duties include:–

- Control of vendor assessments relative to ILS.
- Control of vendor supplied support information.
- Production of line item networks against each equipment vendor
  – their primary objective is to identify items of equipment that will become Phased Support Candidates.
- Planning and controlling the introduction into service of Phased Support Items.

Programmes and Budgets Group

Finally, we have the Programme and Budgets Group. They plan, monitor and report progress on ILS matters both to management and, on behalf of the management, to the customer.

They also issue the work directives to the ILS disciplines and manage the ILS budgets.

To achieve this they are split into 3 areas:

- Programming and Reporting.
- Budgets and Directives.
- Meeting and Briefings.

Let us look at how the work packages for the Integrated Logistic Support disciplines are issued and how they link in with the programmes that are used to monitor the overall ILS progress.

Statement of Work (SOW) and Work Packages

Initially, a "Statement of Work" (SOW) is issued from the customer detailing work packages that need to be undertaken for the project to be completed.

The SOW consists of various work packages, all required to ensure that the required tasks are fully completed on time. These packages are then discussed with the relevant disciplines and their contents and time scales agreed. Finally, the work package is issued as a formal Directive.

As tasks are completed and the project progresses there will be a need to update the directives and issue new ones as targets and requirements change. Once the Directives have been issued it is necessary to monitor their progress and ensure that they are completed by the required dates.

Integrating the Support Elements

We have outlined the main objectives and some of the short falls of previous projects. We have also demonstrated an organisation that can be set up to implement ILS and manage the support activities. It is now necessary to discuss the system that will integrate, discipline and structure support planning activities.

This system is called: Logistic Support Analysis.

The aim of this section is to give you a working level view of Logistic Support Analysis. it will not be an explanation on how each discipline should carry out Logistic Support Analysis in their particular area or a guide on which computer systems you may need to employ. It will be an overview of how LSA works; how the information is generated, what happens to it once it has been compiled and how each of the disciplines fits into the process.

Logistics Support Analysis

Logistic Support Analysis is used to:–

- Add discipline to the ILS task.
- To integrate the support disciplines, and
- To provide a structured process to achieve optimum support-ability.

Logistic Support Analysis is the means of achieving the objectives of Integrated Logistic Support.

Systems Breakdown Structure

An analysis is carried out on, for example, the aircraft system breakdown structure. The aircraft is divided into systems. These are divided again into sub-systems, sub-sub-systems and then, through the LRI's (Line replacement items), down to Module level. If you imagine a matrix over the whole aircraft then every item on the aircraft will be identifiable.

Candidate Item Identification

For any part of this breakdown structure to become a candidate for the LSA process it must be classified as either:

- A Maintenance significant item or a
- Functionally significant item.

That is, it must be potentially repairable or cause a maintenance task to be carried out for example an inspection, a removal or replacement, a functional test.

Candidates for LSA have now been identified, but how do we keep track of each of them?

Logistic Control Number

Each candidate is assigned an individual Logistic Control Number; an LCN. The LCN is made up of up to 10 digits depending on the level of system under examination.

Firstly, a letter identifies the aircraft. The next two digits represent the appropriate system. Following that the sub-system and then the sub-sub-system. The next two digits represent the individual LRI's in the sub-sub-system. Following that the modules within that LRI can be identified, and, finally, the last is the submodule, which is normally a character.

Logistics Control Number and System Breakdown Code

If a typical system is examined, for example the Crew Escape and Safety System, it can be seen just how a system breakdown code and numbering conventions work.

At the top there is the system, numbered in this example 95. Below that there is the sub system, designated the "Ejection Seat and Survival Kit". As it is the first sub-system in the "Crew Escape and Safety System" it is designated 951.

The first sub-sub-system is the "Ejection Seat" (single seat and twin seat rear) and is therefore numbered 9511. The 4th LRI is identified by its LCN which is 951104 and in this example this corresponds to the "Parachute".

So, it can be seen how each LRI has its own individual Logistic Control Number and how that number is generated.

Below this level, modules within the LRI would have the same LRI LCN but they would have two further identifying digits. Finally, a sub-module would have the full LCN for the module but it would normally have a character rather than a digit at the end.

This system breakdown structure and numbering system gives traceability – we can easily identify where an LSA candidate belongs within the aircraft.

So, this gives a list of candidates and they have all been numerically identified but how does this Logistic Support Analysis work?

The easiest, and only, way to imagine LSA is to think of the most logical way in which you would analyse an item of equipment in order to identify what its support requirements will be.

Support Requirement Identification

If an item of equipment is selected and tabulate all the basic information that is available for it. This information will come from the items' specification, the information supplied by the manufacturer of the item – the Use Study. The next step is to analyse this information.

It is necessary to identify maintenance tasks because it is only through knowing how to maintain the aircraft that it can be decided which support requirements will be required.

Support Requirement Identification

To identify a maintenance task for an item it is important to anticipate how the item will fail. To this end it is necessary to carry out a Failure Modes, Effects and Criticality Analysis (FMECA) on the item and predict how it will fail and how critical that failure will be. It cannot be stressed enough how important the role of FMECA's play in any support requirement identification process. If the potential failure modes of a particular item is unknown maintenance tasks cannot be identified.

If the mathematical part of the analysis is incorrect then the reminder of our Support analysis, and that of the Provisioning activity that is based on "Mean Time Between Failures" and "Mean Time Between Maintenance Actions" will be incorrect. Provisioning is, in essence, calculating the quantity and type of spares required. The result of an RMECA allows identification of essential maintenance tasks to prevent failures occurring.

Even if no preventative tasks are identified the fact that a failure mode exists means that at some point the item will fail and have to be replaced by a serviceable item. This action is called "Corrective Maintenance" because it's sole task is to restore the system to a serviceable state. Having identified the maintenance tasks that are applicable to the item through analysing the Failure Modes Effects the next logical step taken in identifying support requirements is to group all the tasks identified together so that each one can be considered in further detail.

Sequential Tasks

It is now possible to take each task and carry out an in depth analysis on it. Each step of the task is itemised so that a sequential description is documented. Obviously, as this procedure is carried out, it is possible to identify the need for support requirements.

For example: If a Transfer Isolate Valve is to be changed when it fails the tools to remove it will be needed – these would be identified. If the valve needed to be functioned after it had been fitted it would not be unreasonable to identify a training requirement if the function involved new test equipment.

So, this gives a list of tasks, described in full, sequentially, and a list of proposed support requirements.

In Depth Analysis

Now the remaining support disciplines can become involved and analyse the support requirement, as applicable to their own areas.

For example: Support Equipment can look at the requirements for tools for work on the removal of the valve and training can analyse the need for new courses to train tradesmen in the use of new test equipment to function the valve. Facilities will look at the requirements for providing the buildings and support to carry out the work.

So, to re-cap:–

- The Maintenance requirements for the equipment under consideration have been itemised.
- Potential Failure Modes can be highlighted. From these it is possible to identify the corrective tasks and the preventive tasks after carrying out the Maintenance analysis. The tasks that are applicable to that item are listed together.
- And finally each task can be analysed in full and the support requirements needed identified. The remaining support disciplines can now carry out their in depth analysis on their own particular areas and in doing so the complete support package for the valve will be generated. Part of this support package will be the level of repair required. Given industry's general inability to effectively manage repairs, this area of analysis is particularly important.

Level of Repair Analysis (LORA)

From the end of the support requirement identification, a basic supportability trade-off is carried out that will identify whether it is more economical to repair the item in service or to just discard it when it fails. Should the fact that the item will be discarded when it fails to be identified, then, the LSA process will be stopped here – there is obviously no need to carry out further in depth analysis to identify support requirements when as soon as the item becomes unserviceable it is thrown away!

Assuming the item is repairable, a more in depth Level of Repair

Analysis can be carried out if an item is identified as being more economical to repair then, as industry would provide all the support facilities, the LSA process will be stopped here. Normally it would be most unusual to find industry cheaper for a repair option over the life cycle of an aircraft because the customer has extensive repair and overhaul facilities. But should this be the case then the most economic support option will be implemented.

LORA determines the most cost effective maintenance policy for each item in the system over the whole life cycle of the aircraft. Each combination of support options is examined for each item, both as an individual and as part of the overall system. In the absence of any overriding customer policy constraints the option showing the least life cycle costs is chosen.

Undesirable Design Features

At times such as this the justification can be provided, through LSA to the design engineers, that an alternative approach on their behalf is needed. If the undesirable areas can be highlighted and the savings that can be made pointed out they are altered and the ability to influence the design process is created. This is one of the main objectives in Integrated Logistic Support.

Life Cycle Costs – Early Design Influence

The need for early design influence by Support is clear. The major support decisions are made as the item is designed due to the inherent designing-in of support requirements. In doing so they are committing the majority of our costs at an early stage.

Unfortunately, although these costs are committed at an early stage they are not actually paid out until the items go into service and it is at this time everybody starts complaining about the costs of support.

That is why it is *vital* to influence design to reflect the organization's supportability requirements.

Whether the design has been changed or it is necessary to come up with an alternative approach or data is updated, the data must be re-entered and the analysis re-considered.

At least with an LSA system it is possible to reconsider the situation and view the consequences over the whole of the support disciplines quickly and with a relative amount of ease. This process of refining data, known as iteration, enables the optimum support solution to be achieved.

Logistic Support Analysis

To recap on the objectives of LSA.

- Discipline can be added to the requirements of the Integrated Logistic Support tasks by providing a process that is common to all disciplines.
- The support disciplines can be integrated.
- A Structured Process can be produced using the Analysis Steps that will ensure that all decisions are recorded and that an audit path exists for each decision.

This has been a very basic and broad overview of the LSA process. Large areas of information have been discussed in a very short period and much of this has been stated in a very simplistic manner so as to ensure that an insight into all the different areas of LSA has been provided.

LSA is new method of carrying out what has gone on for many years but it is designed to make the organisation more efficient and the product sold more supportable.

Integrated Logistic Support is a structured, co-ordinated and disciplined approach that will:-

- Harmonise all aspects of support or a product.
- Optimise support levels to customers policies at minimum costs.
- Ensure that the product is fully supported to the required level of Logistic Supply Date.
- Produce a more reliable and maintainable product.
- Ensure that the support costs are a much smaller proportion of the total costs and that recurring costs are as smaller a percentage of initial costs as possible.
- Lower the product life cycle support costs.

The adoption of ILS, working within its structure and co-operation between the respective functions will lead to greater Customer satisfaction.

Logistics Information Systems

It would not be prudent to recommend a specific information system or database primarily because each business entity has its own needs. To effectively manage a concept such as ILS, each entity needs to establish its information needs; a method of establishing such needs is to carry out an Information Strategy Planning Project.

The purpose of the Information Strategy Planning (ISP) project is to examine the information needs of the business and to develop a plan to ensure that the Logistics function is effectively served with information systems that match both the business and its needs and provide clear business benefits.

Information Strategy Planning (ISP)

It is fundamental that the ISP is driven by the business, this will be achieved through the following approach:–

- Development of a partnership between the Information Technology (IT) function and business management who will direct and steer the process.
- Development of a clear understanding (by the IT community) of the business, it's needs and priorities, as identified by the businessmen.
- Identification of the business systems and supporting equipment infrastructure required by the business.
- Development of an approved investment plan for the provision of the system identified, together with the respective costs and benefits.

Methodology: Workshops and Questionnaires

It is important to allow everyone within the Logistics chain to discuss what they do, how they do it and ideas for improvement. Following the workshop, questionnaires covering objectives strategies and information needs must be completed by the same group of people. This is the key to prioritisations.

Detailed Analysis of Results:
This will involve:

- Identification of all the business systems required by the Business.

This will be achieved by detailed analysis of the results from the Workshop and Questionnaires using formal systems analysis techniques for structuring information.

- Identification of the coverage of current systems against the business systems required.
- Deficiencies between the business systems required and those already in place will be highlighted and taken forward into detailed plans for the enhancement or replacement of existing systems.
- Equipment infrastructure required to support the findings will be identified and plans developed for its implementation.

It should be noted that the purpose will not be to replace the existing infrastructure and systems across the board. While in some areas this may be necessary, it is envisaged that the plans resultant from the ISP will build on and enhance much of what is already in place.

Now that a brief summary of what is required has been provided, it is necessary now to look at the methodology most viable for the workshop.

The purpose of a workshop is to gain a collective understanding of the linkages between the business plan and the business information needs in the areas that the Workshop is examining. Not surprisingly, these linkages are expressed using the same terminology of business plans and strategy, (such as Mission Statement, Objectives) but it should not be thought that they are redefining these elements.

Mission Statement

The Business plan contains a mission statement briefly defining the overall purpose and direction of the organisation. This statement will not be changed as a result of the ISP analysis. A Mission Statement is "To provide the Customer with a total quality service and secure continuing and expanding profitable business to year 2000 and beyond".

There may be lower level Mission Statements to give a particular group of business activities focus. For Human Logistics the Mission Statement could be identified as:

"To provide a Quality pro-active Logistics Service to enhance and support the programme aims to the customer".

However, a local Mission Statement is optional.

Objectives

The business objectives are defined as the long term results that the organisation wishes to achieve. Topically, objectives relate to the financial, market, customer services, quality, products, services and people aspects of the organisation. They are likely to be represented in the form of a hierarchy.

For example; for logistics, a key objective is:

"To secure a measured improvement in the quality of Logistics services provided to the Customer".

This has Supporting Objectives:

"Comply with the Customers' Support requirement both in terms of quality and timeliness in the supply of spares".
"Work towards a marked improvement in the clearance of repairs".

Typically, 10 to 20 key objectives would be identified at each Workshop.

Strategies

The strategies will define existing, or planned initiatives, deploying the organisation's resources, to achieve one or more objectives. Strategies are the "means" by which objectives are achieved.

The more specific the strategy, the more useful it is to the formulation of the IT plans. For example, the strategy "To improve clearance of repairs" is rather vague. The strategy "To improve clearance of repairs by wider product inspection and more selective testing" is stronger, pointing to specific information needs and activities and indicating where IT could provide support.

For example, in relation to the logistics objective above:

"Expand the content of 'hands on' training through extending the time operatives spend on the actual product".
"Examine the speciality training standards and make adjustments where appropriate".

There should always be at least one strategy supporting an objective and, in many cases, more than one.

Performance Measure

Progress in the achievement of objectives and the implementation of strategies is monitored by performance measures.

For example, for the Logistics objective above:

"Number of Customer Warranty Claims"
"Products delivered against products found faulty on delivery"

It is possible for an objective or strategy to have many performance measures and a performance measure to support many objectives and strategies. It is a characteristic of a mature business strategy plan that a high proportion of objectives and strategies have performance measures.

It is envisaged that in the region of 20 Performance Measures will be identified at each Workshop.

Critical Success Factors

A Critical Success Factor is a key area where things "must go right" for the organisation to achieve it's objectives and goals and implement its strategies.

Examples of typical Critical Success Factors are:

"Must clear repairs within one month for all Customers"

By definition, the number of Critical Success Factors is small. It is envisaged that in the region of 10 CSF's will be identified at each Workshop. Their main use in the ISP process is to understand the overall priorities of the organisation.

Critical Assumptions

Associated with every business plan there are critical assumptions. It is essential that they are made explicit and fully understood. Critical Assumptions will usually relate to the organisation's structure, competitor activity, technologies, market economic conditions and legislation. For example, "It is highly probable that the Customer will move more and more towards incentive contracts to minimise defects found on product delivery".

Business Activities

The high level activities (functions) performed by the organisation will be identified. The activities will implement the strategies identified, support the operations of the business and generate the information need requirements. It is anticipated that, initially, 50 to 80 activities will be identified.

Example activities associated with Logistics are Repairs and Spares Management, Employee Administration, Manpower Planning and Monitoring, Logistics Strategy and Policy Management, Recruitment Management, Employee Development, Employee Relations Management, Health and Welfare Management. These can be divided into sub-activities.

It is anticipated that 30 to 50 business activities will be documented at each Workshop.

Information Needs

Information Needs are unstructured statements defining the data required to support the organisation. Information Needs relate to a range of strategy planning objects including:

- Objectives
- Strategies
- Critical Success Factors
- Performance Measures
- Business Activities

This is why it is so vital to identify these and gain an understanding of how they relate to one another.

Information Needs will be categorised by the type of need they satisfy, such as strategic, planning, analysis, monitoring or transaction requirements.

Examples of information needs for the logistics area are:

- "Number of repairs received in any given period".
- "Number of new spares orders received in any given period".
- "Number of vacancies to be filled, broken down by position and skill".

It is anticipated that approximately 100 to 150 information needs will be documented at each Workshop.

Issues and Problems

These will include:

- Current systems support for the business strategy.
- Major planning concerns and issues raised by management.
- Areas of business plan which are incomplete or are lacking in detail.
- Conflicts between departments within the business, including incompatible strategies.
- Major areas of uncertainty and risk regarding the business plan.
- Differences in perceived priorities. (From the objectives and strategies priority Questionnaire).

Each Workshop will be run by members of an ISP Core Team, with a further ISP Team member documenting the results. These will be issued to all Workshop attendees immediately following completion of the session.

The ISP team members will ensure continuity between Workshops and more than one workshop may well be needed in order that the results from each Workshop are progressively built upon.

End Product

An information system that will meet the needs of the business and not the desires of a salesman.

Logistics and Other Organisational Functions

The principal inter-relationships between logistics and other organisational functions are:

- The relationship between the marketing function (or non-commercial equivalent) and the physical distribution sub-function of logistics.
- The relationship between the manufacturing function and the physical procurement and materials management sub-functions of logistics.

However, for the organisation to be properly served by an effective logistics system then rather similar co-ordination problems have to be solved in both inter-relationships.

Logistics is concerned with activities from throughout the enterprise. These activities interact for purposes which are to the enterprise's benefit. Materials flows affect all parts of an organisation and its relations to other organisations.

The major difficulty is that the traditional functional orientation of managers put organisational activities into departmental boxes – production, marketing, purchasing – which tends to limit an overall appreciation of the management issues which affect the entire organisation.

Logistics can only be efficiently and effectively conducted if it is seen by managers as being concerned with the totality of related functions within the organisational systems:

- Production;
- Marketing;
- Purchasing;
- Finance;
- Personnel and;
- Information Processing.

Also, logistics can only be efficiently and effectively conducted if it is seen by managers as being concerned with the total sub-functions within the logistics system:

- Materials Handling;
- Transport;
- Warehousing;
- Inventory Control;
- Unitisation;
- Packaging and;
- Information Processing.

The twin objectives of logistics are:

- To minimise logistics costs and;
- to optimise customer Service Levels (and ideally to do both simultaneously.)

These objectives are achieved by 'trade-offs' between these sub-functions and functions so as to minimise total logistics costs and/or optimise total logistics service levels.

To take the first objective, costs may be deliberately incurred in one function or sub-function in order that the performance across several

functions or sub functions may be optimised. To put it more simply –
total logistics costs can be minimised by balancing individual logistics
costs. For example, the more depots a company owns the less its
transport costs BUT the more its depot investment and running costs.

Examples of possible trade-offs are:–

Trade-offs between elements of logistics sub-functions

- Choice between more sophisticated and expensive packaging
  against reductions in other handling and warehousing costs.
- Choice between improved efficiency in prediction of demand for
  inventory against the holdings of inventory levels sufficient to cope
  with the uncertainties of demand.
- Choice between the firm's own road freight transport ('own
  account') against bought in ('hire and reward') road freight
  transport. ("Own account" is more expensive per mile travelled
  but much more flexible so it could reduce overall logistics costs).

Trade offs between logistics sub-functions

- Choice between improved warehousing facilities and reducing
  materials handling costs and improved flexibility in modal choice.
- Choice between improved cost control procedures in ware-housing
  and reduced difficulties and costs in total logistics planning.
- Choice between improved information processing facilities and
  reduced costs and improved service levels elsewhere through
  greater organisational intelligence.

Trade offs between organisational functions

- Choice between more selective and distribution cost-conscious
  marketing initiatives and a rationalised physical distribution effort.
- Choice between improved materials planning and control and
  rationalised requirement for warehousing space and materials
  handling.
- Choice between improved order processing facilities and
  rationalised manufacturing planning procedures.
- Choice between research and development investment in producing products which can easily be distributed and reduced logistics
  costs.

Trade offs between the organisation and its sources and customers;

- Choice between promoting improved materials handling facilities on the part of customers and improved possibilities for unitisation and palliation.
- Willingness of suppliers to make deliveries within a 'time window' convenient for the organisation and reduced costs for delivery.
- Willingness of suppliers to deliver 'just-in-time' and reduced organisational requirements for inventory holding and control.

Total logistics management needs to be built around the search for cost and service trade-offs to improve efficiency. There is a clear need for the development of information systems sophisticated enough to support the demands of comprehending the detail of cost trade offs, cost versus service level trade offs, and, trade-offs within varieties of service. Equally as important is having the skilled personnel logistics management.

Bibliography

Ammer, D *Materials Management*, 3rd edition. Irwin, Homewood, Illinois, 1974.

Audit Commission *Reducing the Cost of Local Government Purchases*. HMSO, London, 1984.

Bailey, P *Purchasing Systems and Records*. Gower Publishing, Aldershot, 1983.

Baily, P and Farmer, D *Purchasing Principles and Management*. Pitman, London, 1985.

Baily, P *Purchasing and Supply Management*, 5th edition, Prentice Hall, London, 1991.

Bain, J S *Industrial Organisation*. Wiley, New York, 1959.

Branwell Report *The placing and management of contracts for building and civil engineering works*. HMSO, London, 1964.

Bauer, P T and Yamey, B S *Markets, Market Control and Market Reform*. Weidenfeld and Nicholson, London, 1968.

Bolton, J F *Small firms*, Cmnd 4811, HMSO, London, 1972.

BS5750/ISO 9000 *A positive contribution to better business*. BSI, London, 1987.

Buckner, H *How British Industry Buys*, Hutchinson, London, 1967.

CBI *Transport and distribution in the Single Market*, TNT Express. Mercury Books, London, 1992.

Croell, R C *Measuring purchasing effectiveness*. Journal of Purchasing and Materials Management, 13 (1), 3–4, 1977.

Cyert, R M and March, J G *A Behavioural Theory of the Firm*. Prentice-Hall, Englewood Cliffs, New Jersey, 1963.

Dickie, H F *ABC Analysis shoots for dollars not pennies*. Factory Management and Maintenance, July 1951.

Economist Intelligence Unit *Retail Business*, No. 338, London, April 1986.

Edwards, R S and Townsend, H *Business Enterprise, its Growth and Organisation*, Macmillan, London, 1985.

Farmer, D H *Source decision-making in the multi-national company*. Journal of Purchasing, 8 (1), 5–18, 1972.

Fearon, H E *Purchasing research in American business*, PhD thesis, Michigan State University, 1961.

Gattorna, J *The Gower Handbook of Logistics and Distribution*, 4th edition, Gower Publishing, Aldershot, 1990.

Ghemawat, P *Commitment: the dynamic of strategy*, The Free Press, New York, 1991.

Heinritz, S F and Farrell, P V *Purchasing: Principles and Applications*. Prentice-Hall, Englewood Cliffs, New Jersey, 1981.

Institute of Purchasing & Supply *Electronic Data Interchange*, IPS, Easton, 1990.

Institute of Purchasing & Supply *Just In Time The Purchasing Viewpoint*, IPS, Easton, 1990.

Johnson, G and Scholes K *Exploring Corporate Strategy Text and Cases*, Prentice-Hall, London, 1992.

Kostishack, J D and South, J C *The composition of industrial buyer performance*. Journal of Purchasing, 9 (3), 50– 63, 1973.

Kotler, P and Balachandrian, V *Strategic remarketing, the preferred response to shortages and inflation*. Sloan Management Review, August 1975.

Kotler, P and Levy, S J *Buying is marketing too*. Journal of Marketing, January 1973.

Lauer, S *Westinghouse Plant X. In Purchasing Problems* (eds Baily and Farmer) POA, London, 1967.

Lee, L and Dobler, D *Purchasing and Materials Management*, McGraw-Hill, New York, 1977.

Leenders, M R *Improving Purchasing Effectiveness through Supplier Development*, Harvard University Press, Cambridge, Mass., 1965.

Lewis, C D *Scientific Inventory Control*, Butterworth, London, 1970.

Little, D and Barclay, I *Materials Management: the technologist's role in controlling materials costs*. Purchasing and Supply Management, IPS Easton, January 1986.

Lock, D *Project Management*, Gower, Aldershot, 1989.

Meopham, B *ICE Conditions of Contract – a Commercial Manual*, Waterlow Publishers, London, 1985.

Moos, S *Research Report 13, Committee of Enquiry on Small Firms*, HMSO, London, 1971.

Muhlenmann, A, Oakland, J and Lockyer, K *Production and Operations Management*, Pitman, London, 1992.

Newman, R G *Validation of Contract Compliance under Systems Contracting*. Journal of Purchasing and Materials Management, summer 1985.

Pagonis, WG *Moving Mountains: lessons in leadership and logistics from the Gulf War*, Harvard Business School Press, Boston Massachusetts, 1982.

Porter, M E *How competitive forces shape strategy*. Harvard Business Review, March–April 1979.

Quayle, M *Prime Contractship*. Purchasing and Supply Management, IPS Easton, April 1991.

Quayle, M *Developing Industrial Purchasing Policy*. Purchasing and Supply Management, IPS Easton, February 1992.

Rees, G *St Michael, A History of Marks and Spencer*, Weidenfeld and Nicholson, London, 1969.

Rook, A *Transfer Pricing*, British Institute of Management, London, 1972.

Rowe, D and Alexander, I *Selling Industrial Products*, Hutchinson, London, 1968.

Strauss, G *Tactics of lateral relationships: the purchasing agent*. Administrative Science Quarterly, 7 September 1962.

Tse, K K *Marks and Spencer*, Pergamon Press, Oxford, 1985.

Webster, F E and Wind, Y *Organisational Buying Behaviour*, Prentice-Hall, Englewood Cliffs, New Jersey, 1972.

Welford, R and Prescott, K *European Business An issue-based approach*, Pitman, London, 1992.

Index